WHERE THE BODIES ARE

*Final Visits to the
Rich, Famous & Interesting*

Patricia Brooks

The
Globe
Pequot
Press

GUILFORD, CONNECTICUT

Book design by Casey Shain

Photo Credits: pp. vi, x (middle and bottom), 27: Jackie Curtis; p. vii: the Savannah Area Convention and Visitors Bureau; pp. 26, 30: Barbara and Charles E. Marchant; p. 31: Thomas Berg; p. 70: Frank Gillespie; p. 76: Richard A. Gerweck; p. 85: Phillip Lovell, Historic Oakland Foundation; p. 106: Allegheny Cemetery; p. 108: The Andy Warhol Museum; p. 111: Christopher Berg; p. 117: Washington and Lee University; p. 118: © Virginia Tourism Corporation; pp. 120, 122: Maureen Baxter; p. 126: the Chicago Architecture Foundation; p. 130: Carl Sandburg State Historic Site; p. 133, 134: Illinois Historic Preservation Agency; pp. 137, 138: © Marty N. Davis; p. 140: Oakdale Memorial Gardens; p. 143: Pat Richardson, Frankfort Cemetery; p. 146: Louisana Office of Tourism; p. 147: Spring & Quinn; p. 151: Phillip La Grandeur; p. 152: Sinclair Lewis Foundation, Sauk Centre, Minnesota; · pp. 157, 159: Kathie Sutin/St. Louis Convention & Visitors Bureau; p. 163: Lake View Cemetery; p. 167: Used by permission © Elvis Presley Enterprises, Inc.; p. 177: Dwight D. Eisenhower Library; p. 179: Girls and Boys Town; p. 189: South Dakota Tourism; p. 191: Texas State Cemetery Photo Archives; p. 194: Whitehead Memorial Museum; p. 199: Sandra Bond. All other photographs by the author.

Library of Congress Cataloging-in-Publication Data

Brooks, Patricia, 1926-
    Where the bodies are ; final visits to the rich, famous, interesting/Patricia Brooks.-- 1st ed.
      p. cm.
    Includes index.
    ISBN 0-7627-2337-8
    1. Celebrities—United States—Biography. 2. Celebrities—Tombs—United States—Guidebooks. 3. Cemeteries—United States—Guidebooks. 4. United States—Biography.
    I. Title.

CT215 .B76 2002
920.073--dc21   [B]2002027112

Manufactured in the United States of America
First Edition/First Printing

DEDICATION

To Lester Brooks, my lifelong companion and fellow writer, for his endless support and encouragement, his research expertise and invaluable critique of my manuscript, and—no small matter—his willingness to provide chauffeur service and cheerful company, slogging along with me through soggy grass and bumpy burial grounds in search of elusive gravestones day after day after day.

Contents

ACKNOWLEDGMENTS

In the course of researching and writing this book, I received encouragement and invaluable assistance from many people. First of all, heartfelt thanks and appreciation belong to the helpful, dedicated team at The Globe Pequot Press who shepherded this book from concept to completion. Special thanks to executive editor Mary Norris for her sensitive advice, patience, and enthusiastic encouragement; to associate editor Imee Curiel, who cheerfully navigated me and the manuscript through the production maze; and to Casey Shain for his text design and inspired photo layouts and arrangements.

I am deeply grateful to my son Christopher Brooks for his witty and wise editorial suggestions and thoughtful review of my manuscript. Without my son Jonathan Brooks this book probably wouldn't exist; years ago in Los Angeles, his teasing words, "Want to visit some celebrities?" led me to my first Hollywood cemetery, which planted the seed of an idea that eventually grew into this book. He also helped enlarge my list of "rich and famous" spirits with a veritable "who-was-who" inventory of noteworthy names.

Warm thanks also to Jackie and John Berg for helpful suggestions about specific bodies to include in these pages; to Frances Salant Barker and Pat Nivakoff for their willingness to drive me to distant burial grounds; Richard Gerweck, who made a special trip to West Point to take pictures for me at a time, just after 9/11, when the post was off limits to civilians; and Mary Ellen Johansen for keeping me company on other grave searches. Mary Billingsley of the National Trust Historic Hotels of America was especially kind in making my Washington, D.C. research trip easier.

So many people in cemetery offices around the country provided me with useful information and stories of interest, there's not space to thank them all, but here's a special nod of appreciation to Barbara Held at Allegheny Cemetery, Pittsburgh; Beverly Jeffers at Mount Hope Cemetery, Peru, Indiana; Michelle Lefevbre at the Will Rogers Museum; and Joyce Lyng at the Sinclair Lewis Foundation.

For some of the book's photographs, I am immensely grateful also to the following helpful souls and organizations who rallied from far away places to my call for photographic "body snatching." They include:

Maureen Baxter; Christopher Berg; Thomas Berg; Marla Bexley-Lovell, Oakland Cemetery, Atlanta; Sandra Bond; Chicago Architecture Foundation; Jackie Curtis; Marty Davis, Crown Hill Cemetery; Dwight D. Eisenhower Library; Frankfort Cemetery; Frank Gillespie; Girls and Boys Town; Steve Holden, Carl Sandburg Historic Site; Katherine Keena, Juliette Gordon Low Birthplace; Philip LaGrandeur; Phillip Lovell; Clint Lynch, Texas State Cemetery, Austin; Charles E. Marchant; Nancy Milton, St. Louis Convention and Visitors Bureau; Molly Mitchell; Marion Nenstiel; Oakdale Memorial Garden, Davenport; Oak Hill Cemetery, Battle Green; Oak Ridge Cemetery, Springfield, Illinois; Terry Cody Spring; Jenny Stacy, Savannah Convention and Visitors Bureau; Louise Uffelman, Washington and Lee University; Virginia Tourism Corporation; Andy Warhol Museum.

INTRODUCTION

"A book on burial grounds? How ghoulish!" was one friend's reaction to this project. "Weird!" said another. "I never thought you were a necrophiliac," a third exclaimed.

Fortunately most people I discussed my current passion with were downright enthusiastic. "What fun!" was a frequent comment. Cemeteries seem to be on many people's "must-see" list—a nonsubversive underground movement, you might say—when visiting a specific locale. The popularity of cemeteries as tourist attractions is evidenced by how many cemeteries now provide maps to help visitors locate their famous permanent boarders.

And when you think about it, tourists have always visited graves. Consider: What else is the Taj Mahal but the most elaborate, beautiful tomb in the whole world? Yet a tomb it is, a tribute in stone of ruler Shah Jahan to his favorite departed wife, Mumtaz Mahal, in the seventeenth century, as well as the magnet that lures visitors to India as one of the world's major tourist sights, a true wonder of the world. Visitors to the pyramids in Egypt may be thinking more of the architecture than that these are tombs of Egyptian kings. In Rome crowds queue up to go down into the catacombs, where ancient Christians were disposed of, spooky as these underground chambers are.

Napoleon's tomb in Hotel des Invalides in Paris is another tourist destination. So is the English Cemetery in Rome, where English majors flock to pay their respects to John Keats and Percy Bysshe Shelley. And some of the very people who might say, "A cemetery—how odd!" are the first off the Metro to wander through Cimetière du Pere Lachaise, the Parisian graveyard that is the final home of Isadora Duncan, Oscar Wilde, Sarah Bernhardt, and, more recently, Jim Morrison, and scores of others.

There are many reasons why the living are so intrigued by the final addresses of the dead. Celebrity worship takes many forms, and an admirer of a movie star, author, musician, statesman, general, president, or some other notable wants to know everything about the admired one, even the final port of call. Visiting is a way of saying you're sorry—sorry they're gone, sorry you are older, sorry about life's passing. It's nostalgia: a remembrance of persons past who had some significance in your life.

There's also a sociological interest: How is it that someone as famous in life as, say, Rudolph Valentino, is permanently confined in a modest wall crypt in a mausoleum in Hollywood? Or why does director John Huston, whose movies filled the screen with vitality, lie so semianonymously beneath an inconspicuous plot of grass? It is fascinating, at least to me, that Judy Garland, gone since 1969, still receives bouquets of fresh flowers from her Great Britain fan club and that the grave of James Dean in Fairmount, Indiana, is covered with lipstick smears almost every day; if alive, he'd be over seventy.

These silent cities are also places in which to contemplate the vagaries of wealth and fame and how short-lived celebritydom can be. In many cemeteries the most elaborate tombs belong to people whose names are mere footnotes in history: city builders, industrialists, mayors, governors, generals, all celebrated in their time, now long forgotten. At the same time one can meditate over the graves of those to whom fame caught up too late, mere markers at the time, now sites of revered pilgrimages: jazzman Bix Beiderbecke and architect Louis Sullivan come to mind.

Observing the changes in burial styles could be the subject of a doctoral thesis (and probably already has been). The simple austerity of colonial times, with the naive engraved tombstones and their sprightly epitaphs ("Here lies Ann Mann; she lived an old maid but died an old Mann"), gave way to the ornate, often Baroque monuments, obelisks, and mausoleums of the keeping-ahead-of-the-Joneses Victorian era, with tomb messages rich in flowery epitaphs ("Jesus, in his bosom wears, the flower that once was mine"). These in turn gave way to the huge, impersonal cellblock mausoleums of today with their wall crypts and columbariums, where simple, speeded-up messages summarize an entire life ("Beloved mother • wife • sister").

Much statuary in a Victorian-era cemetery seems overwrought to "cool" twenty-first-century sensibilities, but objects then had a special "vocabulary" that the Victorians understood. For instance, a carved hand on a gravestone wasn't just a hand, it symbolized "taking leave." A sculpted sheaf of wheat suggested God's harvest, a stone daisy meant purity and youth, a lily resurrection, a rose unfailing love. Granite shaped into a tree trunk or broken column spoke of a life cut short too young, and carved drapery, whether on a figure or folded over a gravestone, represented sorrow and mourning.

Burial grounds are fascinating in and of themselves. In the mid-nineteenth century, cemeteries changed. Formerly spooky places where Washington Irving's Headless Horseman—or his real-life equivalent—was feared to be riding at midnight and ghostly things went bump in the night metamorphosed into rural parks, arboretums, and gardens, where a regular Sunday pasttime was to take a buggy ride through the beautiful grounds. Even today a visit to these parklike graveyards, such as Mount Auburn in Cambridge, Massachusetts; Woodlawn in the Bronx, New York; or Graceland in Chicago, Illinois, can be a restful and relaxing getaway. In our noise-saturated age, there is nothing more peaceful than a cemetery for cool-down time to meditate, sit and read, bird-watch, jog, or hike.

Just savoring the varied trees and shrubbery can be a reason for a graveyard visit. To our forebears certain trees, like statuary, had significance, and those at burial sites were often chosen for what they "said." This explains why burial grounds are such repositories of oak trees, symbols of "loyalty and faith." In Greek mythology the cypress tree represented the god Apollo's transformation of his dead human friend Cyparissus into a long-living cypress. This may be why so many European burial grounds are surrounded by these tall, silent guardians, which seem to be watching over those who were loved in life. The very word cemetery derives from the Greek koimētērion: a place to sleep.

Graveyard protocol, I learned during visits to hundreds of burial grounds across the country, is to maintain respect for the (unstated) rights of the inhabitants. That means (a) using walkways and paths rather than stepping on graves, (b) being relatively quiet (no loud boom boxes in hand), (c) keeping hands off flowers and plants (no souvenirs, please), and (d) parking along roadsides, not hogging access roads. Another thing I learned in my grave hopping was how helpful and cheerful most cemetery employees are, whether office personnel or groundskeepers. Perhaps this is because their full-time charges never shout, argue, talk back, question their authority, quibble over charges, or demand a refund.

One of the challenges of this book was deciding which worthy sleepers to include and which to let lie. I wanted the book to be as diverse as life—or death—itself. That's why you will find people as obscure today as Hetty Green and as omnipresent as Marilyn Monroe. Doctors, lawyers, Indian chiefs, they're all here, along with rogues and saints as well. There wasn't the ghost of a chance of doing biographic sketches of every body mentioned, but at least you'll know where to find many of those footnoted and can—ahem—unearth more about them on your own. In the course of writing this book I initially included more obituaries than there was space to accommodate them all. This meant that a number of departed had to be deleted—re-buried, so to speak. If there are any egregious omissions, in your view, let me know. Speaking up, or writing down, may not raise the dead, but it will be helpful for an afterlife in future editions.

Meanwhile, happy hunting on your own undertaking, and wherever you go, give the gang my best.

New England

For the grave seeker New England is, dare I say it, a happy haunting ground. The earliest headstones are well-carved and sometimes fanciful examples of naive folk art, and often the epitaphs convey messages that are poignant or, at the other extreme, downright hilarious. Books have been compiled featuring many pithy and mirthsome comments from New England cemeteries, like "Tears cannot restore her: therefore I weep" and the classic, "I told you I was sick."

New England burying grounds have another important distinction: They are often inhabited by people we know from our histories and from their literary works. Not all New England cemeteries are the final destinations of the rich and famous, but almost all of the really old ones shelter "interred-esting" people from all walks of life. Stumbling (sometimes literally) across a familiar name is one of many serendipitous rewards of a cemetery visit in this part of the country.

Connecticut

Mountain Grove Cemetery

BRIDGEPORT

Beautiful old-fashioned Mountain Grove Cemetery is just a minute from the roaring traffic of I-95 (exit 25), but it is so quiet and peaceful even the wild turkeys that cluck-cluck around the grounds think it, the pond, all the shade trees, and marvelous monuments are their private preserve. The cemetery was established in 1849 on land donated by P. T. Barnum. *Dewey Street at North Avenue, Bridgeport. Tel. (203) 336-3579. Grounds open 7:30 A.M.–6:30 P.M. Office located inside the gate beyond the chapel on the right; hours: 8:30 A.M.–4:00 P.M. Monday–Friday; map and pamphlets, rest room.*

PHINEAS TAYLOR BARNUM
1810–1891

"There's a sucker born every minute" was one of the most famous quotes attributed to this master showman and circus entrepreneur, who called himself "the prince of humbugs" and was a pioneer in the art of publicity and ballyhoo. He introduced soprano Jenny Lind to the United States as "the Swedish nightingale" and made her name and that of midget General Tom Thumb household words. Many of P. T. Barnum's sideshow acts and exhibits were fakes, but his larger-than-life personality and a credulous public's willingness to be fooled over and over again made him world famous, as did his three-ring circus, which was, in his words, "the greatest show on earth." Bridgeport's most celebrated son and mayor gave the city the flamboyant building that is now the Barnum Museum (820 Main Street; 203–331–9881), full of exhibits and examples of his trickery, hoopla, and feats. The inscription "Not my will but thine be done" on Barnum's grave (inside an attractive gray granite border, to the left of his towering granite monument) suggests a modesty rarely evident in life.

TOM THUMB
1838–1883

Carrying "the last shall be first" idea to a new height, this towering 40-foot-high white marble tribute (see opposite) to one of the world's smallest human beings (40 inches high) is, probably intentionally, one of the tallest monuments in the cemetery. Tom's real name was Charles S.

Stratton. A Bridgeport native with a pituitary deficiency, he was four years old when Barnum discovered him, publicizing him as eleven and later calling him "General" Tom Thumb. Barnum's hoopla brought the perfectly formed midget fame, fortune, overseas travel, and several visits to Queen Victoria. At twenty-three, he married Lavinia Warren, a petite 32 inches tall, and their much-publicized nuptials — attended by 2,000 — ended with a visit to President and Mrs. Lincoln in the White House. Today Stratton's life-size statue stands tall atop its column, staring across time (and a narrow roadway) at his mentor.

The Burying Ground

F A R M I N G T O N

The Burying Ground is the oldest cemetery extant (circa 1661) in one of Connecticut's appealing smaller towns. The imposing wooden gate, modeled after that of Grove Street Cemetery in New Haven, bears the words Memento Mori at the top. All the headstones (mostly made of red stone, which flakes and disintegrates) face the road, easier for the passerby to read—except one, which faces the hill in the opposite direction. This belonged to a Tory whose property was confiscated. He wanted to be buried backward, so that on Judgment Day he wouldn't have to face his tormentors. His stone tells the story: "In memory of **Mathias Leaming** who has gott beyond the reach of persecution. The life of man is vanity." Also here is **Samuel Hooker** (1633–1697), the town's second pastor and son of Thomas Hooker, one of Hartford's founders. One of my favorite stones reads in its entirety: "In memory of **Nodiah Bird** who was killed by an insane person May 17, 1835." *123 Main Street, Farmington. Grounds open all the time.*

Riverside Cemetery

F A R M I N G T O N

Dating from 1838, Riverside Cemetery is located on a quiet road above the old abandoned Farmington Canal. The burial grounds shelter no flashy names, but many intriguing ones, such as **William Gillette** (1853–1937), Broadway actor whose interpretation of Sherlock Holmes modernized the role for all time; **Lambert Hitchcock** (1795–1852), who invented the Hitchcock chair (still being produced in Riverton, Connecticut); **John Treadwell Norton** (1795–1869) and his wife, **Elizabeth Cogswell Norton** (1803–1876), who were active in the Underground Railroad; and **Winchell Smith** (1871–1933), a playwright who persuaded Lillian Gish to film *Way Down East* in Farmington. *160 Garden Street, Farmington. Tel. (860) 674–0280. Grounds open all the time. Office hours: irregular; map available, but not very specific. It is better to ask a grounds worker for precise grave locations. If you enter the gate on the far right, follow the curving drive down to a garage. The office is inside. The local Heritage Trails Sightseeing Tours offers a Halloween Graveyards Tour of both these local cemeteries. Tel. (860) 677–8867 for information.*

FOONE
–1841

Although the words incised on this small upright stone have faded with time, a new bronze marker at its base reiterates the original inscription: "Foone, a native African who was drowned while bathing in the Center Basin August 1841. He was one of the company of slaves under Cinque on board the schooner Amistad who asserted their rights and took possession of the vessel after having put the captain, mate and others to death, sparing their masters, Ruez and Montez." Foone, one of fifty-two surviving slaves vindicated by a trial in New Haven, at which John Quincy Adams was their defense lawyer, had to work to gain money for his passage back to Africa. Unfortunately, he didn't make it, drowning in the newly built Farmington Canal. The gray stone column with bronze marker next to his simple grave designates his headstone as part of Connecticut's Freedom Trail. Grave and column are just to the left of the road that leads from the cemetery's South Gate.

SARAH PORTER
1813–1900

Porter is a name to be reckoned with in Farmington, as a family that traces its ancestry back to the town's beginnings in 1640. Unusual for a female of her era, Sarah—fluent in Greek, Latin, French, and German, with knowledge of history, mathematics, and other studies—taught school in Springfield, Massachusetts; Philadelphia; and Buffalo. In 1843 she returned to her hometown and opened Miss Porter's School, which became one of New England's most distinguished preparatory schools. Jackie Bouvier Kennedy Onassis was an alumna. Sarah's father, **Noah Porter** (1781–1866), was for sixty years pastor of the town's Congregational church. His nearby red granite stone, far more imposing than Sarah's simple gray granite rec-

tangle, bears a green-patina-etched bronze oak leaf wreath with the inscription: "Them also, which sleep in Jesus, will God bring with him." Sarah's accomplished brother, Noah, became president of Yale and is buried in New Haven.

Cedar Hill Cemetery

H A R T F O R D

Even if Cedar Hill Cemetery were bereft of heavenly bodies, it would be worth a visit for the beauty of the grounds, serene little lake (Llyn Mawr), scenic walkways, and a chapel at the entrance gate. Within its 270-acre boundaries lie such people as **Samuel Colt** (1814–1862), inventor of the Colt revolver, whose arms factory was at one time the world's largest; **Thomas Gallaudet** (1787–1851), founder of the American School for the Deaf; **Isabella Beecher Hooker** (1822–1907), ardent abolitionist and suffragette, sister of Harriet Beecher Stowe; the poet **Wallace Stevens** (1879–1955); and **Charles Dudley Warner** (1829–1900), publisher and coauthor with Mark Twain of *The Gilded Years*. *453 Fairfield Avenue, Hartford. Tel. (860) 956-3311. Grounds open sunrise to sunset; jogging permitted. Office hours: 8:00 A.M.–4:00 P.M. Monday–Friday; map and other information available from helpful staff; rest rooms. A free* Guide to the Notable Trees of Cedar Hill Cemetery *identifies the park's many rare old trees. Walking tours (fee).*

JOHN PIERPONT MORGAN
1 8 3 7 – 1 9 1 3

At first sight the glowing pink granite oblong on top of a small hillock resembles a huge safety-deposit box — fitting for America's best-known banker. But viewed close-up, the message on the handsomely incised stone calls it an interpretation of the biblical Ark of the Covenant. J. P. Morgan, the prototype of a Wall Street financier, was a Hartford native. The son of a banker (**Junius Spencer Morgan**, buried here in the same family vault), Pierpont, as he was known, was educated at the University of Gottingen,

Sweden. By 1895, as head of his own banking firm, he was also one of the richest men in the world. His name still epitomizes wealth. An enthusiastic sailor, he was once asked the cost of a yacht and supposedly replied, "If you have to ask, you can't afford one." Morgan was also a generous patron of New York's Metropolitan Museum of Art and Museum of Natural History. His former home, now the **Pierpont Morgan Library** in New York City (29 East 36th Street; 212–685–0610), houses much of his vast collection of books, illuminated manuscripts, and art objects.

Old North Cemetery

HARTFORD

Old North Cemetery, on the northern edge of Hartford, may be the best possible argument for funding graveyard upkeep. Formerly a place of pride and grandeur, where many Hartford VIPs, such as **Horace Bushnell** (1802–1876), theologian and Congregationalist minister, were buried, it is now a ghostly ruin, beset by weeds and poison ivy, surrounded by a rundown neighborhood. Headstones have been overturned and vandalized, and the asphalt road is rutted and decayed. It is especially dispiriting that **Frederick Law Olmsted** (1822–1903), America's first great landscape architect, lies here with his family in a metal vault built into a hillock, with a large imposing pink granite memorial above it. Surrounded by unmowed grass, it is a far cry from Central Park in Manhattan, Prospect Park in Brooklyn, Fairmount Park in Philadelphia, and other of his landscaping triumphs. He must be spinning in his grave. *1821 Main Street, Hartford. Grounds open all the time. Do not visit alone or after dark.*

Spring Grove Cemetery

HARTFORD

Spring Grove Cemetery, at Hartford's north end, is located to the left of and behind the AME Zion church. The thirty-five-acre burial grounds date back to 1800. Note the gigantic Vermont marble Celtic cross, belonging to relatives of J. P. Morgan— so large it took a team of thirty-four horses to drag it from the train station. *2035 Main Street, Hartford. Tel. (860) 525-8502. Grounds open 8:00 A.M.–5:00 P.M. weekdays, 8:00 A.M.–6:00 P.M. weekends. Office hours: 8:00 A.M.–12:00 P.M. Monday–Friday; map, rest room.*

FREDERICK EDWIN CHURCH

1826–1900

One of America's most celebrated nineteenth-century painters, represented in all major U.S. museum collections, Church was born in Hartford. Having studied with Thomas Cole in Catskill, New York, he made his name as the leading painter of the Hudson River School. Best known for his technical dexterity, use of color, and his luminous landscapes, Church also painted scenes of the Andes, based on two visits to South America. In 1872, after extensive travels abroad, Church built **Olana**, a faux Moorish fantasy home, high above the Hudson River (5 miles south of Hudson, New York, on New York Highway 9 G; 518-828-0135). It is open to the public and is a unique reflection of Church's artistic sensibility, far more so than his unassuming family grave here.

Lakeview Cemetery

NEW CANAAN

Tiny Lakeview Cemetery is less than a mile off the Merritt Parkway (exit 38). Its winding roads, set among ponds and flowering trees, make for pleasant walking or jogging. Among its residents are **William Attwood** (1919–1989), author, editor of *Look,* publisher of *Newsday,* and U.S. Ambassador to Guinea and Kenya; **John Robert Gregg** (1864–1984), inventor of a widely used shorthand system; **Peter van Steeden** (1904–1990), orchestra leader of the mid-twentieth century; and **John Rogers** (1829–1904), whose "Rogers group" sculptures were the rage of middle-class American households in the nineteenth century (his studio is part of the **New Canaan Historical Society** complex at 13 Oenoke Ridge Road; 203-966-1776). *South Main Street, New Canaan. Tel. (203) 966-1861. Grounds open 7:00 A.M.–dusk. Office hours: 7:00 A.M.–3:30 P.M. Monday–Friday; map, rest room.*

MAXWELL EVARTS PERKINS

1884–1947

What do Thomas Wolfe, Ernest Hemingway, and F. Scott Fitzgerald have in common? They were all discovered by the same editor, Max Perkins. Editors are usually unsung, but Perkins was widely praised for his skills in nurturing and encouraging authors. Perkins edited, cut, trimmed, and restructured Wolfe's unwieldy works into readable, popular novels. To Fitzgerald, Perkins became a financial advisor, helping the spendthrift author manage his money. Perkins also edited Ring Lardner, Marjorie Kinnan Rawlings's *The Yearling*, and was working on James Jones's *From Here to Eternity* when he died.

Grove Street Cemetery

Grove Street Cemetery dates back to 1796, but its imposing, and rare, Egyptian Revival gate was an 1845 addition. The grounds look small, surrounded on three sides by brownstone walls, but encompass eighteen acres and some 15,000 people. This was one of the first burial grounds to be laid out in a grid pattern. Among the many luminaries buried along the lanes shaded by oak, copper beech, birch, and dogwood trees are **Lyman Beecher** (1775–1863), abolitionist and father of Harriet Beecher Stowe; **Charles Goodyear** (1800–1860), inventor of the process of vulcanizing rubber; **Jedediah Morse** (1761–1826), the father of American geography; various Yale University presidents, including **Noah Porter** (1811–1892), the eleventh; **Roger Sherman** (1721–1793), judge, senator, and the only founding father to sign all four great documents of the new Republic; and **Eli Whitney** (1763-1825), inventor of the cotton gin, which resulted in the prolongation of slavery in the South. A memorial to the left of the office commemorates six *Amistad* slaves who died in 1839 (where they are buried nobody knows, but it's not here), never making it back to Sierra Leone. The grounds are easy to explore, with lanes named for trees: sycamore, spruce, laurel, and the like. *227 Grove Street, New Haven. Tel. (203) 787-1443. Grounds open 8:00 A.M.–4:00 P.M. daily. Office hours: 9:00 A.M.–12:00 P.M.; map and brochure, rest rooms. Free guided tours 11:00 A.M. Saturdays, but call in advance.*

WALTER CAMP
1 8 5 9 – 1 9 2 5

If football fans don't recognize this name, a polished black granite marker, with his picture etched into it, should help. It lies in front of Camp's classical headstone and commemorates him as the "father of American football, an outstanding athlete and coach, and the single most important figure in the development of American football, recognized as the final authority on football rules in his lifetime." A successful businessman and prominent New Haven civic leader, Camp selected his first All-American team in 1889.

BARTLETT "BART" GIAMATTI
1938–1989

Latinist, Renaissance scholar, and full Yale professor at age thirty-three, Giamatti was such a Boston Red Sox fan that when he was elected Yale University's nineteenth president (1978–1986), he said, "Actually, the only thing I want to be is president of the American League." The youngest Yale president in the university's 200-year history, Giamatti inherited a $2 million deficit, but managed to balance the budget in four years. After retiring, he indulged a lifelong interest in baseball by becoming president of the National League. Two years later (1988) he was Commissioner of Major League Baseball. An extended controversy and subsequent stress over the gambling activities of player-manager Pete Rose and whether or not he violated league rules by betting on baseball led to Rose's lifetime ban from the game and, some believe, to Giamatti's sudden heart attack and death.

NOAH WEBSTER
1758–1843

Lawyer, judge, member of the Connecticut House of Representatives, teacher, grammarian, journalist—all these, but this West Hartford native's main claim to lasting fame is as the compiler of the first American dictionary. He first published *A Grammatical Institute of the English Language* over a two-year period (1783–1785). Its huge financial success helped him support his family for the twenty years it took to write his major opus, *The First American Dictionary* (1828). (One story goes that when Webster was working on this book, his wife discovered him in his study, locked in an embrace with a young servant. "Noah, I am surprised," said his wife. "No, my dear," he replied, "I am surprised, you are astonished.") He finished a revision of the appendix to the second edition a few days before his death. The birth and death dates on Webster's gray granite cenotaph are effaced—an ironic finale for a man obsessed with words. The Noah Webster birth house (227 South Main Street, West Hartford; 860–521–5362) is now the **West Hartford Historical Society** and is open to the public.

Long Ridge Union Cemetery

STAMFORD

On a narrow shaded road in North Stamford, you'll find the Long Ridge Union Cemetery, a classic country graveyard abutting woodlands. Too small to have an office, the oak-and-pine-shaded cemetery is nevertheless large enough to make a grave hunt time consuming, unless you happen to visit when the helpful grounds crew is present. Though lacking monumental mausoleums and cenotaphs, this burying ground has five notable twentieth-century graves, all in the vicinity of the center and right entrance gates. Less famous now is **Kenny Delmar** (1910–1984), comic radio actor whose "characters" contributed to the popularity of *The Fred Allen Show* in the 1940s. *Erskine Road, Stamford. Grounds open from dawn to dusk.*

BENNY GOODMAN
1 9 0 9 – 1 9 8 6

The contrast between Goodman's modest gravestone (inscribed "Benjamin David Goodman"), almost buried in the grass, and the stature of one of the twentieth century's greatest jazz musicians couldn't be greater. Goodman, born in Chicago, was playing the clarinet professionally at age twelve and carried a union card at thirteen. His first big success as a band leader-cum-performer came in 1934, the beginning of the swing era. Internationally known as the "King of Swing" for the magic fluidity of his clarinet and the smoothness of his sound, Goodman was the first to mix the races in his band and the first to play jazz at Carnegie Hall. His unusual ease with both jazz and classical music led to gigs as a soloist with many classical orchestras later in life. Though criticized as a tough task master, he let the end results speak (or sing) for themselves. "Sing Sing Sing," Benny.

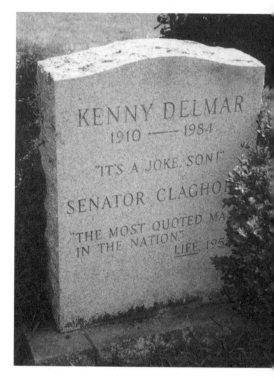

GILDA RADNER
1 9 4 6 – 1 9 8 9

The life of this talented comedienne was unkindly cut short by ovarian cancer, but broadcasts of her hilarious characterizations (Rosanna Rosannadana, Emily Laetella, and Baba Wawa, a take-off of Barbara Walters) live on. She was one of the first stars of the television comedy show *Saturday Night Live,* which was at its most successful when she, Chevy Chase, Bill Murray, and John Belushi were part of the repertory company. She was married

to comedian Gene Wilder and lived in Stamford. While her tombstone—bordered with small rocks, faced by a little bench, shaded by a fruit tree, and marked by a pink azalea bush—reads "Comedienne-Ballerina," few fans would consider her anything but a very funny lady.

WALTER "RED" SMITH
1 9 0 5 – 1 9 8 2

The large gray granite rectangle proclaiming "Walter Wellesley Smith" seems curiously pretentious for a man known for his informal writing and offhand approach to fame. Considered one of the best sportswriters in the United States, he received a

Pulitzer Prize in 1976 for the colorful commentary in his column "Sports of the Times" in the *New York Times*. It was only the second time a Pulitzer was given to a sportswriter. In a long career Smith worked for many newspapers, beginning with the *Milwaukee Sentinel* in his home state of Wisconsin. During the Depression, when newspaper work paid little, he remembered, "I was attached to newspapers like an undernourished barnacle." He remained a reporter/columnist all his life, also authoring several books in his deceptively simple writing style. He once described how he wrote: "I just open a vein and bleed."

GENE TUNNEY
1897–1978

James Joseph Tunney was better known as "Gene" to thousands of boxing fans in the early twentieth century. One of three sons in a large New York Irish family, as a kid Gene liked acting and Greek and Roman history. He was a gawky ten-year-old when his father gave him boxing gloves to learn to defend himself. Young Gene grew to love the strategy of boxing, becoming the thinking man's boxer. His ambition, after he won the U.S. light heavyweight title in 1922, was to someday beat Jack Dempsey, the reigning heavyweight champ. It seemed unlikely at the time, but just four years later he did, only to repeat the feat the following year in a fight known for its controversial "long count." Tunney retired as world champion and millionaire in 1928. He married, made a second fortune in business, traveled widely, became friends with literary figures like George Bernard Shaw, lectured at Yale, and saw one of his four children (John) become a U.S. senator from California. It was a classic only-in-America success story, which ended fittingly in toney Greenwich, Connecticut.

West Cemetery

AMHERST

West Cemetery is the kind of unassuming, old-fashioned, eighteenth-century New England village burial ground in the center of town where you'd expect to find Amherst's most famous native, along with many other Dickinson relatives. *The entrance is off Triangle Street, Amherst. Grounds open from dawn to dusk.*

EMILY DICKINSON
1 8 3 0 – 1 8 8 6

Widely considered one of America's best poets, this homebody was born, lived, and died in the same house in Amherst. There was only one hint of mystery in her life. In 1854, after a family visit to Washington, D.C., Emily stopped by herself to visit a friend in Philadelphia. When she returned home she suddenly began writing love poems and became increasingly reclusive. What happened? Did she meet and fall for a mysterious stranger? Only Emily knows for sure and she's beyond telling. To her family and friends, she was known for her wit, sense of fun, and her love of gardens and music—traits obvious in her brief poems, which are surprisingly timeless. Only two were published during her life, but some 800 of them filled five volumes afterward. The inscription on her white tombstone is suitably pithy: "born December 10, 1830, called back May 15, 1886." Called back, yes, but she is still in the midst of her family, in a plot separated from the rest of the residents by a wrought iron fence. **The Dickinson Homestead** (280 Main Street; 413–542–8161), her birthplace and lifelong home, is open to visitors.

Granary Burying Ground

B O S T O N

Granary Burying Ground is a Boston landmark and a must stop for history buffs, even those without a mania for cemeteries. Established on property that was once the town granary, this burial ground dates back to 1660 and is one of the oldest in America. Nowadays it has been almost smothered by high-rise buildings on three sides, which is the price it pays for being in the center of the city's business district. On this turf are scores of early patriots, governors, and three signers of the Declaration of Independence. Residents include **Benjamin Franklin's parents** (remember, he was from Boston); **Mary Goose** (died 1690), dubbed Mother Goose by the folks who stop by her ancient, decorated headstone; **John Hancock** (1736–1793), a wealthy merchant and nine-term governor of Massachusetts; and **Robert Treat Paine** (1731–1814), Revolutionary War leader. *Tremont Street, opposite the Suffolk County Courthouse. Grounds open from dawn to dusk.*

SAMUEL ADAMS
1 7 2 2 – 1 8 0 3

One of the sparks who ignited the American Revolution, Adams was a Boston-born, Harvard-educated lawyer, considered a firebrand for his anti-compromise positions in the revolutionary councils. He wrote scores of articles for newspapers, under a variety of noms de plume, urging that a Continental Congress be called. When it was, he was a delegate (from 1774 to

1781) who forcefully opposed concessions to Britain. Though not a gifted orator, he was an effective writer with a logical mind, who had a flair for epigrams and appeals to action. After the Boston Massacre, he arranged for the British soldiers to be removed without incident to a fort in the harbor. He was also an effective manager of the Boston Tea Party. In a life dedicated to public service, he was a signer of the Declaration of Independence, member of the Massachusetts delegation to ratify the U.S. Constitution, lieutenant governor (1789–1794), and then governor (1794–1797). Eclipsed in history by his second cousin, John Adams, Samuel played his role in the American Revolution to the hilt. Few could ask for anything more.

CRISPUS ATTUCKS
1 7 2 3 – 1 7 7 0
To the right of the cemetery gates is a huge rough-hewn stone commemorating the five men who were killed in the Boston Massacre. One was Crispus Attucks, the leader of the protest mob that precipitated the massacre. Although he is featured in history books as the first African American to fight for his country, so little is known about him that historians aren't even sure he was a black man. Some believe he was an Indian, a member of the Natick tribe from nearby Framingham; others think he was a mulatto who had run away from his owner, Deacon William Browne of Framingham. Another theory is that he was a sailor on a whaling vessel; and still another is that he was of mixed African and Indian heritage. What is known is that it was a stressful time. Locals did not like the presence of British troops in Boston, and on that fateful evening of March 5, 1770, Attucks led fifty or sixty men, mostly sailors, on a march from Dock Square to State Street. They were accosted by a small contingent of nervous British troops. Shots were fired and three of the mob, including Attucks, were killed instantly. Two more died later. This episode fueled the fires of rebellion that led to the American Revolutionary War five years later. Thus are heroes—and legends—born.

PAUL REVERE
1 7 3 5 – 1 8 1 8
There's more to this Boston-born patriot than his famous midnight ride from Charlestown to Lexington (April 18–19, 1775) to warn the countryside of the British troops coming from Boston (as depicted in Henry Wadsworth Longfellow's poem). Revere, trained as a goldsmith and silversmith, was a leader of the Boston Tea Party; induced the citizens of Portsmouth, New Hampshire, to attack and capture Fort William and Mary (one of the first acts of military force in the war); commanded Castle William, which defended Boston Harbor; and served in an expedition to Rhode Island in 1778. Then, of course, there is all that beautiful silver he produced—a legacy that lives on. His monument, like his silver, is simple and straightforward, stating only: "born in Boston January, 1734, died May 1818." **The Paul Revere House** (19 North Square; 617–523–2338), circa 1680, the only structure from the seventeenth century that still exists in downtown Boston, has family memorabilia and is open to view.

Cambridge Cemetery

A municipal burial ground on sixty-six acres, Cambridge Cemetery opened in 1854 and shelters veterans of the many wars that have ensued since then. Here also are several members of Cambridge's cultural elite. **William Dean Howells** (1837–1920), a literary light of the late nineteenth century, whose best-known novel is *The Rise of Silas Lapham*, rests here, along with his family. Nearby, in a site similarly defined by low redbrick walls that separate their family plots from others, are members of the cerebral **James** family. *76 Coolidge Avenue, Cambridge. Tel. (617) 349–4890. Grounds open 8:30 A.M.–5:00 P.M. daily. Office hours: 7:00 A.M.–3:00 P.M. Monday–Friday; map, rest room.*

HENRY JAMES
1 8 4 3 – 1 9 1 6

For decades this author's ornate, oblique style has limited the reading of his novels to English majors and literary enthusiasts. Mark Twain once said, "I would rather be condemned to John Bunyan's heaven" than finish reading James's *The Bostonians*. But recent movies and television plays adapted from *Portrait of a Lady*, *Wings of the Dove*, and *The Golden Bowl* have renewed interest in this master's works. Born in New York City, James spent much of his adult life in England and died there. Most of his novels subtly depict the relationships between upper class Americans vis à vis titled Europeans. Considering his affinity for England, and the fact that he became a British citizen as a gesture of support during World War I, James's fans may be surprised to find his final address this side of the Atlantic. At his funeral in London's Chelsea Old Church, friends who mourned included Rudyard Kipling, John Singer Sargent, and actress Ellen Terry. James was cremated and the ashes smuggled back to the United States (it was wartime and his sister-in-law was afraid of trouble with U.S. Customs) and placed in an urn buried beside his father. His gravestone reads: "Henry James O.M. Novelist-Citizen of two countries—Interpreter of his generation on both sides of the sea." (O.M. stands for Order of Merit,

the highest award in Britain, given only by the monarch and only for outstanding artistic or intellectual achievement.) James's distinguished relations, including father **Henry** and sister **Alice**, are now within the same brick borders, in whispering distance of one another.

Mount Auburn Cemetery

C A M B R I D G E

Mount Auburn Cemetery, Cambridge's other graveyard, located just across the road, is its most famous and was consecrated in 1831. Inspired by Pere Lachaise in Paris, it served as a model for many of the garden-style burial grounds built across the United States in the nineteenth century, with 172 acres of hills, ponds, a Gothic chapel, gardens, winding roads, fastidious landscaping, paths named for trees and birds, monuments, sculptures, rare trees, shrubs, and flowers. Mount Auburn is the last known address of a veritable who-was-who list of notables prominent in Boston's cultural and civic life. The well-manicured grounds welcomed **Jean Louis Agassiz** (1807–1873), Swiss-born biologist-naturalist, and Harvard professor of zoology; **Nathaniel Bowditch** (1773–1838), mathematician and navigational expert; **Dorothea Dix** (1802–1887), philanthropist; **Felix Frankfurter** (1882–1965), U.S. Supreme Court justice appointed by Franklin Roosevelt; **Charles Dana Gibson** (1867–1944), illustrator who created the popular "Gibson Girl"; and **Oliver Wendell Holmes** (1809–1894), writer, physician, Harvard professor, and author of a popular essay series called the *Autocrat of the Breakfast Table*. There are more, lots more, to be discovered as you wander along the paths and over the undulating hills, including **Julia Ward Howe** (1819–1910), leading abolitionist, suffragette, and poet who wrote "The Battle Hymn of the Republic"; **Amy Lowell** (1874–1925), poet, critic, and lecturer who received the Pulitzer Prize for poetry in 1926; and **Bernard Malamud** (1914–1986), novelist. *580 Mount Auburn Street, Cambridge. Tel. (617) 547-7105. Grounds open 8:00 A.M.–5:00 P.M. Office hours: 8:30 A.M.–4:30 P.M. weekdays, until 12:30 P.M. Saturday; map, rest rooms, brochures on trees, birds, special programs, seasonal talks, walks, and tours.*

EDWIN BOOTH
1 8 3 3 – 1 8 9 3

The nineteenth century's leading Shakespearean actor, Booth learned his craft touring with his father, Junius Brutus Booth, but far surpassed him in ability and fame. Older brother of John Wilkes Booth, Edwin was loyal to the Union cause and didn't suffer professionally from his brother's ignominious act, perhaps because his reputation was already well established. In 1869 Edwin opened his own theater, Booth's, in New York and triumphed for years as Hamlet, Macbeth, Benedick, Romeo, and Othello. The words beneath his bronze funereal bas relief, with its theatrical profile, read: "I will turn their mourning and will comfort them and make them rejoice from their sorrow—Jeremiah XXX, 13." A trouper to the end.

CHARLES BULFINCH
1763–1844

As a privileged fourth-generation Bostonian, Bulfinch enjoyed a youthful, post-Harvard Grand Tour of Europe. On this trip he was befriended by Thomas Jefferson and the Marquis de Lafayette, but it was the beauty of Europe's many neoclassical buildings that really caught his fancy. A leading architect of postcolonial America, Bulfinch changed the face of Boston and became even more famous as the architect of the U.S. Capitol, a work that took twelve years to complete. He also designed the Old State House in Hartford, Connecticut, and many other splendid neoclassical buildings. The ornate English urn at the top of his grave pedestal is adorned with the graceful Renaissance-style detailing he so obviously loved.

MARY BAKER EDDY
1821–1910

Mrs. Eddy was nearly seventy when she founded the Church of Christ Scientist; she was eighty-seven when she followed up with the newspaper, the *Christian Science Monitor*. For much of her earlier life, she was chronically ill with nervous seizures, spinal problems, and other disorders. Things turned around dramatically for her after she met Dr. Phineas Quimby, a clockmaker-turned-doctor

and mesmerist who used faith healing and mental persuasion to heal patients. Sparked by his help in her recovery from a bad accident, Mrs. Eddy became convinced that one could heal oneself through prayer and positive thinking. The words that rim her burial pavilion—a colonaded Greek temple overlooking a small lake (see above) —proclaim "MARY BAKER EDDY • DISCOVERER AND FOUNDER OF CHRISTIAN SCIENCE • AUTHOR OF SCIENCE AND HEALTH WITH KEY TO THE SCRIPTURES." The power of positive healing had its limits: She died of a severe cold two days after one of her daily carriage rides. But then, living to age eighty-nine in 1910 wasn't half-bad.

FANNIE MERRITT FARMER
1857–1915

This energetic Boston lady edited the first *Boston Cooking School Cook Book* in 1896, which, over the course of twenty-one editions, found its way into more kitchens than she ever did. In 1902 she established Miss Farmer's School of Cookery to train housewives in the art and craft of cooking. Difficult as it is to imagine now, in her day cooking was not a science and recipes were, to say the least, inexact. She brought system and an ambitious array of recipes to a newly middle-class public that had enthusiasm but little culinary knowledge. If you have trouble finding her grave even with the map, no wonder. It's a large ivy-smothered gray granite boulder, bearing only three family names: "MERRITT • FARMER • PERKINS." Very cryptic.

BUCKMINSTER FULLER
1895–1983

Author, inventor, architect, mathmetician, cartographer, engineer, poet, philosopher, futurist—Fuller was as close to a Renaissance man as seen in the twentieth century. One of his ideas was to enclose a maximum amount of space and usable surface with a minimum of materials. Presto: In 1948 the geodesic dome was born. It made a hit as the American pavilion in the Montreal World's Fair in 1967 and seems ubiquitous today. "You can't re-order the world by talking to it," he once said. But according to colleagues, he was a great conversationalist and his talk was always worth listening to. It's one of life's (or death's) ironies that Fuller, with his futuristic visions, now lies forever under the same sheltering giant oak tree as Charles Bulfinch, a fellow architect whose creative inspirations were always of the past.

ISABELLA STEWART GARDNER
1840–1924

There are almost as many stories about Mrs. Jack Gardner as there are works of art in her fabulously idiosyncratic art museum. The difference is the art is authentic and many of the stories are not. She was a beautiful socialite and art collector who, after the death of her baby son (not quite two years old), turned her grief into a passion for art and socializing. Her salon was the gathering place in the 1880s and 1890s for artists, musicians, and writers. In 1903 she turned her magnificent home into the **Isabella Stewart Gardner Museum** (280 The Fenway, Boston; 617–734–1359). The Gardner has its own rules, as individualistic as its donor: No art works can be lent and no displays can be changed—ever. These restrictions are as permanent as her imposing family mausoleum.

WINSLOW HOMER
1836–1910

Boston born and world famous, Homer is much loved for his watercolor seascapes, mainly painted in Gloucester. *Inside the Bar, Wrecking of a Vessel,* and *Lost on the Grand Banks* are among the best known. Earlier works, many of battle scenes during the Civil War, were done when he was at the front sketching for *Harper's Weekly.* It's a rare major art museum that lacks some watercolors, paintings, or sketches by this prolific artist. In contrast to the vitality of his art, the Homer family plot seems oddly austere and plain.

HENRY WADSWORTH LONGFELLOW
1807–1882

With longevity befitting his name, the Maine-born, Bowdoin-educated poet spent eighteen years as a professor of

French and head of Harvard's modern language program. In his words, his "poetic dreams were shaded by French irregular verbs," a reference to the fact that so much of his working life was spent teaching French rather than composing poetry, as he might have preferred. Even so, he managed to produce poems, travel sketches, novels, and other writings. His most famous works were the long narrative poems: "Evangeline," "The Song of Hiawatha," "The Wreck of the Hesperus," and "The Courtship of Miles Standish." Although rarely read today, during the nineteenth century he was the country's most beloved poet, admired at home and abroad for the easy accessibility of his verse. The Georgian-style **Longfellow home and garden** (105 Brattle Street; 617–876– 4491) are open to the public.

ROBERT GOULD SHAW
1 8 3 7 – 1 8 6 3

Thanks to the movie *Glory*, which told the story of the young colonel in the Union army in charge of the African American 54th Massachusetts Infantry, we know a little something about this brave young man who fought and died in the Civil War at Fort Wagner, South Carolina, and was buried there July 19, 1863, in a mass grave. The Greek-style monument erected to his memory states: "Greater love hath no man than this. That a man lay down his life for his friends."

Diagonally across the road from his memorial is a mammoth sphinx by Boston sculptor Martin Milmore, dated 1872—one of Mount Auburn's most spectacular works. The words on its pediment are a tribute to the Union cause in the Civil War: "American Union preserved, African slavery destroyed by the uprising of a great people, by the flood of fallen heroes." Although the sphinx has no direct connection with Shaw, the juxtaposition of the two Civil War memorials seems fitting.

Sleepy Hollow Cemetery

CONCORD

Sleepy Hollow Cemetery, in the center of town, nestles into more than one hollow. It's a series of hollows, hills, ridges, and narrow roads heavily shaded by oaks and pines, and punctuated by hydrangeas. The "Authors' Ridge" section is the object of most pilgrimages here, as it is home to many of Concord's past luminaries, including the visionary **Bronson Alcott** (1799–1888), Father of Transcendentalism, educator, idealist, and father of **Louisa May Alcott**; and sculptor **Daniel Chester French** (1850–1931), whose monumental public works include the seated Lincoln within the Lincoln Memorial in Washington, D.C. Here also is French's *Mourning Victory*, honoring the three Melvin brothers who died fighting for the Union in the Civil War. *Bedford Street, Concord. Tel. (978) 318-3230. Grounds open 7:00 A.M.– dusk. The office is an old frame house located inside the new cemetery section, first entrance on the left; hours: 7:00 A.M.–3:30 P.M. weekdays, but erratic, as the office is manned by the maintenance staff who are often outside; map, rest room.*

LOUISA MAY ALCOTT
1832–1888

Although *Little Women* was written in 1868, the autobiographical novel's upbeat cheerfulness and pathos continue to speak to generations of American girls, both in book and movie form. The author (obviously Jo, the heroine) was one of four sisters whose family lived in genteel poverty. Louisa May worked hard at any job that would bring in money for the family, from doll dressmaker and nurse to writer of potboilers. Success finally came with *Little Women.* Devoted to the causes of abolition and women's suffrage, suffering from poor health and overwork, she died at age fifty-six, just two days after her father, who is buried within the same modest enclosure. The ground in front of her tiny granite marker (with initials L.M.A.) is often covered with pebbles and pine cones, tributes from visitors. **Orchard House** (399 Lexington Road; 978–369–4118), the Alcott home where she wrote *Little Women,* is open to the public and is considered one of the most appealing of nineteenth-century New England houses.

RALPH WALDO EMERSON
1803–1882

In the 1870s and 1880s, when Concord was a den of literary life, Emerson was one of its lions. The town was so renowned that Louisa May Alcott satirized it as a "modern Mecca," with visitors flocking there on pilgrimage. Emerson came from a line of preachers. Writer, poet, essayist, lecturer, teacher (Thoreau was his student), abolitionist, minister, mystic, he was intrigued by the relationship between nature and the mind of man, which led to his espousal of a philosophy called Transcendentalism. Emerson's *Threnody* is considered one of the finest elegies in English and his *Nature* and *Essays* are still read and respected. His tombstone, in the rear of a grassy enclosure bursting with twenty-two Emersons, is a large yellow-rose quartz rock, bearing a bronze marker decorated with art nouveau flourishes (see following page). It reads: "The passive Master lent his hand, to the vast soul that o'er him planned" (from his poem "The Problem"). **Emerson's Concord home** (28 Cambridge Turnpike; 978–369–2236), with many of his belongings, is

open to the public, as is the **Old Manse** (Monument Street at the North Bridge; 978–369–3909), the eighteenth-century parsonage where Emerson's grandfather Reverend William Emerson lived.

NATHANIEL HAWTHORNE
1 8 0 4 – 1 8 6 4

Hawthorne was born and spent much of his early life in Salem, not a jolly place at the time. Haunted by the early death of his father and by a mother who thrived on sorrow, shutters, and a life of grieving, Hawthorne did his own hiding in his works, with such bewitching themes as sin, guilt, evil, and repentence. Surprisingly for such a reclusive spirit, he joined the utopian Brook Farm community, leaving a few months before his late (he was thirty-eight at the time), happy marriage to

Sophia Peabody. Fame if not financial success followed with *The Scarlet Letter, The House of Seven Gables, Mosses from an Old Manse,* and *The Blithedale Romance* (based on his experiences at Brook Farm). In 1860 Hawthorne, his wife, and three children moved into **The Wayside** (455 Lexington Road; 978–369–6975), the Concord house where the Alcotts had lived when Louisa May was a child. But Nathaniel didn't have long to enjoy it: He died of cancer four years later. The house is open to the public.

HENRY DAVID THOREAU
1 8 1 7 – 1 8 6 2

This poet, essayist, naturalist, and supreme individualist continues to exert influence far beyond his simple grave. His essay *Civil Disobedience* fueled Mahatma Gandhi and Martin Luther King, and many consider him the grandfather of environmentalism. His most famous book, *Walden, or Life in the Woods,* was the result of two years spent in a cabin he built on Walden Pond just outside Concord. It continues to inspire environmentalists and naturalists. Ever the iconoclast, while a student at Harvard, Thoreau wore a green coat to chapel instead of the required black one. In 1842 he refused to pay the poll tax and spent a night in jail. His entire life was spent in Concord, which, according to his friend and mentor Ralph Waldo Emerson, he knew as well as a fox or bird. He was only forty-four when he died of tuberculosis, and his grave, alongside his parents and siblings, is what you'd expect—simplicity itself.

Forest Hills Cemetery

J A M A I C A   P L A I N

Even if Forest Hills Cemetery didn't have its share of famous residents, it would be worth the trip for cemetery fans and sculpture and garden lovers. The Gothic entrance gate (see above) is a work of art and the grounds are gorgeous, with rolling hills, roads, paths named after trees and flowers, and some striking funereal sculptures, the most notable being Daniel Chester French's *Death and the Sculptor,* honoring fellow sculptor **Martin Milmore.** The cemetery was opened in 1848 and spans 275 acres. Among numerous luminaries here is **William Lloyd Garrison** (1805–1879), ardent abolitionist, reformer, and publisher. *95 Forest Hills*

Avenue, Jamaica Plain. Tel. (617) 524-0128. Grounds open 8:30 A.M.–dusk. Office hours: 8:30 A.M.–4:30 P.M. Monday–Friday, 8:30 A.M.–1:00 P.M. Saturday; map, rest rooms, brochures about seasonal walks and talks, sculptures, art shows, special events.

e. e. cummings
1 8 9 4 - 1 9 6 2

To find cummings's grave stone, flat in the ground as it is, look for his full name: Edward Estlin Cummings, to the left of a large monument that says "Clarke." It is tempting to use lower case exclusively (as he did) in writing about this poet, playwright, artist, and novelist, who was known for his unique typographic forms. His life was a blend of the conventional and bohemian: magna cum laude graduate of Harvard, ambulance driver in France during World War I, recipient of a Guggenheim Fellowship and Bollingen prize in poetry, Charles Eliot Norton Professor at Harvard, contrasted with three marriages, three months in a French prison (due to a clerical error), being an art student in Paris, resident of Greenwich Village, visitor to Soviet Russia in 1931, avant garde poet. Among his best-known works are *The Enormous Room*, *him*, and *1 x 1*. peace be to him.

EUGENE O'NEILL
1 8 8 8 - 1 9 5 3

Did O'Neill's birth in a Broadway hotel room foreshadow his long career as a playwright? Probably not. But having a father who was a prominent actor may have sparked his poetic fire. Basic to O'Neill's muse was a dysfunctional family whose problems and conflicts were fodder for his plays and provided a sense of gloom, doom, and dramatic realism that pervaded most of his work. Between 1918 and 1928 he wrote more than twelve major plays, but those considered his finest—*The Iceman Cometh, Long Day's Journey into Night, A Touch of the Poet,* and *Moon for the Misbegotten*—were his last, written between 1935 and 1943. Though his work went into eclipse after his death, his plays are in vogue again, and he is widely praised as a (some would say "the") major American playwright of the twentieth century. He is buried with his third wife, Carlotta, beneath a single, large, irregular headstone, with the prescient words, "Rest in peace." By now maybe he does.

Abel's Hill Cemetery

M A R T H A ' S   V I N E Y A R D

On a quiet country road in Chilmark, behind a split rail fence, lies Abel's Hill Cemetery, whose oldest grave is dated 1717. The burial ground is a mere six or seven acres, occupying the site of Chilmark's first meeting house (erected before 1701). The more celebrated occupants of this pine-dotted, grassy landscape reflect the Vineyard's popularity as a summer escape hatch for people with high-pressure jobs. One permanent resident is **Joseph P. Lash** (1909-1987), a close advisor of

Franklin Roosevelt. Modern architect **Eliot Noyes** (1910–1977) lies nearby. *South Road, near Chilmark Pond, Chilmark. Tel. (508) 645-3414. Grounds open all the time.*

JOHN BELUSHI
1 9 4 9 – 1 9 8 2

Behind a white-gated little enclave next to the entrance road and fence is a massive boulder in which is carved the name Belushi, nothing more. This commemorates the star of *Saturday Night Live, Animal House,* and the first *Blues Brothers* movie, who owned a summer home on the island. The boulder is often garlanded with flowers ("and beer bottles and girls' panties, too," said Basil Welch, the caretaker) by those who remember this talented comedian's impersonations of Henry Kissinger, a Japanese samurai, and others. A director said, "If he doesn't burn himself out, his potential is unlimited." But burn he did. Larger than life in both his work and his lifestyle, Belushi died smaller—of an overdose of heroin and cocaine in a Hollywood hotel, a long way from Wheaton, Illinois, where he was born.

LILLIAN HELLMAN
1 9 0 6 – 1 9 8 4

To the right of the white frame utility building in the parking area, a path leads to the grave of one of the country's most prominent playwrights, located near a Japanese maple. Etched into the upright black slate stone are her dates and a quill pen. Pebbles encircle the headstone in the traditional

Jewish burial custom ("the stones play havoc with my lawn mower," Mr. Welch said). Hellman is best known for her plays, *The Little Foxes, The Children's Hour, Watch on the Rhine* (which won the New York Drama Critics Circle Award), and *Toys in the Attic.* She also wrote several memoirs, like *Scoundrel Time,* which relates her experience testifying before the House Un-American Activities Committee in the Joe McCarthy-witchhunt era. Her best-selling memoir *Pentimento* was adapted as the movie *Julia.* The memoir later turned out to be an invention, which left her veracity in doubt. Nevertheless, her plays are still powerful. She is also remembered for her thirty-year-long affair with, and devotion to, mystery writer Dashiell Hammett.

United First Parish Church

QUINCY

The old (1828) United First Parish Church has four graves in its crypt, those of two U.S. presidents and their wives: John and **Abigail Adams** and their son **John Quincy Adams** and his wife **Louisa**. *1306 Hancock Street, Quincy. Tel. (617) 773-1290. Open mid-April to mid-November, 9:00 A.M.–5:00 P.M. Monday–Saturday, 12:00 P.M.–5:00 P.M. Sunday; tours offered.*

JOHN ADAMS
1735–1826

In a term of office sandwiched between those of giants Washington and Jefferson, our second U.S. president has often been overlooked and underrated. But thanks to a recent biography, he is in fashion again (despite his role in the infamous Alien and Sedition Acts) and respected for his intelligence, honesty, and moral courage. He first demonstrated these traits by undertaking the unpopular defense of British soldiers charged with causing four deaths in the Boston Massacre. His contributions to the formation of the United States were formidable, beginning with his membership in the Continental Congress from 1774 to 1778. George Washington's vice president for eight years, he was elected president in 1796. But his suspicious, sometimes cantankerous nature and unpopular policies led in 1800 to his defeat for a second term by his longtime rival Thomas Jefferson. In one of life's great coincidences, he and Jefferson died the same day, July 4, hours and miles apart. **The John Adams and John Quincy Adams birthplaces** (133 and 141 Franklin Street; 617–770–1175), both seventeenth-century saltbox houses, are open to visitors.

Stark Cemetery

D U N B A R T O N

Stark Cemetery is pocket size, maybe 20 feet by 30 feet. Behind a cast-iron fence and gate, edged by aged trees, it is pure New England. Generations of Lowells are isolated within a black cast-iron fence with concrete posts. *Mansion Road near Barnard Hill Road, Dunbarton. Grounds open all the time.*

ROBERT LOWELL
1 9 1 7 – 1 9 7 7

Not always the proper Bostonian, Lowell led a restless, complex life, punctuated by three marriages to fellow writers, imprisonment (in 1943–1944) as a conscientious objector in World War II, and hospitalization for manic-depression. Even so, he received Guggenheim Fellowships in 1947 and 1974 and a Pulitzer Prize for poetry in 1947. Among his highly praised works are *Life Studies,* called confessional poetry for its autobio-graphical elements; *Near the Ocean;* and *For the Union Dead.* He taught at Yale, Harvard, and as a visiting fellow at Oxford. No ivory tower dweller, he was also involved in political action; in 1965 he refused President Lyndon Johnson's invitation to a White House Arts Festival as a protest against the Vietnam War. He was in a taxi in New York, on his way to reconcile with his second wife, Elizabeth Hardwick, when he suffered a heart attack and died. Life, like poetry, can be fraught with surprises.

Old Burying Ground

J A F F R E Y

Old Burying Ground is, as its name implies, a tiny, venerable cemetery located behind the original meetinghouse, less than 2 miles from the center of Jaffrey Center. Also buried here is **Amos Fortune** (1710–1801), a former slave, tanner, successful businessman, and patriot, who bought freedom for himself and his wife and helped endow the meetinghouse. *Route 124, Jaffrey Center. Tel. (603) 532-8541. Grounds open 7:00 A.M.–dusk. A carriage shed to the right of the grounds has a map on the side.*

WILLA CATHER
1873–1947

Death Comes for the Archbishop and eventually it came for its author, Willa Cather, too. She was born in Winchester, Virginia; moved to a Nebraska ranch as a child; graduated from the University of Nebraska; and then traveled widely. She spent many summers in the crisp New Hampshire air and wrote her Pulitzer Prize-winning novel *One of Ours* (1922) here. The best books of this prolific writer are considered *O Pioneers* (1913), *My Antonia* (1918), *Shadows on the Rock* (1931), and the aforementioned demise of a cleric (1927). Although she lived her later life in New York City and died there of a cerebral hemorrhage, she chose this as her final address. It seems fitting, too, that part of her final gravestone message are words from a book she had worked on while in Jaffrey Center,

My Antonia: "That is happiness, to be dissolved into something complete and great." Look for her upright square granite headstone, down a slight hill in the far southwest corner of the graveyard. A well-marked path helps direct you to it.

Rhode Island

Island Cemetery

N E W P O R T

As you'd expect in a town as old as Newport, Island Cemetery dates back to the 1800s, though it is a mere stripling compared to the **Common Burying Ground,** circa 1640, which is adjacent to it, separated only by a fence. Island Cemetery is the final home of millionaires, naval heroes, and other gilt-edged Newport names. The windswept hill, guarded by two beautiful spread-winged stone angels and overlooking the water, should make Newporters residing on the grounds feel right at home. *Intersection of Farewell Street and Warner Avenue, Newport. Grounds open from dawn to dusk. Haunted New England tours available April-October (fee). Tel. (401) 845-9138 for information.*

HUGH DUDLEY AUCHINCLOSS, JR.
1897–1976

Some people are known for the company they keep, but in Auchincloss's case, it was the company he married. His second wife, **Nina Gore Vidal**, was the mother of novelist Gore Vidal, and his third, **Janet Lee Bouvier Auchincloss** (1907–1989; also buried here), was the mother of Jacqueline Bouvier Kennedy Onassis and Lee Radziwill. In England, this patrician stockbroker-lawyer would be a classic country squire. The first Auchincloss came to America in 1803. Through two centuries the family was allied through marriage and/or commerce with the Rockefellers, Tiffanys, Vanderbilts, and other blue-chip families. Hugh was born at Hammersmith Farm in Newport, where the Bouvier sisters, Jackie and Lee, grew up in an atmosphere of unostentatious "old money." Groton, Yale, Kings College, Cambridge, Columbia, the New York Stock Exchange, were all part of Hugh's provenance. His other family home was Merrywood in McLean, Virginia, which Gore Vidal expropriated for the setting of his novel, *Washington, D.C.* Hard times in the stock market forced "Uncle Hughdie," as Jackie and Lee called their stepfather, to sell Hammersmith Farm. The fun days by the sea were over. Hidden by evergreens, Hughdie's grave is a simple one with a cross and the inscription: "BELOVED, WISE AND NOBLE MAN."

AUGUST BELMONT
1816–1890

In the stuffy Newport society of his time, Belmont must have been an anomaly: a German-born Jew, an immigrant, and a Democratic supporter of Tammany Hall. But he had several assets: money, charm, and cultivated tastes. At age thirty-three, he was one of the richest men in New York. As a banker who had been an agent of the Rothschilds in Europe, he amassed a fortune and crowned it by marrying Caroline Perry, the daughter of a naval hero, Commodore Matthew Perry. During the Civil War, Belmont was an ardent Unionist. He was also a horse racing fan; for many years he

was president of the American Jockey Club. The Belmont mausoleum is on a smaller scale than the family's Newport mansion, naturally, but still impressive: a Greek temple with two statues and a polished rose marble sarcophagus, surrounded by other Belmonts in a fenced-in, exclusive compound of their own.

RICHARD MORRIS HUNT
1827-1895

As a Paris-trained architect who favored French Renaissance Revival, Hunt left his mark on Newport—in the monumental "cottages" he built for the resort's millionaires, whose philosophy seemed to be: "If you've got it, flaunt it." Marble House, The Breakers, Belcourt Castle, Ochre Court—he did them all. He was also a founder of the American Institute of Architects. Considering his ostentatious building style, his grave is surprisingly simple: flat in the ground like a small layer cake, inscribed with the Latin phrase *Laborare est orare* ("Work is prayer"). That might sum up his life.

MATTHEW CALBRAITH PERRY
1794–1858

Near the end of a respectable naval career (in which he took part in the War of 1812 and the Mexican War), Perry—the younger of two brothers, both in the U.S. Navy—had a once-in-a-century opportunity. In 1853 he was chosen by President Millard Fillmore to lead a fleet to the Far East in a show of force designed to secure a treaty of peace and trade with Japan. At the time Japan was a completely closed society, hermetically sealed off from the western world. Perry parried (ahem) with suspicious Japanese officials; after a brief standoff, he won a commitment that Fillmore's letter to the emperor of Japan would actually be delivered. Perry returned the next year (things moved slowly in those days) and signed a treaty of peace, goodwill, and commerce, which opened Japanese ports to trade and permitted American vessels to enter and secure supplies—all done without firing a shot. This treaty has forever linked Perry's name with the opening of Japan to the West, recognized as one of the major diplomatic achievements of the nineteenth century. Perry died in New York City, but he was buried in Rhode Island, his birth state. His lofty memorial, erected by his widow, is head and shoulders above others, a statement of sorts.

OLIVER HAZARD PERRY
1785–1819

Son of one naval officer and brother of another, this Perry won a decisive battle in the War of 1812, commanding a superior force that defeated a British squadron on Lake Erie. He then proclaimed: "We have met the enemy and they are ours." His was a short life: He died of yellow fever at Port of Spain, Trinidad, at age twenty-four. His hillside obelisk, with a black iron fence around it, overlooks the water—a fitting finale for a naval man.

Vermont

Immanuel Cemetery

BELLOWS FALLS

Located on two levels behind and above the Immanuel Episcopal Church in the center of town is the low-key Immanuel Cemetery, which dates back to the early 1800s. Scattered among its curved, sloping roads are several Civil War brigadier generals. *12 Church Street, Bellows Falls. Tel. (802) 463-3100. Grounds open from dawn to dusk, April–October. Walking the grounds is possible in winter, but the road to the entrance is closed. Office is in the church, on the left side; hours: 9:00 A.M.– 12:00 P.M. Monday–Friday; map, rest rooms.*

HENRIETTA "HETTY" GREEN
1834–1916

Known as the richest woman in the world in her day, New Bedford–born Hetty Howland Robinson Green inherited much of her great wealth from her Quaker father—successful in whaling and the China trade—and from a New Bedford maiden aunt, Sylvia Ann Howland, whose fortune also came from shipping and trading. Wealth begets wealth: Hetty married a successful man, Edward Henry Green, and, through acumen, miserliness, and true grit, accumulated so much more that when she died she left her two children over $100 million. She made money on the stock market when this was male turf, and was called "the Witch of Wall Street," only partly because she dressed in black. She survived the panic of 1907 by converting many holdings to cash and railroad and real estate investments. Her eccentric, penny-pinching ways were good copy in the tabloid press, which reported that she lived in Hoboken because rents were cheaper than in New York City and carried her lunch to avoid restaurant prices. Green once told someone why she needed a gun: "Mostly to protect myself against lawyers. I'm not much afraid of burglars or highwaymen." In this peaceful setting there's nothing for her to fear either. The tall obelisk bearing her name is easily found.

Prospect Hill Cemetery

BRATTLEBORO

Very near the center of town, Prospect Hill Cemetery, on the east side of South Main Street, is as pretty as can be, with plantings, fountains, trees, and Victoriana. Among its occupants are **William Hunt** (1824-1879), artist-member of the Barbizon school in Paris and Civil War Congressional Medal of Honor recipient **George Hooker** (1838-1902), who was Jim Fisk's brother-in-law and shares the same family plot. *South Main Street, Brattleboro. Grounds open from dawn to dusk.*

JAMES FISK
1 8 3 4 – 1 8 7 2

Few people in the history of American capitalism have epitomized "rags to riches" more dramatically than Jim Fisk, a bold, flashy, boastful entrepreneur of Brobdingnagian proportions. From modest Vermont beginnings, with a skimpy education, he parlayed an early life as waiter, ticket-seller in a circus, and salesman into a career as stock speculator and broker. Through dubious dealings and stock manipulations, he earned a reputation (deserved) for double-dealings on a mammoth scale. With Jay Gould, another greedy speculator, he cornered the gold market in New York, which caused the financial panic of 1869 (Black Friday). All the while he lived like a corrupt Roman emperor with a string of showy mistresses and brassy opulence rarely seen on this continent up to that time. In the end he quarreled over a mistress with an equally depraved competitor, Edward Stokes, who shot and killed him in New York's Grand Central Hotel. At Fisk's baroquely ornate funeral, the cortege included the Ninth Regiment and a 200-piece band, proof that dying well is the best revenge. As you would expect, Fisk's tall white marble monument—with four seated stone ladies, naked to the waist, embellishing it—is the largest one here, easily spotted on the east side of the grounds, as marked by excess as was his life.

Bennington Center Cemetery

OLD BENNINGTON

The Bennington Center Cemetery, the town's old colonial burying ground, is tucked behind Old First Church, a mile west of town. It is the town's oldest landmark (1762); occupants include many American and British soldiers from the Battle of Bennington in 1777, five Vermont governors, and **Ellery Channing** (1780–1842), founder of the Unitarian Church. Through the white picket fence to the left of the church a sign with an arrow leads to Robert Frost's grave, very near the rear of the church. Beside the grave is a small stone bench, ideal for sitting and contemplating the beauty of the peaceful countryside. *Route 9, 1 mile west of the town center, Bennington. Grounds open from dawn to dusk.*

ROBERT FROST
1 8 7 4 – 1 9 6 3

While his down-to-earth verse extolls New England country life, Frost was actually born in San Francisco (though his father was a New Englander). That was not the only anomaly in his long career. Frost's poetry and public persona (especially later in life) suggested a kindly, grandfatherly type, but his personal life was marked by unhappiness: a stressed marriage, insecurities, and jealousy. Although he did some farming, he also taught at Amherst and Harvard; was a fellow at Michigan, Yale, and Dartmouth; and a founder of the Bread Loaf School at Middlebury College. Although credited for revolutionizing blank verse, it was forty years before his first book was published. He received the Pulitzer Prize for poetry four times and the Bollingen in 1963, just twenty-four days before his death. His lines "But I have promises to keep, / And miles to go before I sleep" are part of the American vocabulary, although they are not, as might be expected, found on his headstone. Many Americans know him best for his recitation from memory of his poem "The Gift Outright" at the inauguration of President John F. Kennedy in 1961, the first time a poet was ever asked to participate in a presidential inauguration. Frost's white hair and rugged New England face marked him as a survivor, an image perpetuated in his

poetry, which he once described as "taking life by the throat." (Another of his wry observations: "You can be a little ungrammatical if you come from the right part of the country.") On his and his family's shared headstone, with a border of stone leaves, situated in a spacious opening dotted with squat evergreen bushes, are the words "I HAD A LOVER'S QUARREL WITH THE WORLD" from "The Lesson for Today." Beneath his wife **Elinor Miriam White's** dates (1873–1938), is "TOGETHER WING TO WING AND GAR TO GAR" (*gar* being a mild oath), from the sonnet "The Master Speed."

Plymouth Cemetery

PLYMOUTH

Plymouth Cemetery is a modest colonial burial ground, established before 1800, with fieldstone walkways, white wooden gate, and steep, terraced hillsides with steps and railing. The Coolidge family plot, with Calvin's simple granite head-stone—and eight generations of Coolidges—is well marked and easily visible, about fifty feet from the road. A wreath is laid on his grave each July 4, his birthday. *Off Route 100 A, Plymouth. Tel. (802) 672-3773. Grounds open 9:30 A.M.–5:00 P.M. daily, late May to mid-October.*

CALVIN COOLIDGE
1872–1933

From humble, rural Vermont beginnings, descendant of a long line of farmers and storekeepers, this laconic man rose to become the thirtieth president of the United States. Lost among many stories about his frugality and taciturnity is the fact that he had common sense, integrity, a capacity for hard work, administrative ability, and a dry Yankee wit. (The wit is evident in one of my favorite "Silent Cal" stories: A woman guest at a White House dinner gushed, "I've bet so-and-so that I can get you to say more than two words, Mr. President." His response: "You lose." Then he spent the rest of the meal in silence.) These attributes served him well in his climb from college days at Amherst; years as a lawyer and mayor of Northhampton, Massachusetts; legislator; two-term governor; and finally to vice president under Warren Harding, who died in the third year of his administration. Coolidge had the good fortune to serve his single full presidential term (1924–1928) during a period of prosperity—the Roaring Twenties—leaving office a popular man, before the 1929 crash, when the country's "ceiling" fell in. **The Calvin Coolidge Homestead** (1 mile northeast on Vermont Highway 100 A in Plymouth Notch; 802-672-3773) is open to visitors.

New York

Most of the old nineteenth-century burial grounds in New York State patterned themselves on the French Pere Lachaise model, with wide boulevards, ancient trees forming canopies over access roads, and a variety of hospitable plantings. All of these accessories were aided by the natural topography of the state, which favors rolling hills, valleys, and meadows that provide sweeping vistas; a welcome sight for visitors and perhaps also for those who now have rooms with a permanent view. The number of notables—movers, shakers, and deal makers—for whom New York is an eternal address would fill several volumes all by itself.

Fort Hill Cemetery

AUBURN

The original ground here was a fortified Cayuga Indian village in the sixteenth century. The first cemetery inhabitant of this tree-shaded eighty-acre property was **Elijah Miller** (1772–1851), a local judge, partner in the New York law firm Cravath Swain & Moore, and William Seward's father-in-law. Civil War generals and local industrialists are here, as well as **Theodore W. Case** (1888–1944), inventor of the first successful soundtrack for talking pictures; **Allen Macy Dulles** (1854–1930), professor at Auburn Theological Seminary, father of Allen and John Foster Dulles; **Jerome "Brud" Holland** (1916–1985), Cornell football star, ambassador to Sweden, and first African American director of the New York Stock Exchange; and **Myles Keogh** (1840–1876), a U.S. Cavalry captain killed at Little Big Horn; *19 Fort Street, Auburn. Tel. (315) 253-8132. Grounds open from sunrise to sunset daily. Office hours: 9:00 A.M.–1:00 P.M. Monday–Friday; map and walking tour brochure, rest room. Tours (fee) conducted by the Cayuga Museum (315-253-8051) and Willard Memorial Chapel (315-252-0339).*

WILLIAM SEWARD
1801–1872

Seward is best known as Abraham Lincoln's secretary of state, but his contributions to our history go well beyond holding this office. A lawyer with strong political ambitions, he was an ardent abolitionist and a man of high principles and humanitarian impulses, willing to challenge those he considered wrong. While governor of New York, he refused to extradite to Virginia three seamen who had helped a fugitive slave. Virginia responded by ordering a ban of New York shipping, but Seward held firm. As a senator he championed the admission of California as a free state and tried to abolish slavery in Washington, D.C. When he lost the Republican nomination for president in 1860, he gamely campaigned for Lincoln. His reward was to be chosen secretary of state, a job he handled with lawyerly shrewdness, parrying British and French anti-Union agitation with great skill. The night John Wilkes Booth shot Lincoln, another conspirator attacked and almost killed Seward, who was left partially crippled, and severely wounded other members of his household. Even so, Seward continued as secretary of state under Andrew Johnson and was just as helpful to him. Though opposed to slavery, he advocated conciliation with the South. He also helped negotiate the purchase of Alaska from Russia. Occupying the same quarters here with Seward is his wife, **Francis Miller Seward** (1805–1865), a Quaker like her husband and a great influence on his liberal views. **Seward House** (33 South Street; 315–252–1283), open to visitors, is a comfortable Victorian home with many period artifacts and some fascinating history about both Sewards.

HARRIET TUBMAN
1 8 2 1 – 1 9 1 3

Born as Araminta Ross, a slave, on the eastern shore of Maryland, Harriet Tubman early on took her mother's first name. The name Tubman came from a man her master forced her to marry in 1844. Five years later, now a spunky woman of twenty-eight, she escaped from slavery, following the north star to freedom. Her husband declined to join her. Though unable to read or write, Tubman had great strength and endurance, acquired during her years as a field hand, and she soon joined the Underground Railroad, working as a cook and housemaid to get money to bring members of her family and others out of the South. On an estimated nineteen trips, she guided more than 300 slaves to northern states and Canada. Nicknamed "Moses" for leading people to the "promised land," Tubman possessed great daring, resourcefulness, and strategic skills. She was a fearless guide, using disguises and carrying a gun. Large bounties were on her head, but it is believed she never lost a fugitive. She rescued her own aging parents and brought them to Auburn. During the Civil War, she assisted the Union forces as cook, nurse, laundress, scout, raider, and even as a spy behind Confederate lines. From the end of the war until her death, she continued to work for her people. She bought a little house (with the profits from *Scenes in the Life of Harriet Tubman*, written and published for her by Auburn neighbors), where she lived, but soon converted it to a home for poor African American children and elderly. **The Harriet Tubman Home** (180 South Street; 315–252-2081) still exists and is open to visitors, but erratic hours make it wise to phone ahead to schedule a visit.

Saint Raymond's New Cemetery

T H E   B R O N X

Old and new Saint Raymond's cemeteries are related but are not contiguous. The older, smaller one, no longer in use, dates back to 1875 and is located at East Tremont and Whittemore Avenues. Its most notable inhabitant is **Father Francis Patrick Duffy** (1871–1932), the chaplain of the famous "Fighting Sixty-ninth" Infantry Regiment, which endured some of the most brutal fighting of World War I. The new Saint Raymond's—near the water, with a view of the Bronx Whitestone Bridge—broke ground in 1953. It is vast, with rows of headstones and wide oak-tree-lined drives, but is so carefully laid out that particular graves are easy to find. Within each section, most having names, graves are identified by designated "range" numbers. In a given range the bases of the headstones are etched with plot and grave numbers. It's a model system other cemeteries would do well to emulate. At home on the ranges here are many entertainers. Among them: **Jackie Jackson** (1941–1997), singer with the Chantels; **Hector Lavoe** (1946–1993), known as "El Cantante," salsa star of the 1950s; **Frankie Lymon** (1942–1968), whose meteoric rise as a teenage doo-wop star ended just as dramatically in a heroin overdose; and **Guadalupe Yoli** (1939–1992), called "La Lupe," a Cuban salsa singer who accompanied Tito Puente, the top Latin performer of all time. *East 177th Street and Lafayette Avenue, Bronx. Tel. (718) 792-1133. Grounds open 8:00 A.M.–4:30 P.M. daily. Office hours: 9:00 A.M.–4:00 P.M. Monday–Friday, 9:00 A.M.–12:00 P.M. Saturday, closed Sunday; map, rest room.*

BILLIE HOLIDAY
1915–1959

With a soulful, jazzy contralto that was so recognizable and arresting it could stop conversation in a crowded room, Billie Holiday sang of love expectant ("Our Love Is Here to Stay") and love thwarted ("But Not for Me"), hope ("I Wished on the Moon"), suicide ("Gloomy Sunday"), and racism ("Strange Fruit"), and even when despair and drugs slurred the words, she kept on singing. Hers is one of the saddest stories in the history of jazz. Born Eleanora Fagan Holiday, she was the illegitimate child of a teenage mother. As a young girl, Billie ran errands for a

bordello in her native Baltimore, was raped at age ten, and quit school after fifth grade. Her mother moved to New York and Billie later joined her, but she was arrested for prostitution at fifteen and jailed on Welfare Island for four months. At some point she discovered she had a voice that people would pay to hear, and by the early 1930s she was recording with Benny Goodman, Count Basie, Red Norvo, and others. Saxophonist Lester Young dubbed her "Lady Day," which stuck as a lifelong nickname. The 1940s and 1950s were a seesaw: up (great fame and success) and down (marriage to a drug addict who got her hooked too). A drug bust led to a year in a federal penitentiary. Once released, she continued to suffer the racial indignities endemic to that time, such as having to ride the service elevator in fancy hotels where she was the featured performer. She married again, there were more drug charges, and finally death came at age forty–four from kidney problems and cardiac arrest. "She died of everything" one obituary report read. A proud, intense woman, she was a unique interpreter and improviser of jazz for the ages. "They Can't Take That Away" from her. Here, with her mother **Sadie Holiday Fagan** (1896–1945), "Comes Love" or at least peace—at last.

Woodlawn Cemetery

THE BRONX

One of the most otherworldly spots in New York City is right here in the Bronx. The planners of this necropolis intended it to be so, back in 1863 when the first "guest" arrived. The undulating hills and meticulously landscaped banks are stippled with some 4,000 shade trees, which include European cutleaf beech, umbrella pine, white pine, golden rain trees, Kentucky coffee trees, hackberry, katsura, cork trees, and a giant white oak that is more than 240 years old. Trees attract birds, and some 100 species have been spotted on the grounds, bathing in the ponds, waterfalls, and lakes as well. Many of the numerous stately mausoleums, built for prominent "lifers," are architectural wonders, the work of Richard Morris Hunt, McKim, Mead and White, James Renwick, James Gamble Rogers, and Louis Comfort Tiffany. Note the splendid manses of **William A. Clark** (1839–1925), Montana senator and patron of Washington's Corcoran Gallery of Art; **Clyde Fitch** (1865–1909), prolific playwright; **Harry Helmsley** (1910–1997), controversial hotelier and billionaire real estate broker; **Collis P. Huntington** (1821–1900), entrepreneur, land developer, and railroad magnate; and **Dr. Jokichi Takamine** (1854–1922), Japanese aristocrat and

"father of modern biotechnology," who donated the cherry trees to Washington, D.C. Woodlawn was one of two places fashionable nineteenth-century New Yorkers sought a permanent state of grace (Green-Wood in Brooklyn was its chief rival), and the roll call reads like a more egalitarian version of Mrs. Astor's 400, with noblemen and nouveaux riches, philanthropists and philanderers, cultural royalty and robber barons, tycoons and tyrants. Included on the rolls are **Roscoe "Fatty" Arbuckle** (1887–1933), one of the most popular comic actors of the silent screen, until a 1921 sex scandal killed his career; **Irving Berlin** (1888–1989), popular songwriter whose works live on and on; **Nellie Bly** (1864–1922), newspaperwoman famous for her exposés; **Irene** (1893–1969) and **Vernon Castle** (1887–1918), a celebrated ballroom dance team of the early twentieth century; **Miles Davis** (1926–1991), innovative progressive jazz trumpeter and composer of fusion style, whose sarcophagus is one of the most unusual and modern ones here; **Admiral David Farragut** (1801–1870), renowned for his defeat of the Confederate fleet at Mobile Bay and his order: "Damn the torpedoes! Full speed ahead"; **James Montgomery Flagg** (1877–1960), artist and magazine illustrator, who created World War I's famous recruiting poster "Uncle Sam Wants You!"; **Frankie Frisch** (1898–1973), the "Fordham Flash," baseball player and manager with the New York Giants and St. Louis Cardinals; and **W. C. Handy** (1873–1958), known as the "father of the blues." Also here are **Coleman Hawkins** (1904–1969), jazz saxophonist, whose recording of "Body and Soul" is one of the all-time great jazz singles; **John Held** (1889–1958), whose illustrations encapsulated the "Jazz Age"; **Victor Herbert** (1859–1924), conductor and composer of popular comic operas, such as *Babes in Toyland*; **Charles Evans Hughes** (1862–1948), much respected Chief Justice of the Supreme Court; **Augustus Juilliard** (1836–1919), textile magnate, philanthropist who endowed what became the Juilliard School of Music; **Samuel Kress** (1863–1955), merchant, philanthropist, and art collector; **Fritz Kreisler** (1875–1962), Austrian-born, world-famous concert violinist; **Robert Moses** (1888–1981), public works administrator, master builder responsible for most of New York City's highways, bridges, and redevelopment projects of the twentieth century; **Thomas Nast** (1840–1902), political cartoonist who created the Democratic donkey and Republican elephant symbols; **Hideyo Noguchi** (1876–1928), Japanese bacteriologist; **J. C. Penney** (1875–1971), founder of J.C. Penney chain of retail stores, whose middle name was, truly, Cash; **Antoinette Perry** (1888–1946), actress and director, for whom Tony awards (theater version of Oscars) were named; **Adam Clayton Powell, Jr.** (1908–1972), charismatic African American minister and U.S. congressman; **Grantland Rice** (1880–1954), one of the all-time great sportswriters; and **Joseph Stella** (1877–1946), Italian-born futurist painter. *Webster Avenue and East 233rd Street, Bronx. Tel. (718) 920–1469. Grounds open 8:30 A.M.–5:00 P.M. daily. Office hours: 9:00 A.M.–4:30 P.M. Monday–Saturday, closed Sunday; map, rest rooms. Weekend tours (fee).*

RALPH JOHNSON BUNCHE
1904–1971

Considered one of the most intelligent and principled U.S. diplomats of the past century, Ralph Bunche, a Detroit native, had a distinguished academic career before he joined the United Na-tions and became an undersecretary-general. A grandson of slaves, Bunche was an honors graduate of the University of California, a faculty member at Howard University, recip-ient of a Harvard Ph.D., and chief assistant on Swedish sociologist Gunnar Myrdal's book *An American*

Dilemma: The Negro Problem and Modern Democracy (1944). An analyst in the Office of Strategic Services (OSS) in World War II, he became an expert on Africa. This led to a State Department job, and in 1947 he joined the UN as a mediator in territories under UN trusteeship. He negotiated a cease-fire between Arabs and Israelis at the end of the first Arab-Israeli War, for which he was awarded the Nobel Peace Prize. He was the first black to achieve this honor. Although high-level positions in the U.S. government eluded him because of race, he earned great recognition abroad for his UN work. Late in life he advised Martin Luther King, Jr.; like King, he favored a peaceful resolution of the United State's racial problems. His small headstone and those of his wife **Ruth Harris Bunche** (1906–1988), and daughter, **Jane Bunche Pierce** (1933–1966), lie in front of a large rough-hewn granite memorial with the single name "Bunche" on it beneath two gracefully carved olive branches. Nothing could be more appropriate.

GEORGE M. COHAN
1 8 7 8 – 1 9 4 2
Born in Providence, Rhode Island, Cohan really was a "Yankee Doodle Boy," as one of his most patriotic songs put it. From age seven he was one of "The Four Cohans" vaudeville act, which consisted of him, his older sister, Josephine, and their parents. While Cohan was actor, singer, and dancer, he also began writing songs for the troupe at age thirteen. His first hit was "Hot Tamale Alley" in 1895, and his musical comedy, *The Governor's Son,* came six years later. This was followed in 1904 by *Little Johnny Jones,* which featured "Give

My Regards to Broadway" and "The Yankee Doodle Boy." In all, between 1901 and 1940, he produced eighty Broadway shows and starred in a number of them. "Over There," written in a burst of wartime fervor in 1917, quickly became the song of World War I and—along with "It's a Grand Old Flag"—won for Cohan a Congressional Medal of Honor. This patriotic spirit was highlighted in Jimmy Cagney's portrayal of him in *Yankee Doodle Dandy.* Cohan's handsome Gothic mausoleum, designed by Louis Comfort Tiffany, has united the Four Cohans again. Note the altar (visible through the Tiffany windows) and ornamented bronze doors, which always sport a fresh American flag—thanks to a veterans' group and his congressional medal. On the doors in small print are the names Cohan and Niblo (Josephine's married name): rather discreet for show business folks.

DUKE ELLINGTON
1 8 9 9 – 1 9 7 4
The career of Edward Kennedy Ellington—nicknamed "Duke" in school days, for his regal manner and stylish clothes—is proof that talent doesn't always burn itself out young. Born in Washington, D.C., to two upward-striving parents who worked two jobs apiece to care for their family, Ellington was initially more interested in art and sports than in music, even though he began studying piano at age seven. At his high school graduation, he received the offer of a Pratt Institute art scholarhip, but by then he was hooked on music, playing ragtime in local bands. This led to work with Elmer Snowden's Washingtonians, a five-man combo that settled in 1923 at

"Duke"
EDWARD KENNEDY ELLINGTON
1899 · · · 1974

the Hollywood Club in New York. Before long, Ellington was the leader, the group doubled in size, and they were signed by the Cotton Club, the premiere jazz venue in the city. The Cotton Club years (1927–1931) made Ellington a "name," with the chance to play everything, from dance music to blues to jazz instrumentals. His most fertile period musically, as composer and recording artist, was 1932–1942, which brought forth "Mood Indigo," "Sophisticated Lady," "It Don't Mean a Thing," and "Black and Tan Fantasy." Billy Strayhorn joined the band in 1939 as arranger and second pianist and is considered the genius behind many of the band's later arrangements. His "Take the 'A' Train" became the band's theme song. Ellington continued growing musically and expanded what was known as the "Ellington effect." There were concerts at Carnegie Hall of his large-scale "Black, Brown and Beige," "Harlem," and "Liberian Suite"; full-length productions like *Jump for Joy;* film scores such as that for *Anatomy of a Murder;* work with John Coltrane, Charles

Mingus, and other avant-garde instrumentalists; and sacred music for Episcopal church services. Probably the most prolific composer in jazz history—with an estimated 2,000 compositions—the Duke was also a nice guy, family man, and deeply religious, as the stately eight-foot-tall granite cross at his graveside, sheltered by a huge Katsura tree, attests.

JAY GOULD
1836–1892

The financial and audacious roguery of Gould and his buddy Jim Fiske make the savings-and-loan and Enron debacles of our age seem almost picayune. In an era of anything-goes finances, Gould epitomized the "robber" in the phrase robber baron. Born in Roxbury, New York, brought up in Fairfield, Connecticut, he worked as a blacksmith, clerk, and surveyor, and at twenty-one, with savings of $5,000, he and another man opened a tannery in Pennsylvania. Gould, through chicanery, wrested control away from his partner. He then began speculating in small railways. Gould, Fiske, and a third partner, Daniel Drew, became partners in the directorship of the Erie Railroad. By a series of court-defying moves, outright bribery, and stock watering, they looted the railroad and got away with it. Heady with their success, Gould and Fiske then manipulated the country's credit, export, and produce markets. Emboldened, they tried to corner the gold market, but this caused the panic of Black Friday (September 24, 1869), bringing an uproar of public outrage, which forced Gould out of the Erie Railroad. Nevertheless, $25 million richer, he turned westward, bought control of several other railroads, and ventured into other fields. These included part ownership of the *New York World* newspaper and control of the Western Union Telegraph Company. Called the "most hated man in America," Gould was both despised and feared. Money may not buy happiness, but for Gould it bought a magnificent hilltop mausoleum—a Greek temple with Ionic columns, sheltered by an enormous weeping beech tree, designated in 1985 one of the 113 great trees of New York City. Interestingly, his name does not appear on the facade.

BARBARA HUTTON
1912–1979

The phrase "poor little rich girl" might have been custom tailored to Barbara Hutton. Granddaughter of F. W. Woolworth and daughter of the man who founded the E. F. Hutton brokerage firm, little Babs was a chubby, lonely child with a nanny but no friends. Her father ignored her, her mother may have committed suicide (the medical records mysteriously disappeared), and Babs believed no one loved her nor ever would. She may have been right. When she was twelve, Babs inherited $28 million from her grandparents' estate. Her father invested it and by twenty-one, when she came of age, she had $50 million to play with. That was the beginning of her search for love and acceptance, a hunt that led to seven marriages, mostly to fortune-hunting men, many of them minor European nobility. Only one, marriage number three to Cary Grant, seems to have been a love match, but it didn't last either. Anorexia, a custody battle over her only child, bouts with depression, alcohol, and drugs, these were the tabloid outlines of her life. In 1972 her son's death in a plane crash at the age of thirty–six may have pushed her over the edge: She died five years later, bedridden and with only $3,500 left of her enormous fortune. She reclines now, along with her grandfather, in the Woolworth faux-Egyptian mausoleum she had ridiculed as the "pyramid."

FIORELLO LAGUARDIA
1882–1947

Funny, scrappy, and bursting with self-confidence, the "Little Flower"—as LaGuardia was called—was the perfect fit for New York and New Yorkers, who elected him three times as their mayor, beginning in 1933. He made his reputation as a reformer against the corrupt Tammany Hall machine, which had dominated city politics for decades. LaGuardia, short (barely five feet) and stout, is remembered for the time, during a newspaper strike, when he read comic strips to the kids on radio. More significantly, he was scrupulously honest and boasted (which he did relentlessly) of many real accomplishments: cleaning up slums; building parks; creating public housing and airports; revising the city charter; and developing a civil service free of politics. He had reason to boast: These were big accomplishments for any man, little or not. His ambitions for higher office were cut short in 1947 by the cancer that quickly killed him.

BAT MASTERSON
1853–1921

William Barclay Masterson, known by everyone as "Bat," had what may be the most unusual career path of anyone in these sacred grounds. After all there weren't many people anywhere who went from a life of action in the West— as a buffalo hunter, sheriff, peace marshal, killer of dangerous outlaws, and gambler—to a career as a sportswriter for a New York newspaper at age forty-nine. Masterson did and seems to have been successful at it. No one today thinks of him as a writer, remembering him instead as one of the good guys of the West, known for bravery and a cool head. These served him well in 1878 when he captured a notorious bandit, Dave Rudabaugh, and later killed two outlaws after they had gunned down his brother, the acting marshal of Dodge City. Bat's granite headstone states, "Loved by everyone." Rudabaugh might have argued about that, but not President Teddy Roosevelt, who appointed Masterson a federal deputy marshal in 1905. He gave up that job two years later because it interferred with his sportswriting at the *Morning Telegraph,* where he eventually became sports editor. He died at his desk, pen in hand (not his boots on).

HERMAN MELVILLE
1819–1891

The blank scroll on Melville's rough-hewn granite headstone, covered with bas relief ivy, is unnerving. It suggests either nonproductivity on the author's

part or nonrecognition by the public. The first is anything but true, the latter partially so. In the first eleven years of his life as an author, Melville was extraordinarily productive. Based on his true life adventures with cannibals in the South Seas, he wrote *Typee* (1846), which brought him instant fame. *Omoo* followed the next year, and in quick succession came *Mardi, Redburn, White-Jacket,* and, in 1851, *Moby-Dick,* which was deemed a failure at the time but is now considered his masterpiece. More was still to come: *Pierre: or The Ambiguities, Israel Potter, The Piazza Tales,* and *The Confidence Man,* all by 1857. Then followed a dry spell and relative obscurity. But let's turn the page back to the beginning. Melville came from distinguished stock on both sides of his family, with roots traceable to thirteenth-century Scotland. Both his grandfathers fought in the American Revolution, but his immediate family hit hard times. Melville left his New York City home at seventeen to go to sea as a cabin boy. Then came nearly four years of wandering the world on the whaler *Acushnet*, which provided rich material for writing. When his later books did poorly, Melville worked as a customs inspector for nineteen years, while his literary reputation sank out of sight. At his death in 1891, he left unfinished Billy Budd, his "last writes," as it were. Though incomplete, the book ranks with *Moby-Dick, Typee,* and *Omoo* among his major works. Don't call him Ishmael, call him genius. To the right of Melville's headstone is that of his wife **Elizabeth Shaw Melville**.

JOSEPH PULITZER
1847–1911

The annual Pulitzer Prizes perpetuate a name that otherwise might be buried in journalism archives. But Joseph Pulitzer is worth remembering as someone who brought an independent, politically fearless approach to newspapers. Hungarian-born, Pulitzer thirsted for adventure, despite a poor physique and bad eyesight. No army in Europe would take him, so, at age seventeen he sailed for the United States and promptly enlisted in the Union army. After four skirmishes he was mustered out. A job at a German newspaper in St. Louis was the beginning of his life's work: buying, publishing, and editing newspapers. First came the *St. Louis Dispatch*, which soon became the highly successful *St. Louis Post-Dispatch,* then a move to New York and the purchase of the *World*, which was also a

winner. Pulitzer advocated workers' rights, taxation of luxuries and inheritance, the reform of the civil service, and punishment of crooked officials as part of the paper's editorial creed. The brief newspaper war between Pulitzer and William Randolph Hearst led to sensationalistic reporting on both sides, but later, under Pulitzer's personal guidance, the *World* again became a respected and accurate newspaper, making its owner wealthy in the process. His will established a school of journalism at Columbia University and a series of awards "for the encouragement of public service, public morals, American literature, and the advancement of education." Thus the Pulitzer Prizes were born and continue to be coveted by writers.

ELIZABETH CADY STANTON
1815–1902

Wife of an abolitionist, Mrs. Stanton had her consciousness raised when female delegates were excluded from the floor of a World Anti-Slavery Convention in London in 1840. First she got mad, then she got even. She went home and, with Lucretia Mott, organized America's first women's rights convention, which was held in 1848 in Stanton's hometown, Seneca Falls, New York. At the convention she presented a woman's bill of rights that outlined the inferior position of women in government, church, the law, and society, and introduced resolutions demanding redress, including voting rights. That same year Stanton helped secure passage in New York State of a law giving married women property rights. Two years later she joined forces with Susan B. Anthony on the issue of women's suffrage. For the next forty years, they worked together, Stanton writing on the subject, Anthony organizing the movement. By the end of the Civil War (after the birth of her seventh child), Stanton was able to work full-time for the movement as president of the National Woman Suffrage Association, a position she held until 1893. Articulate, argumentive, sometimes abrasive, always dedicated, she remains an inspiration to feminists everywhere. The 1830 **Elizabeth Cady Stanton House** (32 Washington Street, Seneca Falls) was her home from 1847 to 1862 and is open to the public, with much of her memorabilia on display.

F. W. WOOLWORTH
1852–1919

For a man who made millions from plebian merchandise, Frank Winfield Woolworth developed extremely patrician taste. A farm boy who failed as a drygoods salesman, he latched on to a merchandising idea that made him so much money he died leaving a fortune of $65 million. It was simple, as good ideas often are: selling fixed-price merchandise of all kinds at 5 cents each. He soon boosted that to 10 cents, developed a chain of these five-and-ten-cent stores and had merchandise produced in bulk just for the chain. His success enabled him to build a fifty–six-room Italian Renaissance mansion on Long Island, sleep in a bed that had belonged to Napoleon, and have solid gold fixtures in his bathrooms. In 1913 he paid cash—$13.5 million—to erect his Woolworth building, the tallest skyscraper of its time, in lower Manhattan. At his death there were more than 1,000 stores in the Woolworth chain. His Egyptian Revival mausoleum, with two busty sphinxes "guarding" its doors, was designed by John Russell Pope, architect of the Jefferson Memorial in Washington.

Green-Wood Cemetery

B R O O K L Y N

Modeled after Mount Auburn in Cambridge, Massachusetts, Green-Wood (which opened in 1840 on 478 acres) was coveted as the life-after-death home for ambitious New Yorkers. Designed by David Bates Douglass, this city of the dead is a paradise of trees, ponds, lake, streams, and some 20 miles of serpentine roads and paths, with distant views of New York Harbor and the Statue of Liberty. The fanciful Gothic main gate (see opposite) was designed by Richard Upjohn, architect of Trinity Church, and the chapel is a lovely Gothic wonder. Tree-graced grounds are peopled by, among others, **George Bellows** (1882–1925), artist of the "Ashcan" school; **James Gordon Bennett** (1795–1872), legendary editor-publisher of the *New York Herald*, who initiated the hiring of foreign and war correspondents; **DeWitt Clinton** (1769–1828), governor of New York; **Asher Durand** (1796–1886), artist of the Hudson River school; **Charles Ebbetts** (1859–1925), onetime president of the Brooklyn Dodgers baseball team; **Frank Morgan** (1890–

1949), character actor, immortalized as the wizard in *The Wizard of Oz;* **Samuel F. B. Morse** (1791–1872), portrait painter and inventor of the telegraph and Morse code; **Margaret Sanger** (1883–1966), pioneer in family planning; **William Steinway** (1836–1896), patriarch of the piano manufacturing company; and **Louis Comfort Tiffany** (1848–1933), artist and master of stained-glass craft. *Fifth Avenue and 25th Street, Brooklyn. Tel. (718) 768-7300. Grounds open 8:00 A.M.–4:00 P.M. daily. Office hours: 8:00 A.M.–4:00 P.M. Monday–Friday, closed holidays; map (fee), rest rooms, tours.*

JEAN-MICHEL BASQUIAT
1960–1988

When he burst onto New York's art scene, which was desperately seeking something new and different, Basquiat seemed a natural: an untrained ghetto-bred graffiti artist with great ability. The truth was something else: He was a middle-class Brooklyn kid whose father was an accountant. From age four Basquiet liked to paint and showed an aptitude for it. To encour-age him, his mother took him to museums to see professional works by modern artists. Basquiat responded to art but not to school, dropping out for good at age seventeen. When he began doing graffiti with a friend, it wasn't run-of-the-subway stuff, but vibrant murals with clever commentary. Shrewdly, he painted where his work would have maximum impact: on walls outside art galleries, nightclubs, places where influential people gathered. He was soon "discovered" and quickly became the poster boy of the New York art scene. By the time he was twenty–four, his paintings were in museum shows and selling for $25,000. His face adorned magazine covers. Andy Warhol was his new best friend. By then Basquiat had a $2,000 a week drug habit, from which Warhol tried to wean him. It worked briefly, but a few months before his twenty-eighth birthday Basquiat was dead of a heroin-cocaine overdose. Whether Basquiat is regarded as a tragic figure of art or just a footnote depends on how time treats his work. He painted fast and furiously, leaving a sizable body of paintings in less than ten years, but much of the later work was repetitive. No question that this African American painter had talent, but as art critic Robert Hughes noted, "it did not develop."

HENRY WARD BEECHER
1813–1887

Because of a presumed illicit affair with one of his parishioners, Beecher is remembered today by many as the Jimmy Swaggert of the nineteenth century, a model of religious hypocrisy. But this popular Brooklyn clergyman was in some ways more a Billy Graham, revered by all who heard his sermons. The Beechers were a family descended from Puritans, and young Henry was destined early for the ministry. His father, Lyman Beecher, was a Connecticut cleric, and sisters were Harriet Beecher Stowe and Isabella Beecher Hooker, both social reformers. Henry was an emotional, sensitive, sometimes unstable young man, and he took a long time to find his niche. When he did, it was as a reformer, not a conventional minister.

Soon his sermons, lectures, and antislavery speeches, delivered in a rich, sonorous voice, brought him attention far beyond his Brooklyn-based Plymouth Congregational Church parish. Now about that affair. The "injured" husband (who had a reputation himself as a rake) charged Beecher with adultery and sued, demanding $100,000 in damages. The trial lasted six months, was tsk-tsked and chuckled at all over the country, and ended with a hung jury (nine for acquittal, three against). Some eighteen months later, a council of Congregational churches examined the charges and vindicated Beecher. Did he or didn't he? is the question. Though he retained his popularity with his church members and continued to lecture on public affairs, Beecher's legacy remains tarnished by the scandal. His and his wife's shared headstone reads, without a touch of irony, "He thinketh no evil."

LEONARD BERNSTEIN
1918–1990

It might be a stretch to call Bernstein the Leonardo de Vinci of music, but he was certainly multitalented, as a composer of both classical music and musical comedy, as a conductor, and as a music educator. Piano lessons as a child, glee club at Boston Latin School, and a music major at Harvard were all preparation for a career in music. Friendships, made at Harvard, with Dimitri Mitropoulos, Adolph Green, and Aaron Copland, also aided his career. For fifteen years he led a series of Young People's Concerts on television, explaining with obvious gusto how various instruments worked in musical compositions. Bernstein was also a masterful, if flamboyant, conductor. He led the New York Philharmonic from 1958 to his death, the first American-born-and-trained conductor to lead a major U.S. orchestra. He composed *Kaddish*, a symphony, and *Trouble in Tahiti*, a modern opera, but he will probably be best remembered for his scores of three Broadway musicals: *Wonderful Town*, *West Side Story* (a smash hit), and *Candide* (not a smash, but arguably the richest of all). Off the podium, Bernstein led almost as complicated a life. Though married to Chilean actress Felicia Montealegre for twenty–seven years, with whom he had three children, Bernstein was widely, if discreetly, known for his homosexual affairs. Yet here Felicia and Leonard are together again, side by side, in a quiet space bordered by ivy and punctuated by evergreens and rhododendrons, at the pinnacle of Green-Wood. No music here, just the twitter of birds.

HORACE GREELEY
1811–1872

Today the name Horace Greeley means little more than his quote, "Go West, young man, go West!" In his heyday, as editor of the *New York Tribune*, from 1840 to 1860, he exercised a voice for morality and integrity and was known for his clear, impeccable writing style. In editing the *Tribune*, New Hampshire – born Greeley wanted it to be, in his words, "removed from servile partisanship." Indeed it set high standards with its straight news reporting. There was no room on its pages for scandals or police blotter stories. Greeley was opposed to monopoly and class dominance, and as an abolitionist, he was against any compromise with slavery. He bolted the Whigs and joined the

new Republican Party. Bitten by the political bug, Greeley ran for office early, often, and usually unsuccessfully, though he did serve in the U.S. Congress for three months in the late 1840s. Efforts to get elected to the Senate failed, and as he became more involved in politics, his influence on the *Tribune* declined. Although he supported General Ulysses S. Grant for president, he soon became disappointed in Grant's policies and in 1872 ran against him as a splinter party's candidate. Despite his personal popularity, intensive campaigning, and rousing rhetoric, Greeley was demolished in the election, winning only six states. He called himself "the worst beaten man who ever ran for high office." To add to his despair, another man had assumed control of the *Tribune*, leaving Greeley editor in name only. This news, his exhausting campaign—waged in poor health to begin with—and the death of his wife just before the election may have tipped him over the edge: He died insane within the month, a tragic ending to a full and constructive life.

WILLIAM MARCY "BOSS" TWEED
1823–1878

You might not expect the son of a Scottish chairmaker to become—before he was forty—the most influential man in New York. From teenage apprenticeships as a saddler, then bookkeeper, young immigrant Tweed graduated to volunteer fireman. Then he wangled a job as an assistant alderman. Soon he worked himself into the inner sanctum of Tammany Hall, the power base of the Democratic party, and in 1860 became chairman—the boss—of Tammany's central committee, a position that

controlled all nominations and appointments. This was a time in New York when money "talked," and people paid the "Boss" generously for jobs, favors, the passage of bills, and access. He opened the gates for the Brooklyn Bridge project to proceed and, as his reward, accepted $40,000 in stock. Tweed's influence was exposed constantly by political cartoonist Thomas Nast in *Harper's Weekly,* and eventually a member of the Tweed gang blew the whistle. Tweed was tried and convicted, sentenced to twelve years in jail and a $12,750 fine, but both penalties were reduced on appeal. Released after a year in prison, he was rearrested in a civil suit and ordered to recover all the money, $6 million, that he and his chums had stolen from the state. He couldn't do so and was reincarcerated, but so casually that he was able to escape, first to Cuba and then to Spain, disguised as a sailor. A Nast cartoon likeness alerted Spanish authorities, who shipped him back to New York and prison, where he died. There have been worse rogues in public life (recently too). By all accounts, Tweed, brazen as he was, was also amiable and generous, which may be why so much of the money he filched during his ten-year reign, estimated to be between $30 million and $200 million, was dissipated. The Tweed family memorial here isn't ostentatious, but it's not shabby either.

Green River Cemetery

EAST HAMPTON

A tiny burial ground on less than three acres, shaped like a horseshoe, this has become such an A list for East Hampton's artistic community that it is oversubscribed. You'll find such star power as **Stuart Davis** (1892–1964), a modern painter whose career spanned several artistic trends; **Elaine de Kooning** (1918–1989), abstract artist, wife of Dutch-born Abstract Expressionist Willem de Kooning; **Jimmy Ernst** (1920–1984), modern artist, son of surrealist painter Max Ernst; **Pierre Franey** (1921–1996), French chef, columnist for the *New York Times;* **A. J. Liebling** (1904–1963), *New Yorker* magazine writer; **Frank O'Hara** (1926–1966), poet; **Alfonso Ossorio** (1916–1990), Abstract Expressionist artist; **Alan Pakula** (1928–1998), stage and movie director, whose films include *To Kill a Mockingbird* and *All the President's Men;* **Steven J. Ross** (1927–1992), telecommunications mogul, CEO of Time Warner; **Jean Stafford** (1915–1979) novelist, wife of Liebling, and winner of a Pulitzer Prize for short stories; and **Stefan Wolpe** (1902–1972), German-born composer of avant-garde music. *Old Accabonac Road, East Hampton.*

JACKSON POLLOCK
1 9 1 2 – 1 9 5 6

Pollock, born on a ranch in Cody, Wyoming, became the symbol of Abstract Expressionism, the leading art movement of the 1950s–1960s. His "action" or "drip" style painting looked simple. His technique was to spread a large canvas on the floor, then splatter paint all over it. There was order in what he was doing—a lifetime of study went into it—but to the public it often elicited the comment that "a child could do that." Not so. Pollock studied with Thomas Hart Benton at the Art Students League, went through a social realism phase, then surrealism and finally his work evolved into the large squiggles of color that adorn museum walls today. He struggled at first to sell his work, but patrons like Peggy Guggenheim, Betty Parsons, and fellow artist Alfonso Ossorio came to his rescue with financial and moral support. But no one could help him control his rage or chronic alcoholism, which only ended when he lost control of his car and crashed into a tree, killing himself and one of two companions. Fame came too late for him to enjoy. His marker here is a gigantic boulder with his signature in bronze. In front of it is a smaller stone, that of fellow painter **Lee Krasner** (1908–1984), his long-suffering wife of eleven stormy years, who kept the Pollock flame alive.

Woodlawn Cemetery

ELMIRA

Well shaded by oak trees, Woodlawn, which has been open since 1858, might seem ghostly to anyone with a vivid imagination, but it is merely sepulchrally peaceful. Like many burial grounds, this one has its surprise residents: **Thomas K. Beecher,** the minister who officiated at Samuel Clemens's wedding, leader of the Underground Railroad in Elmira, and half brother of Harriet Beecher Stowe; **Ernie Davis** (1939–1963), Syracuse University football hero, first African American to win the Heisman trophy, who died at age twenty-three of leukemia; and **Hal Roach** (1892–1992), producer of the Laurel and Hardy shorts, *The Little Rascals,* and other 1930s comedies, who was an Elmira home boy and lies very near the Clemens's site. Adjacent is **Woodlawn National Cemetery**, where 2,000 Confederate soldiers lie, prisoners of war in Elmira during the Civil War. *North and Walnut streets, Elmira. Tel. (607) 732-0151. Grounds open 8:00 A.M.–9:00 P.M. daily. Office hours: 8:00 A.M.–4:00 P.M. (closed 12:00 P.M.–1:00 P.M. for lunch) Monday–Friday; map, rest room.*

SAMUEL LANGHORNE CLEMENS
1835–1910

Why Elmira? Because Elmira was the hometown of Clemens's wife, Olivia Langdon. The Clemenses—or Mark Twains—spent twenty summers at Quarry Farm, the Langdon home. It might not seem to be surprising to find Clemens resting in his hometown of Hannibal, Missouri, which he put on the literary map with *The Adventures of Tom Sawyer* (1876), *Life on the Mississippi* (1883), and *The Adventures of Huckleberry Finn* (1884), perennial favorites among his voluminous works. But though he drew on his early days in Missouri and on the Mississippi, he was a wanderer at heart. As a boy he wanted to be a river pilot, and he later took his pen name from the call used by river pilots taking soundings, "mark twain," meaning two fathoms deep. But river trade dried up after the Civil War, so Clemens/Twain meandered west, briefly mining for gold and writing for newspapers in Nevada. While living in San Francisco, he wrote the humorous story, *The Celebrated Jumping Frog of Calaveras County,* which brought him instant celebrity and money enough to write what he wanted and to wander at will. After marriage, he settled down in Hartford, Connect-

icut, built his dream house, and spent thirty years there. Success gave him the means to travel frequently to Europe and around the world. Every trip, every experience, was fodder for his humor and pen. While *Huckleberry Finn* is considered Twain's masterpiece, his steady output produced books as diverse as *Roughing It* and *A Tramp Abroad, The Prince and the Pauper, A Connecticut Yankee at King Arthur's Court,* and *The Tragedy of Pudd'nhead Wilson.* He once said, "I came in with Halley's Comet ... and I expect to go out with it." And he did. More than 3,000 mourners attended his funeral. The route to his grave is well marked, at the end of a short sloping pathway shielded by a canopy of giant oaks and lined with Langdon and Clemens gravestones. At the end of the path is a twelve-foot-high granite column (erected by Twain's daughter Clara) with a bronze medallion of Twain at the top and that of Clara's husband, a concert pianist, at the bottom. **Mark Twain's study** (Park Place; 607-735–1941), moved from Quarry Farm, is now part of Elmira College and open to visitors. Built like a pilothouse on a Mississippi riverboat, it is where he worked on four of his best-known books.

Flushing Cemetery

FLUSHING

There's nothing pretentious about the seventy-five acres on which this 1853 grave-yard rests. It is a quiet place of trees and gentle slopes, with workmanlike stones and an occasional obelisk and mausoleum. The subterranean inhabitants include **Bernard Baruch** (1870–1965), financier, who cultivated friendships with and offered advice to five U.S. presidents (though there isn't much evidence that any of them took it); **Johnny Hodges** (1906–1970), one of the all-time great jazz saxophonists, a featured soloist with Duke Ellington; **Adam Clayton Powell, Sr.**, minister of the Abyssinian Baptist Church in Harlem and father of controversial congressman Adam Clayton Powell, Jr. (who is buried in Woodlawn in the Bronx); **Mae Robson** (1865–1942), movie actress; and **Hazel Scott** (1920–1981), jazz pianist and enter-tainer, onetime wife of Adam Clayton Powell, Jr. *163-06 46th Avenue, Flushing, Long Island. Tel. (718) 359-0100. Grounds open 8:30 A.M.–4:30 P.M. daily. Office hours: 8:30 A.M.–4:30 P.M. Monday–Friday, 8:30 A.M.–1:00 P.M. Saturday; map, rest room.*

LOUIS ARMSTRONG
1 9 0 0 – 1 9 7 1

The scat singing and exuberant trum-pet playing of Louis Armstrong are so pervasive on CDs, radio, and cassettes that it seems impossible to believe that he's been gone since 1971. This dynamic man, the shape of whose mouth, often formed in an infectious grin, gave him the nickname "Satchmo" (for satchel mouth)—it's even etched into his polished black granite headstone with the white trumpet on top—is the epitome of jazz. Even those who normally don't "dig" jazz, dig him. His bouncy persona and incandescent playing, whether singing duets with Ella Fitzgerald or blasting out trumpet solos, were real. His raspy, ebullient renditions of "Hello Dolly" and "Mack the Knife" made these show tunes his own. His early life on the mean streets of Storyville, the red-light district in his hometown of New Orleans, included time at the Colored Waifs Home for minor brushes with the law, but it was time he put to good use, learning several musical instruments and earning the chance to play in the home's marching band. Later he met Joe "King" Oliver, who helped hone Louis's natural raw talent. Then it was on to Chicago and New York, and wider recognition. Triumphant tours of Europe, Africa, and Asia followed, and the accolade "Ambassador of Jazz" was his for life. He never stopped loving what he did—and it showed. He once said, "Anyone can steal anything but my applause," which may be why he never gave a lackluster performance. Satchmo was no saint marching in—he supposedly smoked marijuana daily most of his life—but he was one of the most extraordinary jazz artists of the twentieth century.

DIZZY GILLESPIE
1917–1993

John Birks Gillespie earned his nickname "Dizzy" for his humor and sense of fun. You might think, though, that the name derived from the lightning speed with which he played trumpet, his syncopated rhythmic phrasing and his great technical facility that carried listeners to Dizzy-ing heights. As a fifteen-year-old in South Carolina, he won a scholarship to Laurinburg Institute in North Carolina, where he studied music theory and harmony, while sitting in with Southern dance bands. Trumpeter Roy Eldridge was his inspiration, but once Gillespie began playing professionally, he hooked up with his contemporaries, musicians like Thelonius Monk, Oscar Pettiford, Kenny Clarke, and, later, Charlie "Bird" Parker, and he began to develop the sound known as bebop. Most of the group had some classical music background and deep roots in the African American musical tradition. With bebop's rise, it brought along a new culture of hip talk and a "uniform" of horn-rimmed sunglasses, beret, and goatee, Gillespie trademarks. But for all the external "look," Gillespie was a serious musician. He immersed himself in other cultures, synthesized jazz and Afro-Cuban rhythms, became the U.S. State Department's first jazz cultural ambassador abroad, performed at the White House for three presidents, launched a "Jazz-America" project for public television, and mentored younger musicians. All the while he was proving himself a dazzling jazz innovator. Many awards and honors and an autobiography, *To Be or Not to Bop: Memoirs*, followed, before diabetes and pancreatic cancer stopped the bopping for good.

Ferncliff Cemetery

Some 30,000 people are buried on Ferncliff's sixty-six acres, though buried is a matter of speech. Most are entombed indoors in wall vaults in the main and newer Shrine mausoleums. There are few headstones outdoors; most of the fresh-air graves have more or less identical bronze markers flush to the grass, making them difficult to find. Among scores of terrestrial tenants here are **Maxwell Anderson** (1888–1959), poet-playwright, author of *Winterset*; **Harold Arlen** (1905–1986), composer of "Over the Rainbow" and other popular songs; **James Baldwin** (1924–1987), African American novelist and essayist much acclaimed for his original prose; **Charles** (1874–1948) and **Mary Beard** (1876–1958), husband and wife historians; **Hattie Carnegie** (1889–1956), fashion designer; **Michel Fokine** (1880–1942), world-famous Russian ballet choreographer; **Karen Horney** (1885–1952), noted psychiatrist; **Jerome Kern** (1885–1945), composer of *Show Boat* and other popular classics; and **Thelonius Monk** (1917–1982), pianist and jazz composer known for his witty, original style. Also be on the lookout for **Basil Rathbone** (1892–1967), British actor who *was* Sherlock Holmes on the silver screen; **Ed Sullivan** (1901–1974), newspaperman and host of a popular television variety show; and **Whitney M. Young, Jr.** (1921–1971), executive director of the National Urban League. Classical composer **Bela Bartok** (1881–1945) was here

and gone (returned to his native Hungary). *281 Secor Road, Hartsdale. Tel. (914) 693-4700. Grounds open 9:00 A.M.–4:00 P.M. daily, except closed on major holidays at 1:30 P.M. The office is in the main mausoleum; office hours: 9:00 A.M.–4:00 P.M. daily, except closed at 1:30 P.M. major holidays; map, rest rooms.*

JOAN CRAWFORD
1 9 0 6 – 1 9 7 7

In a long career Lucille LeSeuer (as Crawford was born, on the wrong side of the tracks, in San Antonio, Texas) emerged from a modest start as a Broadway dancer to the starring role in dozens of dramatic films, beginning in 1925 with *Pretty Lady* and *Sally, Irene and Mary*. In her golden decade (1931–1941), she made many classics, *Rain*, *Grand Hotel*, *The Women*, and *A Woman's Face* among them, and was considered queen of what were called tearjerkers or "four handkerchief" movies. In 1945 *Mildred Pierce* won her an Oscar for best actress. As Crawford's career wound down, she made *Whatever Happened to Baby Jane?* in 1962 with Bette Davis. It was a huge hit, helped along by a public feud between the two aging stars, who detested each other. Crawford lived to the hilt her public life as a glamorous Hollywood star. Her private life, with four adopted children, four marriages, and affairs (including a long one, off and on, with Clark Gable) was something else, as attested to by her daughter, Christina, in a bitter exposé titled *Mommy Dearest*. There is something anticlimactic about la Crawford's final address. No perpetual music, no flowers, no grandiose marble monument here. Au contraire: a large vault, with "Steele" as top billing and below that her name and that of her husband, **Alfred M. Steele**, and that's it. Though the birthdate listed on her vault is 1908, experts believe that 1906 is accurate. Ever the actress, even unto death.

JUDY GARLAND
1 9 2 2 – 1 9 6 9

The Judy Garland fan club is alive and well, still leaving fresh flowers at her unassuming wall vault. The story of the transformation of little Frances Gumm into one of Hollywood's legends is a familiar one. Oldtimers remember her as Mickey Rooney's girfriend in the Andy Hardy series, but *The Wizard of Oz* brought her eternal stardom and *A Star Is Born* proved she could really act. Her tremulous voice and soulful brown eyes gave her a poignancy that fans adored. Add the sad story of her bouts with alcohol, drugs, and failed marriages, and she became larger than life or death. Proof of her eternal popularity is that even today the name "Judy" evokes thoughts of only one star. Her performances, via films and television concerts, go on and on, over the rainbow.

PAUL ROBESON
1 8 9 8 – 1 9 7 6

"The artist must elect to fight for freedom or slavery. I have made my choice. I had no alternative." So speaks this proud man defiantly from beyond the grave, as his tombstone states. Powerful singer, actor, political activist, Robeson lived, and died, in controversy. Born in Princeton, New Jersey, the son of a former slave, he inherited from his Presbyterian minis-

PAUL ROBESON
APRIL 9, 1898   JAN. 23, 1976
"THE ARTIST MUST ELECT TO FIGHT
FOR FREEDOM OR SLAVERY. I
HAVE MADE MY CHOICE. I HAD
NO ALTERNATIVE"

ter father his stentorian baritone, sense of dignity, and devotion to social justice. The last defined his entire life. Robeson might have had it easy; he was a star football player and Phi Beta Kappa at Rutgers, earned a law degree at Columbia, was a successful Broadway actor, concert singer, scholar, and ladies' man. He scored major Broadway successes in *Emperor Jones, Othello,* and *Show Boat.* But his left-wing politics during the 1930s, when he was an apologist for the Soviet Union, did him in professionally. He was blacklisted and persecuted by the FBI, which tapped his phone. Pride and a certain arrogance kept him from recanting earlier idealistic beliefs. He suffered in other ways: from depression and several suicide attempts. Robeson's long sad life finally ended in loneliness and despair.

PRESTON STURGES
1898–1959

Fans of *Sullivan's Travels, The Great McGinty, The Lady Eve, Christmas in July, Hail the Conquering Hero, The Palm Beach Story,* and other films by this writer-director may be disappointed at the minimal final tribute here to his memory. Last seen, the marker, with name and dates only, located in front of the Shrine mausoleum in the Maplewood section, was half-covered by crabgrass. But the movies live on as testament to Sturges's originality, sense of farce, satire, and madcap fun. Born in Chicago, Sturges lived in France as a child, served with the Signal Corps of the U.S. Army in World War I, spent six years in his mother's cosmetic business (where he invented kissproof lipstick—how Sturgesian!), worked briefly on Broadway, and started writing plays. He headed to Hollywood in 1932 and that's when his real career and life's work began, as a screenwriter, then a writer-director. Sturges defined himself as a humorist working in movies, and most of his best work has a wry, witty slant. He was at his best when he could control everything—production, direction, and writing—which is why his best films have his distinctive point of view. His slightly askew look at the world went out of fashion in the late 1950s. While working on his autobiography, *The Events Leading Up to My Death,* at New York's Algonquin Hotel, Sturges had a heart attack and died. He would have loved the irony.

MALCOLM X
1925–1965

Malcolm X, aka Hajj-Malik, had a life fraught with discord, from early beginnings in prison to his murder by members of an opposing Black Muslim sect. In the *Autobiography of Malcolm X*, which he related to Alex Haley, he describes his conversion from street hood to follower of Elijah Muhammad and the Black Muslim movement. At a time, the 1960s, when Martin Luther King was preaching integration, Malcolm X was promoting separatism for African Americans. His red-hot rhetoric inflamed blacks and terrified whites, but after a religious pilgrimage to Africa, he returned to America with a new perspective. Many believe that had he lived he would have reinvented himself one more time. With his intelligence and articulateness, there was the potential for better things ahead. They were not to be. He can be found now outdoors near two dogwood trees in the Pinewood section, next to his wife, **Betty El Shabazz** (1936–1997), a peaceful finale after the horrific shots that ended his life just before his fortieth birthday.

Westchester Hills Cemetery

HASTINGS-ON-HUDSON

Cited as the Memorial Park of the Stephen Wise Free Synagogue, in honor of a respected Reform rabbi, **Stephen S. Wise** (1874–1949), this seventeen-acre burial ground climbs a steep hill around a circuitous drive and down again. It is chockablock with large, austere mausoleums, like one with the name **Barricini**, the candy manufacturer, written in script across the front. Here also are the shades of **John Garfield** (1913–1952) stage and movie actor; **Sidney Hillman** (1887–1946), union leader and head of Amalgamated Clothing Workers of America; **Judy Holliday** (1922–1965), comic actress, best known for her role as the dumb but sensitive blond in *Born Yesterday*, for which she won an Oscar; **Max Reinhardt** (1873–1943), producer and director; and **Billy Rose** (1899–1966), Broadway producer, songwriter, promoter, and showman, known for his small size, now at rest in a spacious mausoleum. *400 Saw Mill River Road, Hastings-on-Hudson. Tel. (914) 478-1767. Grounds and office open 8:00 A.M.–4:00 P.M. daily except closed Saturday; rest room.*

GEORGE GERSHWIN
1898–1937

Torn between an affinity for popular music and admiration of the classics, Gershwin managed the unthinkable: He bridged the gap between them. Beginning with "Swanee," one of his first pop hits, he wrote all the songs in the *George White Scandals,* annual Broadway revues of the 1920s. His ticket to ride the classics train came with a commission from Paul Whiteman to compose a big orchestral work in the jazz idiom. This turned

out to be *Rhapsody in Blue* in 1924, the success of which made Gershwin famous overnight and rich forever. But he was just hitting his stride. *An American in Paris* followed four years later, but concurrently there were his scores for *Lady Be Good, Girl Crazy, Funny Face,* and *Strike Up the Band,* Broadway shows that have become classics too. Then came *Of Thee I Sing,* for which his brother Ira wrote the lyrics and George S. Kaufman the book. His *Porgy and Bess* folk opera, with words by his brother and DuBose Heyward, was not a success at the time (1935) but has become an important part of the Gershwin legacy. Prolific, talented, and inspired, Gershwin did Hollywood musicals too, found time to collect art, and even took up painting, all while savoring the role of man-about-Manhattan. The world was his—until a catastrophic operation for a brain tumor ended it abruptly. He was thirty-eight years old. "Who Could Ask for

Anything More?" We could. Here with George in this large mausoleum is his lyricist brother, **Ira Gershwin** (1896–1983), his frequent collaborator. Note the panels to the right and left of the tomb doors: bas reliefs of musical instruments, interwoven with notes from *Rhapsody in Blue.*

LEE STRASBERG
1902–1982

The common denominator that links Dustin Hoffman, James Dean, Robert De Niro, Anne Bancroft, Julie Harris, Paul Newman, and Marilyn Monroe is Strasberg, a Polish-born actor-director who taught them all, at the Actors Studio in New York, in the style known as the "Method," which encourages actors to use their subconscious to develop their roles. The most celebrated exponent of the Method was probably Marlon Brando. Strasberg's style influenced at least two generations of American actors. Even successful stars like Monroe considered it chic to study with him. Plays were developed there under his aegis too, notably *A Hatful of Rain, The Night of The Iguana, The Zoo Story,* and *The Death of Bessie Smith.* Although Strasberg stopped acting in public 1929, he constantly acted in class as a teaching tool, and eventually Al Pacino, one of his students, per-suaded him to take a supporting role in *Godfather II,* for which he received an Oscar nomination. Several other movie roles followed. That Strasberg is mourned and still missed by devoted students, playwrights, and other theater-connected folks appears to be no act.

Cemetery of Gate of Heaven

HAWTHORNE

When this 250-acre property became a cemetery in 1918, owned and operated by the Catholic Archdiocese of New York, New York architect Charles Wellford Leavitt was hired to create a plan along rural lines, with rolling hills, steep banks, an abun-dance of oak and pine trees, and a Gothic bridge spanning a little lake. The beauti-ful floor-to-ceiling stained-glass windows in the modern circular chapel were designed by Benoit Gilsoul. The privileged residents here are many and include **Bob Considine** (1906–1975), famous sports columnist; **Anna Held** (1872–1918), French musical comedy star, first wife of showman Florenz Ziegfeld; **Dorothy Kilgallen** (1913–1965), well-known syndicated columnist and radio-television per-former on *What's My Line?;* **Sal Mineo** (1939–1976), promising young actor, victim of a mugging and murder; **Fulton Oursler** (1893–1952), religious writer; **Michael Quill** (1905–1966), labor leader, powerful head of Transport Workers Union; **Dutch Schultz** (1902–1935), racketeer and gangster, buried under his real name, Arthur Flegenheimer; and **Jimmy Walker** (1881–1946), affable bon vivant, ineffectual mayor of New York. *10 West Stevens Avenue, Hawthorne. Tel. (914) 769-3672. Grounds open 7:30 A.M.–4:30 P.M. daily. Office hours: 9:00 A.M.–4:30 P.M. daily, except major holidays; map, rest rooms, drinking fountain, Mass 9:00 A.M. every Saturday in St. Francis of Assisi chapel.*

FRED ALLEN

1894–1954

Fans of Fred Allen's nasal voice and deadpan humor in radio's *Fred Allen Show* usually think first of "Allen's Alley," the hit feature of the program, with oddball characters like Mrs. Pansy Nussbaum, a Brooklyn house-wife; Titus Moody; Ajax Cassidy; Falstaff Openshaw, the resident poet; and Senator Beauregard Claghorn. Portland Hoffa, Allen's real wife, was also a regular. Allen—whose birth name, John F. Sullivan, is also etched on his headstone—developed his interest in comedy from a book on the subject that he found in the Boston Public Library, where he worked nights during his high school years. After graduation he headed for the vaudeville circuit, billing himself "The World's Worst Juggler," with an act that juggled tenpins with jokes. An eleven-month tour of Australia and New Zealand gave him time to create a new act and new name, which, on his return to New York, brought him top billing at the Palace. Then came raves for his stand-up monologues in *Three's a Crowd* and several other musical revues. Throughout his career Allen wrote most of his own material; even today, on hearing rebroadcasts, it sounds remarkably fresh and original. Whether he could have made the transition to television is a moot question. His humor was dry and verbal, his voice was grating, and he looked uncomfortable in his few appearances on the screen. He was scheduled to give TV a try in 1952, but a heart attack forced him into semiretirement. He died two years later, after collapsing on the street near Carnegie Hall. A rare example—for him—of bad timing.

JAMES CAGNEY
1899–1986

Jimmy Cagney didn't have the face of a matinee idol, but he played almost everything else in sixty–five years of acting and dancing, which began in vaudeville in 1919 and ended with a television movie, *Terrible Joe Moran* in 1984. To break into show business, Cagney taught himself to dance (with help from actress-dancer Frances Vernon, who would later marry him) and then danced in Broadway chorus lines all through the 1920s. His grace of movement was evident, even when portraying the worst of hoodlums, as

in *Public Enemy* (his break-through movie) and *Angels with Dirty Faces.* (His knowledge of gangsters was first-hand from the rough New York neighborhood in which he grew up.) After years of playing crooks and cops in 1930s movies, he astonished audiences with his rousing, cocky, dancing performance as showman George M. Cohan in the 1942 musical *Yankee Doodle Dandy,* for which he won a best actor Oscar. *Mister Roberts* (1955) revealed his comedy talents, but by then he was ready for early retirement. He retreated to his New York horse farm, raised Morgan horses, farmed, sailed, played classical guitar, painted, puttered, wrote poetry, and worked on an autobiography, *Cagney by Cagney* (with a little help from a ghostwriter). In 1981 he was lured from retirement to play Commissioner Waldo in *Ragtime.* Diabetes and circulatory problems brought down the final curtain in 1986. He and **Frances W. Cagney** (1899–1994), his wife of sixty–four years, now reside here side by side in marble wall crypts in the mausoleum. He was a Yankee Doodle Dandy.

BILLY MARTIN
1928–1989

Around the corner from Babe Ruth is a former Yankee of a very different (pin)stripe. Alfred Manuel Martin's imposing mottled-brown granite, horizontal memorial has real baseballs inserted in recesses at both end. Also featured on it is a white bas relief of St. Jude, patron saint of lost causes, and at the top above the name "Martin" is a white bas relief cross. Considering Martin's dysfunctional life, it is easy to forget that this pugnacious man was a better than average ball player and a canny manager. It was off the field that he had trouble: too many nightclubs, too much drinking, too quick a temper, too many fistfights, too many tabloid headlines. As an infielder, he played on six world championship Yankee teams but was traded after a brawl at the Copacabana nightclub. In sixteen years as a manager—with five different teams—he won five divisional titles, two American League pennants, and one World Series, that one with the Yankees. His Yankee years were fractured by frequent combat with owner George Steinbrenner, who fired and rehired him three times. But Martin's heart was always with the Yankees, who retired his number 1 uniform and hung a plaque at Yankee Stadium in his honor. He died in a car accident on Christmas Day. That's one call he couldn't argue.

CONDÉ NAST
1 8 7 3 – 1 9 4 2

It may come as a surprise that Condé Nast, widely known as a conglomerate publishing company, actually was a real live human being. Condé Montrose Nast was New York born, St. Louis bred, and Georgetown University educated. Though possessed of a law degree, he joined a friend as advertising manager of *Collier's Weekly* in New York and soon left to cofound the Home Pattern Company, which made and sold dress patterns. In 1909 he bought *Vogue*, which he converted from a small society magazine to the arbiter of good taste and fashion for upper-class women and wannabes. Nast's appetite for magazine acquisition continued with *Vanity Fair.* Then came *House and Garden,* a European edition of *Vogue,* and, after a brief setback during

the Depression, *Glamour*. Nast had more success in his choice of editors than in wives: His two marriages failed. He succumbed to a fatal heart attack in 1942, but the empire bearing his name lives on and on and on.

WESTBROOK PEGLER
1 8 9 4 – 1 9 6 9

Anyone who thinks fame isn't fleeting might check the record of Pegler. In full throttle—the 1930s and 1940s—he ruled the roost of journalism and commentary. From simple beginnings as a sportswriter (at which he excelled), he moved on to a national beat with a syndicated column called "Fair Enough." Writing in an acerbic, hard-hitting, often witty style, he spared nothing and no one, ridiculing hero worship, lambasting politicians, sports figures, anyone in public life. Favorite targets were Franklin and Eleanor Roosevelt, author Upton Sinclair, fellow columnist Drew Pearson, Huey Long, and, surprisingly, Frank Sinatra. Labor leaders, Nazis, Communists, gamblers, and the IRS all felt the sting of his words. In his prime his hard-hitting style earned him a Pulitzer Prize for an exposé of a corrupt union leader. But as times changed, Pegler lost his audience and influence. In the process he became embittered and shrilly reactionary, ending up writing for the John Birch Society magazine and other right-wing publications. Finally, he lost a long battle with stomach cancer.

BABE RUTH
1 8 9 5 – 1 9 4 8

No sport has ever been as defined by one man as baseball has by George Herman Ruth, aka the "Sultan of Swat." Record after record for home runs and hits and the visceral joy of

"MAY
THE DIVINE SPIRIT
THAT ANIMATED
BABE RUTH
TO WIN THE CRUCIAL
GAME OF LIFE
INSPIRE THE YOUTH
OF AMERICA"
CARDINAL SPELLMAN

GEORGE HERMAN RUTH
1895 — 1948

CLAIRE RUTH
1900 — 1976

RUTH

playing the game, these are the Babe Ruth legacy. Yet he hardly fit the image of the perfect athlete. Excesses were his signature: drinking, overeating (a pint of ice cream as a between-meal snack), womanizing, fast driving, insufficient sleep, lack of exercise. Even so, he played the game with a zest rarely seen. From shaky beginnings as a truant and reluctant student at a school for underprivileged boys in Baltimore, he could have drifted into adulthood as a small-time loser, but baseball saved him and he never forgot. The Babe began his career as a pitcher (a good one) with the Baltimore Orioles and then with the Boston Red Sox, where he also became a hard-hitting outfielder. After being traded for beans (so it seemed—a mere $125,000 and a loan) to the New York Yankees, he came into superstardom as the Babe Ruth of legend, playing fifteen years in a Yankee uniform, on a team that made seven World Series appearances and won four of them. One of the first five players elected to the Hall of Fame, Ruth held fifty–four major league records when he died. On his large white marble headstone is a bas relief of a full-length Jesus instructing a young boy in modern clothes (the Babe?), with a quote by Cardinal Spellman: "May the divine spirit that animated Babe Ruth to win the crucial game of life inspire the youth of America." The grass in front of the memorial is perpetually strewn with bats, balls, Yankee caps, pennies, fresh flowers, and American flags. For Ruth fans, the Babe will never have a final at-bat.

Franklin D. Roosevelt National Historic Site

HYDE PARK

The graves of both Franklin Roosevelt and his wife, Eleanor, are in the rose garden of the Franklin Roosevelt family home, Springwood, which overlooks the Hudson River from a majestic height. Also on the grounds: the **Franklin D. Roosevelt Library and Museum.** The property is under the supervision of the National Park Service. *U.S. Highway 9, Hyde Park. Tel. (845) 229–8114. Grounds open from dawn to dusk. Grounds and rose garden access free, nominal admission to the house; rest rooms.*

FRANKLIN DELANO ROOSEVELT
1882–1945

Born to a New York family of Dutch descent, Roosevelt was an only child and apple of his mother's eye. An indifferent student at Harvard, a dropout at Columbia Law School (but admitted, nonetheless, to the New York bar), handsome young Franklin was attracted to politics. Marriage to a shy, plain cousin from another branch of the family followed, along with a string of political jobs: state senator, assistant secretary of the navy under Woodrow Wilson, an unsuccessful run for vice president. Then disaster in the form of polio struck, leaving both his legs paralyzed. The promising politician's career seemed over. But through courage, determination, and his wife's encouragement, he learned to stand and, with leg braces, even walk a few steps. He resumed his political career, winning two terms as governor of New York, and, in 1932, the presidency. Our thirty–second president's policies were so popular he easily won an unprecedented four terms. Early on, he repealed Prohibition and introduced his New Deal, which carried the country through the Great Depression with innovative public works and relief programs. He also introduced legislation that established Social Security. Once the Japanese attacked Pearl Harbor, Roosevelt guided the country through a world war. He died of a cerebral hemorrhage on April 12, 1945, when his fourth term had just begun. Like all great leaders he had ardent admirers and a hard core of fierce haters. Today FDR is viewed by most historians as the greatest of our twentieth-century presidents.

ELEANOR ROOSEVELT
1 8 8 4 – 1 9 6 2

Here also is Franklin's independent-spirited wife of forty years. What began as a love match between two cousins, resulting in six children in ten years, evolved, due to Franklin's infidelities, into a detente, and then a solid political partnership. Eleanor traveled the country and the world on behalf of various causes—minorities, working-class women, the poor, the oppressed of all nations—and articulated their frustrations and goals in speeches, a newspaper column, and other writings. Hated by those who felt she had "betrayed her class" (a charge leveled against FDR as well), she was beloved by millions of others. In 1939 she resigned from the Daughters of the American Revolution because the organization refused to let the African American singer Marian Anderson perform at Constitution Hall. **Val-Kill** (2 miles east of Hyde Park; 845–229–8114) is a separate house Mrs. Roosevelt maintained (away from the pressures of Franklin's strong-minded mother, Sara, who ruled Hyde Park with an iron hand). It is open to visitors, offering a fascinating glimpse into Eleanor's lifestyle.

St. Bartholomew's Episcopal Church
MANHATTAN

The simple Memorial Chapel of this beautiful Byzantine-style domed church has mottled-beige marble wall crypts along three sides. Names on all the vaults are nearly impossible to read, being etched into the stone, but in the top row of the wall opposite the altar, the third vault from the left contains the name Gish. Mother **Mary Gish** (1876–1942) gets top billing, next is **Dorothy Gish** (1898–1968), and on the bottom is Lillian Diana. To reach the chapel go to the left side of the church on 51st Street; halfway down the block is the entrance. *109 East 50th Street and Park Avenue, New York. Tel. (212) 751-1616. Chapel is open 8:00 A.M.–6:00 P.M. daily.*

LILLIAN GISH
CA. 1893–1996

By all accounts, including Lillian's, her younger sister Dorothy was the natural talent in the family, with a flair for comedy. Both sisters were beautiful, but Lillian, with her perfect oval of a face, was the eternal childlike innocent and far more serious. "Dorothy got the happy side that God left out of me," she often said. She worked from age nine, outlasting silent films, moving on to a sixty-year career on the stage, radio, television, and talkies. At a graceful ninety-three years, she made her last movie, *The Whales of August*, with Bette Davis. She grew from a star of silent melodramas like *Way Down East, Broken Blossoms, The Birth of a Nation,* and *Orphans of the Storm* into a genuine tragic actress. She also appeared on stage in *Uncle Vanya, Hamlet* (in which at age forty–three she played a believable Ophelia), *Camille,* and opposite John Gielgud in *Crime and Punishment.* Later movies included *Duel in the Sun* and *The Night of the Hunter.* Although Lillian had friendships—believed by many to be platonic—with several men, she never married, claiming she never "found a name I would rather carry than Lillian Gish." Clearly, she made it a distinguished one.

Trinity Churchyard

MANHATTAN

To many who work downtown, this venerable graveyard (part of the old Episcopal Trinity Church), dating back to 1703, is a restful oasis, a place where office workers can spend a quiet lunch hour, munching on sandwiches or reading. No longer an active burial ground, Trinity attracts visitors for its history and historic residents. The grave that garners most attention is that of Alexander Hamilton, but there are many other distinguished full-timers here, such as **William Bradford** (1660–1752), government printer for fifty years or more and exponent of a free press; **Robert Fulton** (1765–1815), prophet and statesman, who recognized the importance of steam navigation to American progress; **Albert Gallatin** (1761–1849), banker, diplomat,

Jefferson's secretary of the treasury; **James Lawrence** (1781–1813), captain of the *Chesapeake*, locked in combat with the British frigate *Shannon* in the War of 1812, famous for his dying words: "Don't give up the ship!"; **Francis Lewis** (1713–1803), a Welshman, signer of the Declaration of Independence; and **John Peter Zenger** (1697–1746), publisher, printer, and advocate of a free press. *Broadway at Wall Street, Manhattan. Tel. (212) 368–1600. Office hours: 8:30 A.M.–4:30 P.M. Monday–Friday; daily services.*

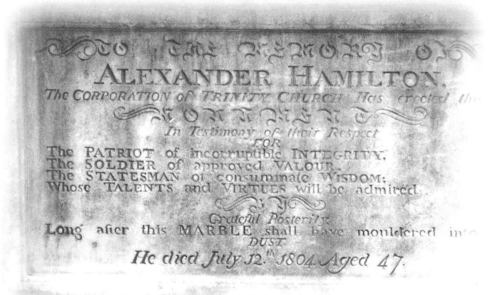

ALEXANDER HAMILTON
1757–1804

We tend to view our founding fathers with rosy lenses, but they were men with both virtues and weaknesses. No one illustrates this better than Hamilton. As George Washington's secretary of the treasury, he put the infant American republic on a sound financial keel, promoted the establishment of a national bank, and did everything possible to strengthen the federal government. His intellect was huge, his courage and integrity beyond reproach. At the same time he meddled in every branch of government, intrigued behind Washington's back, quarreled with John Adams and Thomas Jefferson, and sometimes let personal rivalry interfere with public policy. Yet, in 1800, when the presidential election between Jefferson and Aaron Burr ended in a tie and went to the House of Representatives, Hamilton supported Jefferson, whom he disliked, believing that Burr was dangerous and ill-equipped to be president. Later his successful efforts to keep Burr from being governor of New York led to Burr's challenge of a duel. There was no way Hamilton could refuse, and he was killed by the first shot fired, leaving behind a widow, seven children, and, ironically for a money man, insufficient funds to provide for them.

John Brown Farm Historic Site

NORTH ELBA

Considered part of Lake Placid, this spartan homestead belonged to John Brown. His grave is here, along with those of his two sons and ten followers who fought and died along with him. Brown's simple headstone, etched with his own words, reads, "John Brown, born May 9, 1800, was executed at Charleston, Virginia, December 2, 1859." The stone, intended for his grandfather (whose name is at the top), was brought to the farm by Brown. *John Brown Road (1 mile off NY 73), North Elba. Tel. (518) 523-3900. Open Wednesday–Sunday, May–late October; free.*

JOHN BROWN
1800–1859

Brown, from a family whose lineage supposedly stretched back to the *Mayflower*, wasn't born a revolutionary, but slavery turned him into one. Connecticut-born, Ohio-bred, he tried the tanning business, sheep raising, the wool trade—wandering from Ohio to Pennsylvania and Massachusetts—and finally farming in North Elba. Ardently abolitionist, in 1854 Brown joined five of his sons in Kansas, which was then a battleground between pro- and antislavery settlers. He organized the so-called Pottawatomie massacre, in which five proslavery men were killed in cold blood as retaliation for the murder of five "free-state" settlers. From there Brown became active in the Underground Railroad and established in the Virginia mountains a way station for escaping slaves. By 1858 Brown was almost delusional in his antislavery diatribes, feeling he had a mission from God to free the slaves. This led to his raid on the federal arsenal at Harper's Ferry, Virginia (now West Virginia), on October 16, 1859. With only twenty-two men, he easily captured the arsenal. The next day brought a quick response from a small force of U.S. troops, led by Colonel Robert E. Lee. When the gunsmoke cleared, a wounded Brown and a handful of followers were captured. Twelve days later he was tried by the state of Virginia, convicted of "treason, and conspiring and advising with slaves and other rebels and murder in the first degree" and executed on December 2 in Charlestown. Viewed as a martyr by abolitionists, his death became a rallying cry. "John Brown's body lies a-mouldering in the grave, but his soul goes marching on."

Sleepy Hollow Cemetery

NORTH TARRYTOWN

Tucked around and behind the Old Dutch Church of Sleepy Hollow, this steeply graded old hillside burial ground has two tiers, each representing different eras. The first tier behind the church is the oldest, with weathered headstones crowded together, like the plot belonging to the Irving family. This section is a reminder of the early Dutch heritage in this part of the Hudson Valley. Farther up the slopes, with more space and the luxury of wider drives and grassy inclines, are the graves of later arrivals, such as **Major Edward Bowes** (1874–1946), host of a popular radio show, *Major Bowes and His Original Amateur Hour;* **Walter P. Chrysler** (1875–1940), auto manufacturer and industrialist; **Samuel Gompers** (1850–1924), head of the American Federation of Labor, considered the father of the labor movement in the United States; **Mark Hellinger** (1903–1947), Broadway producer; **Whitelaw Reid** (1837–1912), editor of the *New York Tribune;* **William Rockefeller** (1841–1922), brother of John D., promoter, and financier whose neoclassical mausoleum is one of the most ostentatious gravesites here; **Carl Schurz** (1829–1906), diplomat, senator, writer, and editor; **Henry Villard** (1835–1900), publisher of the *New York Post,* and his son, **Oswald Villard** (1872–1949), editor of *The Nation* magazine. *540 North Broadway, North Tarrytown. Tel. (914) 631-1123. Grounds open 8:00 A.M.–4:30 P.M. daily.*

ANDREW CARNEGIE
1 8 3 5 – 1 9 1 9

Carnegie is often lumped with robber barons of the late nineteenth century, who made millions on the backs of their workers and reveled in opulent lifestyles. But Carnegie was somewhat different. He actually believed in giving back. His Scottish family came to the United States in 1848, settled in Allegheny, Pennsylvania, and little Andrew was soon put to work in a cotton factory as a bobbin boy. From having a salary of $1.20 a week, he was to grow, through daring, organizational skills, and intelligence, into a multimillionaire, making a fortune in railroads and steel. He retired in 1901, early enough to enjoy life: writing, reading, traveling, buying a Scottish castle and building another one, making friends with notables in the English and American cultural and political worlds. But he never forgot his youthful poverty and his early vow to give away as much of his fortune as he could. He was as good as his word. He donated some $350 million to public libraries (a special interest of his), colleges, the Carnegie Institute of Pittsburgh, and the Carnegie Foundation for the Advancement of Teaching, among scores of endowments. His gifts were intended to improve the life of the common man. "Let there be light" was a slogan he placed in his libraries, for he felt that enlightenment was the key to freedom and progress. He died a moderately wealthy man, but no longer, because of all his gifts, the megamillionaire he had been. Money may not buy happiness, but it can buy privacy. The Carnegie gravesite, one of the loveliest here or elsewhere, is a secluded bower, surrounded by a thick circle of ancient rhododendrons. Inside the circle is a clearing and a Celtic cross, half-hidden under pine trees, with Carnegie's name and "born Dunfermline 25 November, 1835, died Lenox, Massachusetts, 11 August, 1919" at its base. His wife, **Louise Whitfield Carnegie** (1857–1946), who supported his charitable giving, is here too, and within the circle are gravestones of three "beloved members of the household" and "lifelong, loyal and devoted" staff.

WASHINGTON IRVING
1 7 8 3 – 1 8 5 9

Author, poet, diplomat, historian, Irving was from a prominent old New York mercantile family with English roots, literary and religious interests. Abandoning a legal career, he enjoyed travel and cultural life and kept notebooks wherever he went. These were grist for his essays, stories, and travel books in years to come. On his first tour of Europe, he was captured by pirates: more grist. His first book, *Salamagundi,* contained satirical poems, which proved a big hit. When *The Sketch Book* was published (in 1819–1820), it included "Rip Van Winkle" and "The Legend of Sleepy Hollow," combining humor with a folkloric quality that charmed readers and added to Irving's reputation as America's "first man of letters." A trip to Spain yielded the respected *History of the Life and Voyages of Christopher Columbus,* followed by the engaging stories and sketches of *The Alhambra.* Stints as a diplomat in London and as American minister to Madrid followed. Irving spent the last thirteen years of his life at Sunnyside, his home above the Hudson River, basking in the affection of family and admiring friends. **Sunnyside** (West Sunnyside Lane, Tarrytown; 914–631–8200) is a delight to visit; it has so many of Irving's belongings and furnishings, it makes you feel he just stepped out for a walk and will return shortly.

Youngs Memorial Cemetery

O Y S T E R   B A Y

This tranquil hillside burial ground was the private quarters of the Thomas Youngs family since 1658. The last male in the line, **William Jones Youngs** (1851–1916), was Thedore Roosevelt's secretary during TR's New York governorship. The area surrounding the cemetery forms the Theodore Roosevelt Sanctuary, the oldest National Audubon bird sanctuary in the country. At the top of the cemetery hill, enclosed by a cast-iron fence, is a graceful headstone with the presidential seal, flanked by Greek pilasters, commemorating Theodore Roosevelt and his second wife, **Edith Kermit Carow Roosevelt** (1861–1948). A boulder nearby bears the inscription: THEODORE ROOSEVELT SAID, KEEP YOUR EYES ON THE STARS AND KEEP YOUR FEET ON THE GROUND. Stones for other Roosevelts trail back down the hill. *Cove Road, Oyster Bay. Tel. (516) 922–3200. Grounds open from dawn to dusk.*

THEODORE ROOSEVELT
1 8 5 8 – 1 9 1 8

No doubt about it, TR or Teddy, as the twenty–sixth U.S. president was called, was a character: exuberant, full of swagger and bombast, but tough, courageous, and dedicated to the public good. His political rise was swift, from his election to the New York legislature at age twenty-three, to mayor of New York, national hero at forty (for his bravery in the Spanish-American War), governor of New York State, vice president and, at forty-two, upon the assassination of William McKinley in the first year of his second term (1901), president. TR roared into the White House, which he termed a "bully pulpit," and used his authority to fight corporate corruption, uphold antitrust laws, pass the Pure Food and Drug Act, set aside 230 million acres for conservation— perhaps his greatest legacy—and create the U.S. Forest Service. In 1905 he won the Nobel Peace Prize for brokering peace between Japan and Russia. Yet he favored an aggressive foreign policy ("speak softly but carry a big stick"), and fomented a revolt in Panama to seize control of the Panama Canal. With untold energy, he found time to write (forty books in all), hunt, hike, travel, read, and play games with his young children. **Sagamore Hill National Historic Site**, TR's summer home (20 Sagamore Hill, Oyster Bay; 516–922–4447), contains many of his artifacts and evokes his spirit better than words can.

Mount Hope Cemetery

R O C H E S T E R

The 196 acres on which Mount Hope lies were dedicated in 1838 as the first municipal Victorian burial ground in the United States. Thick woods, steep hillsides, and twisting roadways offer visual treats of tombs, mausoleums, and obelisks rife with ornamentation carved in stone: angels, lambs, urns, anchors, roses, sheafs of wheat, wreaths, daisies, crowns, crosses, morning glories, lilies of the valley, and tree trunks. Occupiers of this hallowed ground, with its Moorish gazebo and Victorian Gothic gatehouse, include **Dr. Hartwell Carver** (1789–1875), father of the transcontinental railroad; **Elizabeth Hollister Frost** (1887–1958), poet and novelist; **Frank E. Gannett** (1876–1957), newspaper publisher, founder of Gannett newspaper chain; **Myron Holley** (1779–1841), builder of the Erie Canal; **Hiram Sibley** (1807–1888), cofounder of Western Union; and **Margaret**

Strong (1897–1969), flour heiress, whose vast doll, dollhouse, and Victoriana collections form Rochester's Strong Museum. *1133 Mount Hope Avenue, Rochester. Tel. (716) 473-2755. Grounds open from dawn to dusk. Office hours: 8:30 A.M.–3:30 P.M. Monday–Saturday; brochure with map, rest rooms; guided tours by Friends of Mount Hope offered May–October at 2:00 and 3:00 P.M. every Sunday, special tours monthly, actor tour in summer (tel. 585-244-0353; Web site www.fomh.org).*

SUSAN B. ANTHONY
1820–1906

Descended from a high-minded, prosperous Quaker family, Susan Brownell Anthony grew up in a strict, serious household in Adams, Massachusetts, and later resettled in Rochester. A precocious child (she read at age three) with a remarkable memory and hunger for knowledge, she seemed destined to become a teacher, a natural occupation for women in those days. But the classroom was too small a stage for her wide interests and restless intelligence. Before long she was active in the temperance and abolitionist movements, lecturing and participating in campaigns. Soon after the Civil War, she was drawn to the issue of equality — and the vote—for women. Writing, lecturing, and lobbying formed the steady diet of her life. With enormous fortitude, she withstood all kinds of opposition and abuse, physical (eggs and tomatoes thrown at her on lecture platforms) and verbal (hisses and shouts and epithets). But she and her colleagues—Lucy Stone, Amelia Bloomer, Lucretia Mott, and especially Elizabeth Cady Stanton—persevered, through court battles, arrests, trials, opprobrium, vicious editorial attacks. She never married. She didn't live to see the Nineteenth Amendment ratified (1920), giving the vote to women, but somewhere, perhaps even here,

she must be smiling at last. The **Susan B. Anthony House** (17 Madison Street; 716–235–6124), where she lived for forty years, has much memorabilia of the women's suffrage movement and is open to visitors.

FREDERICK DOUGLASS
1817–1895

Many politicians boast of pulling themselves up by their own bootstraps, but few have moved as far up as fast as Douglass, whose life is the stuff of a movie adventure. He spent his first twenty years as Frederick Bailey, a slave on a Maryland plantation. (By age twelve he had taught himself, in secret, to read and write.) In 1838 he escaped to freedom, changing his name to Douglass (from a poem by Walter Scott) to avoid the bounty hunters who were after him. He settled in New Bedford, Massachusetts, married, worked as a laborer, and became an activist in the abolition movement. A powerful orator, he traveled in New England and later in Europe, as an agent of the Massachusetts Anti-Slavery Society, lecturing against slavery. In 1845 he published his first autobiography, *The Narrative of the Life of Frederick Douglass, an American Slave, Written by Himself.* Settling in Rochester, he founded a weekly journal, *The North Star.* By the time of the Civil War, his was the most eloquent black voice speaking in behalf of freedom. He urged President Lincoln to utilize black troops, and in 1863 he became active in enlisting African Americans for the Fifty-fourth and Fifty-fifth regiments. In 1870 he became editor of *The New National Era* newspaper in Washington, and in 1889 President Harrison designated him as minister to Haiti. Until he died at age seventy-eight, he continued to agitate for equality and black voting rights. "There is no Negro problem," he once said. "The problem is whether the American people have loyalty enough, honor enough, patriotism enough to live up to their own Constitution."

Kensico Cemetery

VALHALLA

There are few resting places as halcyon as Kensico, set among the Westchester hills, with circular drives and well-manicured lawns speckled with flowering trees, at its most beautiful in springtime, but serene and contemplative any season. The first interment was in 1891. At that time a private railroad car, luxuriously equipped for funeral parties, brought guests from Grand Central Station in New York directly to the gates at Kensico. From its beginnings Kensico has been a favorite final destination of prominent, high-profile New Yorkers: business tycoons, theatrical stars, authors, and musicians. Here are a few who have found final peace among the trees and graceful slopes: **Peter Arno** (1904–1968), sophisticated *New Yorker* cartoonist; **Vivian Blaine** (1921–1995), musical comedy performer, starred as Adelaide in *Guys and Dolls* on Broadway; **Evangeline Booth** (1865–1950), daughter of the founders of the Salvation Army and the Army's head in the United States; **Marc Connelly** (1880–1980), playwright, winner of a Pulitzer Prize for his play *Green Pastures*; **Danny Kaye** (1913–1987), virtuoso performer and movie comedian, goodwill ambassador for the United Nations Children's Fund (UNICEF); **Guy Kibbee** (1882–1956), comic character actor; **Herbert Lehman** (1878–1963), banker, popular four-term governor, and U.S. senator; **Tommy Manville** (1894–1967), scion of the Johns-Manville fortune, whose sole life achievement was thirteen marriages, mostly to gold-digging showgirls; **Allan Nevins** (1890–1971), Columbia University history professor, prolific author, two-time Pulitzer Prize winner for history; **Harriet Quimby** (1884–1912), first licensed woman pilot; **Jacob Ruppert, Jr.** (1867–1939), beer tycoon and onetime owner of the New York Yankees baseball team; and **David Sarnoff** (1891–1971), radio pioneer, chairman of RCA and later NBC. *Lakeview Avenue, Valhalla. Tel. (914) 949-0347. Grounds open 8:30 A.M.–4:30 P.M. daily. Office hours: 9:00 a.m. 5:00 P.M. Monday–Friday, 9:00 A.M.–4:00 P.M. Saturday–Sunday, closed Thanksgiving, Christmas, and January 1; map, rest rooms.*

BILLIE BURKE
1884–1970
FLO ZIEGFELD
1867–1932

Mary William Ethelbert Appleton Burke is best remembered as Glinda, the Good Witch of the North, in *The Wizard of Oz* (a role she loved). As a shy, young actress in New York, she met Florenz Ziegfeld in 1913 and they soon married. He produced revues called the *Ziegfeld Follies*, which featured beautiful showgirls parading around the stage in extravagant musical tableaux. Ziegfeld was a notorious Lothario, but Billie averted her eyes and stayed married. She juggled her career, mixing stage work and silent films with a comfortable private life at their luxurious Westchester estate. Ziegfeld lost heavily in the Wall Street bust of 1929, and after his death Billie had to cope with his large debts. A real trouper, she did so by turning to Hollywood, the beginning of a long run for her. Specializing in ladylike but scatter-brained roles, she made more than sixty films between 1933 and 1960, among them *Dinner at Eight, Topper, The Man Who Came to Dinner,* and *Father of the Bride.* A touching aspect of the secluded

Burke-Ziegfeld "residence" here at Kensico is the life-size bronze sculpture of a demure lady seated under a beautiful weeping beech tree, which Burke commissioned and dedicated to her mother, Blanche Beatty Burke (1844–1921).

TOMMY DORSEY
1905–1956

In the era of big bands, the Dorsey brothers could really swing. Tommy and older brother Jimmy learned how from their miner father in Shenandoah, Pennsylvania, a self-taught musician determined to keep his sons from having to work in the coal mines. Seeing music as their passport out, he gave them cornet lessons and had them tooting in his part-time band. By the time Tommy was sixteen, the boys had their own Dorsey's Wild Canaries, with Tommy on trombone, Jimmy on sax. They went on to play with Jean Goldkette's jazz band in Detroit and hung with the best of 'em: Bix Beiderbecke, Joe Venuti, Eddie Lang. They joined Paul Whiteman, cut records with Bing Crosby, and formed the Dorsey Brothers Orchestra. That didn't last— too many temperamental differences.

In a dramatic moment before a packed house at the Glen Island Casino in New Rochelle, New York, the brothers had a row, Tommy walked off the bandstand, and the two stopped speaking for eighteen years. Jimmy kept the Dorsey Brothers name, Tommy took over another outfit. By the mid–1940s he was leading the Tommy Dorsey Band, one of the smoothest dance bands in the country, with vocalists like Frank Sinatra, Connie Haines, and, later, Jo Stafford. A perfectionist, Tommy attracted, then lost, a procession of star sidemen: Bunny Berigan, Buddy Rich, Ziggy Elman among them. His theme song, "I'm Getting Sentimental Over You" earned him the nickname "sentimental gentleman," but maybe not by his three wives. In 1953 the two brothers made up, and Jimmy joined his brother's band, taking it over three years

later when Tommy died suddenly. But within seven months Jimmy was dead too. He can be found at home in Shenandoah. Separated again.

LOU GEHRIG
1905–1941

There are some nice guys in sports, and Henry Lou Gehrig was one of the nicest, not a publicity-hyped hero, but the real thing. He was born in the German Yorkville section of Manhattan to a German ironworker and Danish maid. His baseball skills in high school led him to Columbia University, where a New York Yankee scout signed him. Within two years, after a brief stay in the minors, he was with the Bronx Bombers, where he played for the next fourteen years as one of the hard-hitting members of Murderers' Row, so-called because of their slugging ability. Always overshadowed by his showier teammate, Babe Ruth, he considered Ruth a mentor and the two had a friendly home run competition. Although he never won it, he accomplished something Ruth never did: hit four homers in a single game, a rare feat. Shy and unassuming, Gehrig played every game of over thirteen regular seasons: 2,130 games in a row. This steadiness earned him the nickname the "Iron Horse." Although statistics aren't the whole Gehrig story, his record is impressive: a lifetime batting average of .340, 493 career home runs, 1,990 RBIs (runs batted in), winning the Most Valuable Player Award four times. He is also remembered for his fortitude and gallantry in coping with amyotrophic lateral sclerosis (ALS), later called the Lou Gehrig disease, a progressive disease with no known cure. In 1939, after he retired, rules were waived and he was elected to the Hall of Fame without the usual five-year waiting period. He was not quite thirty-eight when he died. That fans remember Lou is evident at his granite headstone, where bats, balls, rain-faded Yankee caps, and gloves are clustered between two little round hedges. With him is **Eleanor Gehrig** (1905–1964), his wife of eight short years.

SERGEI RACHMANINOFF
1 8 7 3 – 1 9 4 3

When we think of Rachmaninoff today, it's his music that floods our minds: compositions like the Second Symphony, the tone poem *The Isle of the Dead,* the Third Piano Concerto, and preludes for the piano (Thirteen Preludes, Six Etudes Tableaux, and Nine Etudes Tableaux). Along with seventy or more songs with piano accompaniment, he wrote a choral symphony (*The Bells*) and a Vesper Mass for male voices. Yet while alive, it was his work as a concert pianist and conductor that sustained him, both during his days in his native Russia, where he came from an impecunious but noble family, and later, after the 1917 Russian Revolution, on tour in the United States, England, and continental Europe. A perfectionist, he seldom felt at the top of his form as a pianist, usually wearing, in Igor Stravinsky's words, his "six-and-a-half-foot-tall-scowl." He yearned for more time for composing. During World War II he left his beloved house in Lucerne, Switzerland, and resettled in Beverly Hills, California. The inner distress he felt through much of his professional life is nowhere evident here, where hedges, rhododendron, and pachysandra provide a serene privacy to the Russian cross and gravestone he shares with his wife, **Natalie Satin Rachmaninoff** (1877–1951), his cousin and life's companion. Their daughter, **Princesse Irina Wolkonsky née Rachmaninoff** (1903–1969), is nearby in the same alcove.

AYN RAND
1 9 0 5 – 1 9 8 2

Too bad she died when she did, Rand would have loved the "me" era of personal consumption: the 1980s and 1990s. Her life philosophy was one of self-centered individualism and unfettered capitalism (does Enron sound familiar?). She promoted this, not through dull economic texts, but in fiction that pulsed with heroes who behaved as she thought. The most famous example is Howard Roark, in *The Fountainhead,* a controversial and successful novel (which as a movie starred Gary Cooper). The book made her name and fortune, while sparking an ultra conservative movement that continues today. (Her most fervent disciple is arguably economist Alan Greenspan, chairman of the Federal Reserve Board.) In a sense Rand created herself as well as her fiction. She was born Alyssa Rosenbaum in St. Petersburg, Russia, and left in 1926, changing her name in the process. The Rand part was lifted from a Remington-Rand typewriter, an omen, perhaps, of the writer she was to become. Although critics give short shrift to her writing style, many of her books, including her novel *Atlas Shrugged*, continue to sell well. Sharing her plot of real estate here is **Frank O'Connor** (1897–1979), her husband of fifty years, whom she met when they both were working as extras in a Cecil B. DeMille movie, her first Hollywood job.

West Point U.S. Military Academy Post Cemetery

W E S T   P O I N T

Although the academy was founded in 1802, the graveyard is even older, with some Revolutionary War soldiers resting in an area marked "unknown." The first "known" grave, that of an ensign, dates back to 1782. Among many stalwarts here are **Lucius Clay** (1897–1978), army general, commander of U.S. forces in Europe, director of the Berlin Airlift 1948–1949; **Glenda Farrell** (1904–1971), the only movie actress buried here, made possible because of her marriage to Dr. Henry Ross, a West Point graduate; **George W. Goethals** (1858–1928), major general, builder of the Panama Canal; **Herbert Norman Schwarzkopf** (1895–1958), general, father of the commander in the Gulf War; **Sylvanus Thayer** (1785–1872), called the "father of West Point"; and **Edward H. White** (1930–1967), lieutenant colonel and astronaut who was the first man to walk in space. The cemetery is located behind the old cadet chapel, but as of September 11, 2001, West Point grounds are off-limits to the public. When West Point Tours (tel. 845–446–4724) resumes its schedule, the two-hour tours (April through October), include a cemetery visit, which is the only way to see the burial grounds. Be sure to phone the tour company—or the Visitor Center—ahead. *West Point Visitor Center, 2107 New South Post Road, West Point. Tel. (845) 446–4731.*

GEORGE ARMSTRONG CUSTER

1 8 3 9 – 1 8 7 6

Idolized, then villified, General George Custer has not benefited from the passage of time and historical research. Fearless he was, without doubt, proving it in well-publicized feats of bravery at Gettysburg and elsewhere during the Civil War, leading the final cavalry charge at Appomattox. He was also reckless, gung-ho, and headstrong, a man who wrote his beloved wife, Elizabeth, from the Virginia battle lines in 1863 about the "Glorious War!" His exploits later in the Indian Wars were sometimes brutal, destroying a largely undefended Cheyenne village in 1868 for instance, but the eastern press loved his derring-do and made his every action seem heroic. That may have been his undoing on the plains of Montana on June 25, 1876, when federal troops converged to put down a gathering of Sioux and other Indians. More attuned to action than to strategy (he graduated last in his West Point class), Custer divided his regiment into three groups, perhaps expecting to encircle the Indian force. As he moved forward with 226 of his center column, they were surrounded by a blizzard of as many as 2,500 warriors. When the fighting ceased, Custer and more than the five companies under his command were dead. Custer's Last Stand was more hubris and folly than heroism, but in the romantic Errol Flynn movie of the same name it's the heroism that survives. Custer's wife, **Elizabeth Bacon Custer** (1842–1933), who did so much to promote his legend, rests here with him.

WINFIELD SCOTT
1 7 8 6 – 1 8 6 6

Arguably the most distinguished military man of the first half of the nineteenth century, Scott was trained as a lawyer, not a soldier, at the College of William and Mary in his native Virginia. When war with England seemed imminent in 1807, he went to Washington and offered his services and, as they say, never looked back. For the next fifty–four years he served his country on the front lines—at the Niagara frontier in 1812, against the Seminoles in 1836—and as a skillful negotiator at the peace table. He arranged treaties after the Black Hawk War; settled a boundary dispute between Maine and New Brunswick, Canada; and mediated a dispute in the northwest between American and British officers who were jointly occupying the San Juan Islands in Puget Sound. Known as "Old Fuss and Feathers," he scored his most celebrated victory in the Mexican War, in which he captured the Mexican capital. This brought him a hero's welcome, a special gold medal from Congress, the nomination of the Whig party for president in 1848 and 1852, and the creation of a special rank, the brevit rank of lieutenant-general. Though a Southerner, his loyalties were to the Union, and when the Civil War broke out, he kept command of the U.S. Army until November 1861, when he retired. In 1866 he died, fittingly at West Point.

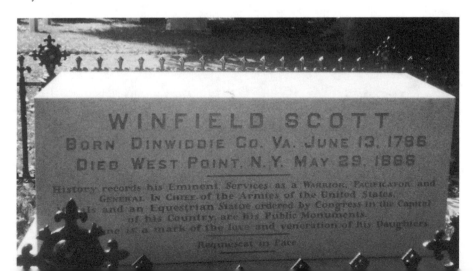

Mid-Atlantic
and the Southeast

In this, one of the most historic regions of America, graves matter. From New Jersey and Pennsylvania through Virginia, the Carolinas, and Georgia, all along the southeast coast, burial grounds are revered for their heroes of bygone eras and, often, for the spirits that may still pervade these quiet places. Nowhere are the contrasts in burial styles more pronounced: simple gravestones (for the most part) lined up in rows for American Revolution soldiers and their neighbors; dashing monuments and cenotaphs in parklike Victorian settings for those of the Civil War and their compatriots. Fashions change; no more so than in burial grounds. Observing these changes is part of the pleasure of visiting this historic area.

District of Columbia

Congressional Cemetery

WASHINGTON, D.C.

Pocked and rutted roads explain why this old place (vintage 1807) is on the list of endangered historic sites. It's a pity because other than the roads, this is a supremely pleasant burial ground near the Anacostia River, easily walkable,

smartly laid out, with brick walkways; graves well delin-
eated; an abundance of magnolias, oaks, and pines; birds chirping; and people walking dogs (they pay for the privilege, which goes toward maintenance). There are cenotaphs for many famous congressmen who are buried elsewhere, but whose families wanted them remembered in the city where they spent so much time, such as **Henry Clay** (1777–1852), **John C. Calhoun** (1782–1850), and **Thomas "Tip" O'Neill** (1912–1994). This hallowed ground is also home to judges and cabinet members, and to **Scarlett Crow** (1825–1867), aka Kangiduta, a Wahpeton Sioux and government scout; **David E. Herold** (1842–1865), an accomplice of John Wilkes Booth; **Belva Lockwood** (1830–1917), suffragette; architect **Robert Mills** (1781–1855), who designed that Washington Monument; and **Push-Ma-Ta-Ha** (1764–1824), Choctaw chief, warrior alongside Andrew Jackson in the War of 1812. *1801 E Street (at 18th) SE, Washington, D.C. Tel. (202) 543-0539. Web site: www.congressionalcemetery.org. Grounds open from dawn to dusk. Office hours: 10:00 A.M.–3:00 P.M. Saturday, other days erratic, best to call ahead; excellent map and historical background, rest room.*

MATHEW BRADY
1822–1896

Considered the father of modern photojournalism for his Civil War photographs, Brady set standards for wartime photography of fearlessness and initiative that are still followed by today's practitioners in the field. Little is known of his early background. He was born in Warren County, New York, had scant education, but was encouraged to draw by William Page, a portrait painter he met in Saratoga. Page later introduced young Brady to Samuel F. B. Morse, who seems to have triggered his interest in photography. By the early 1840s Brady had a portrait studio in New York and was an eager student and experimenter, soon winning awards for his work. Before long he had two studios and was a huge success, photographing almost everyone who was rich or famous or both. When the Civil War began, Brady convinced President Lincoln that photos of battle and camp scenes would make an invaluable record, and the photographer and his assistants soon spread out all over the battlefronts, taking more that 3,500 photos of battles, troops on the march and in bivouac, men at rest, temporarily and permanently. Although his Civil War photos insured his immortality, the time spent and equipment required cost him dearly. In later years, ruined by expenses and the panic of 1873, he lived in virtual poverty.

ELBRIDGE GERRY
1744–1814

Gerry's imposing twelve-foot-high marble monument with a decorative urn on top honors a man who was the only signer of the Declaration of Independence interred in Washington. He was also a governor of Massachusetts and vice president of the United States (under James Madison). As vice president he presided over the Senate and was on his way there when he died, thus, as his memorial states, "fulfilling his own memorable injunction: It is the duty of every citizen, though he may have but one day to live, to devote that day to the good of this country." All of this would merely be ancient history, but Gerry gave one more thing to his country, a gift (of dubious merit) that goes on giving: the term gerrymandering, which means redistricting a district for the political advantage of one party. (The first time this happened, the carved-up district resembled a salamander, hence the nickname gerrymander.)

J. EDGAR HOOVER
1895–1972

A sense of authority and importance fairly bristles from the gravesite of America's most famous twentieth-century G-man. Hoover's large upright headstone, which commemorates his parents and sister as well, is enclosed by a stolid wrought-iron fence, built—it is stated—by a former special agent in 1996 and bearing the official seal of the Federal Bureau of Investigation, of which Hoover was the director for forty-eight years. The sturdy wrought-iron bench facing the fence (for contemplating the director's accomplishments perhaps?) also bears the FBI seal. Hoover put this federal agency on the map, after it had been steeped in scandal, by proving to be an efficient administrator, creating professional standards and stability. He served under eight presidents, from Coolidge to Nixon. In the 1930s, Hoover's FBI agents became heroes for killing gangsters like John Dillinger,

Pretty Boy Floyd, and Baby Face Nelson. Rounding up Nazi spies during World War II brought more luster to the agency. Some of that luster evaporated when it became known that Hoover's obsession with liberals and left-wingers led to illegal wiretaps, disregard of civil liberties, and spying on political enemies. Down a few graves from Hoover on the same side of the narrow road is that of **Clyde Tolson** (1900–1975), Hoover's close friend, longtime companion, and fellow FBIer. There is irony in the fact that Hoover in life was highly critical of homosexuals, but now he lies in a row with several gravestones that declare "gay Vietnam veteran" and similar sexual-choice statements. That sound you hear is Edgar spinning.

JOHN PHILIP SOUSA
1854–1932

It's all silent today at the grave shrouded by evergreen hedges, like rows of marching bandsmen, that shield the Sousa family plot from the cemetery at large. Peacefulness is not what comes to mind at the name Sousa, which suggests bassoons, trombones, trumpets, and the oompah-pah of a military band. Think Sousa and the sounds of his "Stars and Stripes Forever" or "Washington Post March" come bouncing to mind. In 1880 Sousa became the first American-born conductor to lead the U.S. Marine Corp Band, a post he held until 1892, when he formed his own band. For over forty years the Sousa Band traveled the world, over one million miles, giving more than 30,000 concerts and raking in some $40 million.

Rock Creek Cemetery

WASHINGTON, D.C.

Beautifully maintained, Rock Creek belongs to St. Paul's Episcopal Church (often called Rock Creek Church) and is as notable for its plethora of sculpture, obelisks, and mausoleums, set amidst rolling drives, as for its many blue-chip residents, such as **Francis P. Blair, Sr.** (1791–1876), advisor to Abraham Lincoln; **Stephen Field** (1816–1899), justice of the U.S. Supreme Court; **Gilbert Grosvenor** (1875–1966), editor of *National Geographic;* and **Sumner Welles** (1892–1961), F.D.R.'s undersecretary of state. One of the most splendid mausoleums, in Beaux Arts style, supported at each corner by a caryatid, with a Tiffany window, belongs to **Christian Heurich** (1842–1945), a Washington brewer. *Rock Creek Church Road and Webster Street NW, Washington, D.C. Tel. (202) 829-0585. Grounds open: 7:30 A.M.–dusk daily. Office hours: 9:00 A.M.–5:00 P.M. Monday–Friday; map (also available in box to left of office door, in case office is closed), rest rooms.*

HENRY ADAMS
1838–1918

Few people can claim a world-renowned sculpture as their legacy. But visitors to the Adams tomb come as much to admire the mysterious, androgynous bronze sculpture (see right) by Augustus Saint-Gaudens, which dominates the elaborate grave-site, as to visit the author of *The Education of Henry Adams* and *Democracy*. Adams, grandson of John Quincy Adams, had a diverse career, as Harvard professor of European and American history and journalist. His biographies, *The Life of Albert Gallatin* and the more judgmental *John Randolph*, were marked by his partisanship (pro-Gallatin, anti-Randolph). Saint-Gaudens's sculpture, popularly called "Grief," was commissioned for the grave of his wife, who committed suicide just before Christmas in 1885. She was forty-two years old, had been married thirteen years, and suffered from depression. The curved and polished pink granite bench facing the sculpture was designed by Stanford White. The name Adams is nowhere in evidence, but the gravesite is a Rock Creek favorite. Eleanor Roosevelt was one of many who came here to muse and reflect.

ALICE ROOSEVELT LONGWORTH
1884–1980

On the surface, hers was a glittering life: doyenne of Washington galas, arbiter of its social scene (who's in, who's not), gossip par excellence, and mistress of often-quoted bons mots (like her line, "If you can't say something good about someone, sit right here by me"). That was surface only. The truth was less happy. Her mother, Alice, Theodore

Roosevelt's first wife, died within hours of baby Alice's birth; her stepmother disliked her; her father ignored her; and her husband, Nicholas Longworth, was a zealous womanizer and drinker ("He'd rather be tight than president" was one of her quips). When he died, she burned his prize Stradivarius. Buried with Alice, under the same gray granite stone, is her only child, **Paulina Sturm** (1925–1957), who was just as badly neglected by her mother as Alice had been.

UPTON SINCLAIR
1878–1968

An alcoholic Southern father (Upton Beall) and aristocratic mother (Priscilla Sinclair) might not seem promising antecedents for a muckraking writer whose exposé of the meat-packing industry and seamy Chicago politics (*The Jungle*) changed the country. Sinclair, an idealist who became a socialist crusader for the rights of the common man, had struggled with four middling books before he wrote *The Jungle* in 1906. It was a time of public outcry against contaminated food; the book hit a nerve, led to reform of the industry, and became a worldwide best-seller. "I aimed at the public's heart and by accident I hit it in the stomach," Sinclair later said. Although he wrote dozens of books, including juvenile novels and the Lanny Budd series, and won the Pulitzer Prize in 1943 for *Dragon's Teeth*, he is more remembered for his exposés than as a literary stylist. His third wife, **Mary Hard Sinclair** (1882–1967), is buried with him. "A MERRY HEART" is the stone's inscription, more fitting for her, perhaps, than for her deadly earnest husband.

HARLAN FISKE STONE
1 8 7 2 – 1 9 4 6

This New Hampshire native's distinguished career—as lawyer, teacher, law professor, and dean at Columbia University; attorney general of the United States (cleaning up the scandals in the Justice Department left by Warren Harding's cronies); and justice of the U.S. Supreme Court—was crowned by being chosen chief justice by Franklin Roosevelt. Being a Republican selected as the court's chief by a Democratic president was no ordinary event, but Justice Stone had proven himself to be independent and intellectually honest. A conservative who believed in judicial restraint, he realized during the difficult Great Depression years that goverment's role in life was a necessity. His years as chief justice weren't easy; his was one of the most divided courts in history. Fortunately he let off steam in other ways. As chairman of the board of trustees of the National Gallery, he helped to enlarge its collections and helped save European art treasures during World War II. His wife, **Agnes Harvey Stone** (1873–1958), is buried to his right beneath an identical long, flat gray granite stone, decorated with oak leaves and acorns.

Washington National Cathedral

W A S H I N G T O N ,   D . C .

This magnificent Gothic edifice is well worth a visit in and of itself. A bonus is that it is also the final address of notables like **Cordell Hull** (1871-1955), secretary of state under Franklin Roosevelt; **Frank Billings Kellogg** (1856-1937), U.S. senator, secretary of state, judge, and coauthor of the Kellogg-Briand Pact; and Helen Keller's teacher **Anne Macy Sullivan** (1866-1936). *Wisconsin and Massachusetts Avenues NW, Washington, D.C. Tel. (202) 537-6200. Web site: www.cathedral.org/ cathedral. Hours: 10:00 A.M.–4:30 P.M. Monday–Saturday, 12:30 P.M.–4:00 P.M. Sunday; gift shop, a variety of guided tours available (fee).*

HELEN KELLER
1880–1968

There are few true stories as inspirational as this one: A baby, left blind and deaf by a fever, triumphed over both handicaps. She learned to talk, learned to learn, and grew up to graduate with honors from Radcliffe College and become a world-renowned lecturer. That's the bare outline of the Helen Keller story, which has been told in books, movies, plays, and her own autobiography, *The Story of My Life*. She didn't do it alone. Anne Sullivan, a gifted teacher who was also blind, taught the frustrated and unruly little girl how to form words and learn to speak. She interpreted by tapping words into Helen's hand and transcribing books into braille. Helen proved a brilliant student with an inquiring mind. Later she became an advocate for women's suffrage and other causes and helped set up the American Foundation for the Blind. Her ashes are preserved in the columbarium in the cathedral crypt.

WOODROW WILSON
1856–1924

The final resting place of the twenty-eighth president of the United States is as grand and imposing as for that of a cardinal or bishop, which it resembles: a marble tomb tucked into a fretted Gothic bay in the cathedral's right side. On the wall to his right is an inscription about his second wife, **Edith Bolling Wilson** (1872–1961), who lies in a vault below the bay. The location of her inscription suggests that she is peering over his shoulder, as she was reputed to do in life. Wilson suffered a stroke in 1919; some critics speculated that Edith was his éminence grise, making decisions for him behind the scenes. Virginia-born Wilson was a Princeton University graduate, later a professor there, and still later its president. From the presidency of Princeton, he became governor of New Jersey and then president of the United States. He was reelected in 1916 by a small margin, on the slogan, "He kept us out of war." Soon after his reelection, the Germans sank four U.S. ships and his slogan became moot. Although he won the Nobel Peace Prize in 1919, his plan for a League of Nations was rejected by the Senate the next year. Decades later the idea led to the United Nations, too late for Wilson but not for the world. The **Woodrow Wilson House** (2340 S Street NW; 202–387–4062) is a redbrick Georgian Revival house with many family furnishings, where the Wilsons lived after he retired from the presidency.

Martin Luther King, Jr., National Historic Site

ATLANTA

Not a cemetery, this two-block area is managed by the National Park Service with a Freedom Hall complex, chapel, King library, archives, and reflecting pool, and it includes the King sarcophagus. *449 Auburn Avenue, Atlanta. Tel. (404) 331–5190. The tomb is visible day and night.*

MARTIN LUTHER KING, JR.
1929–1968

Son and grandson of preachers, the Reverend King used his oratorical talent to good effect in many civil rights battles. Most successful were his efforts in the Montgomery, Alabama, bus boycott in 1955; the march on Washington in 1963 (when his "I Have a Dream" speech electrified the world); and the passage of the Civil Rights Act of 1964. King's courage, persistence, and commitment to Gandhi-like peaceful protests won him international admiration and, in 1965, the Nobel Peace Prize. He later devoted himself to labor causes and anti-Vietnam War protests, until April 4, 1968, when an assassin's bullet put an end to his life on the balcony of a Memphis motel. King's death triggered riots in 125 cities, leading to forty-six deaths and more than 21,000 arrests, an ironic turn of events for a peace-loving man. His white marble casket, resting on a brick "island" surrounded by a reflecting pool, is serenity itself. "Free at last."

Oakland Cemetery

ATLANTA

Atlanta's oldest burial ground, Oakland dates from 1850. Sprawling on eighty-eight acres, it boasts an abundance of mature trees, gardens with Victorian plants, Gothic Revival and neoclassical mausoleums, and elaborate botanical and religious carvings. Among its 70,000 full-time residents are congressmen, Civil War soldiers and generals, mayors, and others, including **Alexander Hamilton Stephens** (1812–1883), vice president of the Confederacy and governor of Georgia. *248 Oakland Avenue SE, Atlanta. Tel. (404) 688–2107. Grounds open from dawn to dusk*

ROBERT "BOBBY" JONES, JR.
1902–1971

He's been gone since 1971 and was in a wheelchair for twenty years before that, but Atlanta-born Bobby Jones is one of golf's great names. He was a gentleman-sportsman who believed there was life after golf—and proved it. Between 1916 and 1930, while playing competitive golf, he also amassed three college degrees (in engineering at Georgia Institute of Technology, English literature at Harvard, and law at Emory). In his peak years (1923–1930), he won thirteen major championships, while retaining amateur status. He was the only player ever to win the coveted grand slam—the four major championships in the same year—after which he retired to practice law. His later years were plagued by a rare and painful neurological disease, syringomyelia, which made walking impossible, an insurmountable handicap for a golfer. Along the walks to his gravesite are trees, shrubs, and specimen plants, the same kinds that are on all eighteen holes of the Augusta National Golf Course, which Jones designed and where the Masters is played. Note at the grave the golf balls and tees left by visitors.

MARGARET MITCHELL
1900–1949

Everything you may want to know about the Civil War can be found between the pages of a single book, Margaret Mitchell's *Gone with the Wind*. Real history? Not by a long shot! But epic drama, romance, excite-

ment, and the panorama of wartime, this book, the work of an Atlanta journalist-housewife, has in abundance. A feature writer for the *Atlanta Journal*, Mitchell wrote the novel while recovering from a broken ankle. She called it *Tomorrow Is Another Day*, a line made famous by Scarlett O'Hara, the book's heroine. When it was finally sold, the title was changed. That's not all that changed for Mitchell. The book was published in June 1936, and sales by that December topped $1 million. Three years later the book became a movie, and Mitchell was such a celebrity she was afraid to leave her house. Between answering fan mail and taking care of an invalid father and husband, she never wrote again. Though always disdained by the literati, the book is considered a classic: printed in twenty-seven languages in thirty-seven countries, with more than 180 different editions. Her long, imposing memorial, with the name Marsh (for her second husband, John Marsh) in the center and a stone urn gracing the top, is what you might expect of a Southern lady. But frankly, my dear, she no longer gives a damn. **The Margaret Mitchell House** (990 Peachtree Street; 404–249–7015) is open to visitors.

Bonaventure Cemetery

SAVANNAH

Hugging the Wilmington River, Bonaventure—with its elegant tombs; angelic, cherubic, and nymphet statuary; haunting mausoleums; live oaks hung with Spanish moss; and abundance of dogwood trees, camellias, azaleas, and wisteria—has long been a favorite final address of Savannah's aristocracy and wannabes. One of Savannah's first plantations, in 1847 the land became a burial ground. Naturalist John Muir passed by in 1867 and raved: "The grand old forest graveyard, so impressive that almost any sensible person would choose to dwell here with the dead rather than with the lazy, disorderly living." Among the inhabitants are Confederate officers, philanthropists, and governors, as well as **Conrad Aiken** (1889–1973), poet whose works won many awards, including the Pulitzer and Bollinger prizes; **Dr. Brodie S. Herndon** (1810–1886), the first to perform a Caesarean operation in the United States; **Marie Scudder Myrick** (1853–1934), the first Southern woman to own and edit a daily newspaper, the *Americus Times-Recorder*; and **John Walz** (1844–1922), sculptor of reliefs on many Savannah public buildings. John Berendt's book, *Midnight in the Garden of Good and Evil*, brings the old place to new life. *330 Bonaventure Road, Savannah. Tel. (912) 651-6844. Grounds open 8:00 A.M.–5:00 P.M. daily. Office hours: 8:00 A.M.–5:00 P.M. Monday–Friday, 12:00 P.M.–2:00 P.M. Saturday, 12:00 P.M.–4:00 P.M. Sunday; map, rest rooms.*

JOHNNY MERCER
1909–1976

Composer, lyricist, singer, actor, Mercer made it all seem easy. He began writing lyrics as a teenager and continued even as he pursued a career as an actor and singer. During the 1930s and 1940s, he was a vocalist with the Paul Whiteman band, but it was as a songwriter that he *really* sang. His productivity was astounding, first as a lyricist collaborating with others—Jerome Kern, Harold Arlen, Hoagy Carmichael—and then as composer-lyricist. Many of his popular songs have such personality that they have become part of the national vocabulary: "Fools Rush In," "Something's Gotta Give," "Too Marvelous for Words," "Come Rain or Come Shine," "That Old Black Magic," "Blues in the Night." The list goes on: some 1,000 songs. He was the first of only three writers to receive Best Song Oscars four different years. From Broadway shows (*Top Banana, St. Louis Woman*) to Hollywood movies (*Laura, Days of Wine and Roses, Daddy Longlegs*), Mercer composed endlessly. "Jeepers Creepers," Johnny, "I Remember You."

Johnson Square

SAVANNAH

Azalea-framed, brick-lined, and fountain-flanked, this is the largest (and first) of Savannah's twenty-one existing green squares (there were once twenty-four), landmarks that add to this old Southern city's unique charm. King George III was hung in effigy here, and, much later, the Confederate flag was supposedly first displayed. Although not a cemetery, it contains a truncated obelisk, under which lie the remains of a national hero, Nathanael Greene. *Junction of Bull and Julian Streets, Savannah.*

NATHANAEL GREENE
1742–1786

Greene began life in Rhode Island. As a young man, he helped organize a militia company and was drawn into a military life. By 1776 he was a major-general in the Continental Army and spent that memorable Christmas Eve with General George Washington in Trenton capturing Hessian soldiers. Battles and skirmishes throughout Pennsylvania followed. In 1780 Washington chose Greene to head the campaign that would end the war. Tracking Britain's General Cornwallis through the Carolinas, he managed by the end of 1782 to drive the enemy out. In gratitude for his efforts in the South, Georgia presented him with Mulberry Grove plantation near Savannah. For the rest of his life he "commuted" between his homes there and in Rhode Island. He died of sunstroke and was buried in Colonial Park Cemetery, Savannah, only to be reinterred in 1902 to the base of this obelisk, which had been built in his honor.

Laurel Grove Cemetery

SAVANNAH

Once part of a plantation, Laurel Grove, with its sixty acres, was acquired by the city in 1850 and opened for business two years later. Laid out in wide lanes with much shrubbery and green space by Frederick Law Olmsted, it was a favorite meeting place for stylish locals out for a buggy ride on a Sunday afternoon. The impressive mausoleums, statuary, and ornate wrought-iron work are eye catching. Resting here are servicemen from several wars, (most of the Confederate soldiers came from Gettysburg) sea captains and sailors; politicians and statesmen, in all some 37,000 souls. Here also are **John MacPherson Berrien** (1781–1856), U.S. senator and attorney general under Andrew Jackson; **James Pierpont** (1822–1893), the composer of "Jingle Bells"; and **James Moore Wayne** (1790–1867), a U.S. Supreme Court justice. *802 West Anderson Street (at Ogeechee Road), Savannah. Tel. (912) 651-6772. Grounds open 8:00 A.M.–5:00 P.M. daily. Office hours: 8:00 A.M.–4:00 P.M. Monday–Friday; map, rest room, one-hour walking tours by appointment (fee).*

JULIETTE GORDON LOW
1860–1927

"Daisy," as her family called her, was a character with a wicked sense of humor and a love of costumes. There was the time she wore an evening dress to go fishing with Rudyard Kipling; and the shipboard costume party she attended (at age sixty-six) in a sheet with empty liquor bottles attached to it—as "departed spirits." She needed her humor: Her aristocratic English husband was an alcoholic philanderer who left his entire estate to his long-time mistress. Spunky Daisy sued and recovered $500,000, which she later used to found the Girl Scouts. Her life had been a series of scattered good works when, as a widow of fifty, she met Sir Robert Baden-Powell and his sister Agnes. Inspired by his Boy Scout movement and Agnes's Girl Guides, Low called a meeting of eighteen girls and eight leaders in her Savannah home in 1912—and the rest is Girl Scout history. By the time of her death, there were more than 140,000 scouts, testimony to her single-minded focus and inspirational leadership. The **Juliette Gordon Low Birthplace** (142 Bull Street; 912-233-4501) a Regency-style townhouse with a Victorian garden and many family artifacts, is open to visitors.

Monterey Square

SAVANNAH

Another of the city's attractive hubs that doubles as a burial site, Monterey Square is dominated by the Pulaski monument. Across the square is Mercer House, which figures prominently in John Berendt's Savannah novel. *Junction of Bull and Wayne Streets, Savannah.*

COUNT CASIMIR PULASKI
1748–1779

This imposing fifty-five-foot-high Italian Carrara marble column, designed by Robert Launitz, was completed in 1853 to honor Count Pulaski, a nobleman born in the then-subjugated Polish province of Lithuania. A fighter for Polish independence, he was expelled from his own country, but, inspired by the principles of freedom and liberty, he came to America in 1777 to fight against the British. (The figure of Liberty at the tip of the monument is especially fitting.) Volunteering his service, Pulaski received a commission as brigadier-general and fought gallantly side by side with the Americans at Brandywine, Germantown, Trenton, and Charleston. In the siege of Savannah, he led a cavalry unit toward the British line and was killed on October 11, 1779. He was thirty years old. He lies here, very near where he fell.

Maryland

Green Mount Cemetery

BALTIMORE

Completely walled, established in 1839, Green Mount is a terrain of serpentine drives, steep and sloping hills, lovely views, sculpture gardens, and monumental tombstones and mausoleums, set amidst an abundance of cypress, willow, oak, cedar, maple, and chestnut trees. Among the notables here are **Arunah Abell** (1808–1888), founder of the *Baltimore Sun;* **Johns Hopkins** (1795–1873), philanthropist, endower of the famous hospital and university; and **Ross Winans** (1796–1877), engineer who built the Russian railroad from St. Petersburg to Moscow. *1501 Greenmount Avenue, Baltimore. Tel. (410) 539-0641. Grounds open 7:00 A.M.–4:00 P.M. Monday-Saturday, closed Sunday, Thanksgiving, and Christmas. Office hours: 8:30 A.M.–4:00 P.M. Monday-Friday, 8:30 A.M.–12:00 P.M. Saturday; map, rest room. No pets allowed.*

JOHN WILKES BOOTH
1838–1865

To find the grave of the man who killed Abraham Lincoln, look for the Booth family plot, which stars his father, English-born actor **Junius Brutus Booth** (1796–1852). The truncated marble-finished sandstone obelisk has the single large bas relief "Booth" in its granite base; above it in the stone is a medallion with a bas relief profile of Junius encircled by a laurel wreath. All the Booth family members, except famous actor Edwin, lie here together. Fifth son John Wilkes was a late comer. He was first buried at the Naval Arsenal in Washington, D.C. After several requests from the family to President Andrew Johnson, their wish was granted, and in 1869 they quietly brought back the remains of the son who had disgraced the family name. On the backside of the obelisk, under the inscription, "To the memory of the children of Junius Booth and Mary Ann Booth," the names of the five resting here are listed, John Wilkes among them. Note the shiny copper Lincoln pennies often placed at the base of the monument. A silent rebuke?

ALLEN WELSH DULLES
1893–1969

There's no secrecy about the grave of this superspy, director of the Central Intelligence Agency (CIA) for eight years. Dulles, a Princeton graduate, lawyer, and brother of the more famous John Foster, followed the family penchant for government service. After a one-year teaching stint in India, he entered the diplomatic corps in 1916 and served in Europe and the Middle East. He took a break from the government to work in a prestigious New York law firm. During World War II, Dulles joined the Office of Strategic Services (OSS), which later morphed into the CIA. The Bay of Pigs fiasco in Cuba in 1961 was hatched on his watch, so he took the blame, resigned, and returned to private life. He subsequently served on a string of high-level commissions and delegations and wrote eight books, mostly about the craft of intelligence. Talk about spooks; to many he was the archetype.

SIDNEY LANIER
1 8 4 2 – 1 8 8 1

A beautifully striated pink granite rock is a unique grave marker, and completely apt for a creative person. The bronze plaque attached to it, with its green patina, notes, "I am lit with the sun," with an orb etched above the words. Both musical and poetic, Lanier struggled throughout a short life to support his family with mundane potboilers, while writing poetry on the side. He was the epitome of a sensitive soul, kept from fulfilling his early promise by a premature death from tuberculosis. But at least some of his poems, like "Marshes of Glynn" and "Sunrise," have endured.

Loudon Park Cemetery

BALTIMORE

While Loudon Park boasts an attractive landscape of shade trees and woods, its main draw for grave hunters is as the last known address of **H. L. Mencken** (1880–1956), Baltimore's most famous twentieth-century citizen. I went there in search of the curmudgeonly author, but the staff in the office (which is a funeral home) had never heard of Mencken, a world-famous journalist considered the enfant terrible of American letters during his long reign at the *Baltimore Sun* newspaper. "Is he a relative?" was the first question I was asked, followed by "Was he in the military?" and "Do you know his first name?" After a lengthy wait in a bereavement room (I couldn't dispel the notion that I was related), the grief counselor returned with a print-out of the section of the cemetery where the Mencken plot is located. After considerable time spent tracing and retracing stone after stone, I had to move on. But curiosity remains, and I will happily send a copy of this book to the first person to find and send me a photograph of Mr. Mencken's grave. After such neglect, Mr. M. may be dying to get out. *3620 Wilkiens Avenue, Baltimore. Tel. (410) 644-1900. Grounds open from dawn to dusk. Office hours: 9:00 A.M.–5:00 P.M. Monday–Friday, 11:00 A.M.–3:00 P.M. Saturday–Sunday; rest rooms.*

Westminster Cemetery and Catacombs

BALTIMORE

In downtown Baltimore, Westminster wraps around the old Gothic Westminster Church (circa 1852) and itself is enclosed by brick-and-wrought-iron walls and gates. Even if the gates are locked, it is possible to peer in at the tomb and wall memorial of the graveyard's most illustrious guest, Edgar Allan Poe, located in the far right-hand corner from the church. *519 West Fayette (corner of North Greene), Baltimore. Tel. (410) 706-2072. Grounds open 8:00 A.M.–dusk daily.*

EDGAR ALLAN POE
1809–1849

There is irony in the fact that Poe, poor for so much of his life, should now, finally, for evermore, have such an impressive monument: squarish white sandstone embedded with a bronze medallion with his portrait, looking dashingly poetic; behind it in the brick wall is a sandstone plaque in French: a tribute to Poe from a French literary society, recognition of his worldwide reputation. Poe said, "With me poetry has not been a purpose, but a passion." Yet it is his macabre short stories—"The Fall of the House of Usher," "Murders in the Rue Morgue," "The Purloined Letter," "The Pit and the Pendulum," and "The Cask of Amontillado"—that are so admired for their tension-building sense of terror. Many of his poems, "The Raven," "Annabel Lee," "The Bells," and "To Helen," continue to be read as well. For readers who enjoy feasting on sad tales, Poe's life provides a banquet: abandoned by his parents, expelled from West Point, his struggle to scratch out a living, the early death of his child-bride, his own frail health, alcohol addiction, and finally his brief mysterious disappearance, followed by death at age forty, just before his second marriage. Poe's remains have

been twice removed (the original gravesite reportedly had a statue of a raven)—but Nevermore. **The Edgar Allan Poe House** (203 North Amity Street; 410–396–7932), where he lived from 1832 to 1835, is open to view.

Mount Olivet Cemetery

FREDERICK

This quiet burial ground began life, as it were, in 1859. One of its two most celebrated occupants is **Barbara Fritchie** (1766–1862), famous (at age ninety-five) for defiantly waving a U.S. flag as Confederate troops under Stonewall Jackson passed in front of her door. Her feat was immortalized by John Greenleaf Whittier in his poem, "Barbara Fritchie," but it is believed he may have mistaken her for the real heroine, a woman named Mary Quantrill. Fritchie's grave is easy to find, identified by a green marker in the ground. *515 South Market Street, Frederick. Tel. (301) 662-1164. Grounds open 7:30 A.M.–dusk. Office hours: 9:00 A.M.–5:00 P.M. Monday–Friday, 9:00 A.M.–12:00 P.M. Saturday; map, rest room.*

FRANCIS SCOTT KEY
1779–1843

Fittingly, an American flag flies over the grave of Key, the composer of "The Star-Spangled Banner." The grave is clearly visible near the entrance gate (check his green marker). Key practiced law in Frederick, and in 1814 he was sent to secure the release of a noted doctor, William Beanes, who had been seized and held prisoner aboard a British ship, at a time when the United States and Britain were at war. Key accomplished his mission. While returning, he was on an American ship just off Baltimore Harbor when the British launched an attack on the city. After a suspenseful night on shipboard, not knowing the outcome of the bombardment, Key saw at daybreak that the American flag still flew above Baltimore. The rest is history. Author of a few insignificant poems from time to time, he mainly stuck to his day job: the law. Yet every time we open our mouths to sing "our song," we're aware that Key's "fifteen minutes of fame" as a poet have lasted close to 200 years.

St. Mary's Cemetery

ROCKVILLE

This tiny burial ground spreads under umbrellas of shade trees to the left and in the rear of the little steepled Church of St. Mary's, the oldest (early nineteenth century) Catholic church in Rockville. The graveyard is so small that its most famous grave is a cinch to find. Visitor alert: There is another St. Mary's Cemetery, but it is outside of town. This one by the church is the one F. Scott Fitzgerald fans seek. *520 Veirs Mill Road, Rockville. Tel. (301) 424-5550. Grounds open all the time.*

F. SCOTT FITZGERALD
1896–1940

Francis Scott Key Fitzgerald is now where he wanted to be, but it took some doing. At the time of his death, he was a lapsed Catholic, and the church would not allow him to be buried in sacred ground. Times change. In 1975 Scott and his wife, **Zelda Sayre Fitzgerald** (1900–1948), were moved from Rockville Cemetery to this, their final home. Life for both had been a bumpy ride. When Scott, Princeton graduate and budding author, scored his first major success with *This Side of Paradise* in 1920, the world looked golden. And for a while it was, with successes like *The Great Gatsby* (1925) and a wild Jazz Age life in Paris, the Riviera, and New York City. Then came Zelda's breakdown, Scott's alcoholism, odd writing jobs for magazines, and stints as a screenwriter in Hollywood. Washed up too young, he died broke of a heart attack. Zelda's death was unfortunate too, in a fire in the mental institution where she had been hospitalized for years. Buried in the same plot as her parents is **Frances Scott Fitzgerald Smith** (1921–1986), their only child. On Scott and Zelda's large gray granite rectangle is a quote from *The Great Gatsby*: "So we beat on, boats against the current, borne back ceaselessly into the past." In this quiet, restful place, the past lives on.

New Jersey

Harleigh Cemetery

CAMDEN

Dating back to 1885, Harleigh has a spirit that is pure Victorian, as seen in the many obelisks and mausoleums that dot the grounds. Residing among them is **Mother Bloor** (1862–1951), aka Ella Reeve Bloor, labor organizer and social reformer, and **Nick Virgilio** (1926–1989), a haiku master. *1640 Haddon Avenue (at Vesper Boulevard), Camden. Tel. (856) 963-0122. Grounds open 7:30 A.M.–4:30 P.M. daily. Office hours: 8:30 A.M.–4:30 P.M. Monday–Saturday; map, rest room.*

WALT WHITMAN
1819–1892

Admirers often think of Whitman as a poet of cities, and he was, especially New York, Brooklyn (where he grew up), New Orleans, and Washington (where he worked as a nurse during the Civil War). But he was also a poet of the sea, from time spent roaming Long Island, especially Huntington (where he was born). Why, then, is he now in Camden? He came here to live with his brother, trying to recuperate from paralysis caused by a stroke. The last nineteen years of his life were spent in Camden, though his restless spirit could never be tied down nor linked to a single place. It is impossible to pigeonhole this great poet, whose *Leaves of Grass, Song of Myself,* and "When Lilacs Last in the Dooryard Bloom'd" are acknowledged masterpieces. He was—and remains—a study in contradictions: Fastidious in dress, he cultivated the image of a casual workman; big in size, there was something "delicate, womanly in him" (in the words of his friend, the poet John Burroughs). His poetry is fresh and vibrant today, but its veiled homosexuality was scandalous to mid-Victorians, even to many of the writers who admired him, some of whom urged him to tone it down. He designed his own tomb, which resembles a hut of rough-cut stone, with a triangular rooftop bearing his name, arched above a grill-work entrance. The approach to the grave is sepulchral, supposedly inspired by William Blake's poem "Gates of Paradise." Poetic to the end. **The Walt Whitman House** (330 Mickle Boulevard; 856–964–5383), his last home and the only one he ever owned, displays his original furnishings, books, and objects.

Princeton Cemetery

PRINCETON

Perhaps its location in an old university town has caused this cozy burial place, which dates from the eighteenth century, to reap its rich harvest of distinguished guests. Along with most of Princeton University's past presidents, there are: **Sylvia Beach** (1887–1962), publisher of James Joyce's *Ulysses*, proprietor of Shakespeare and Company, a Paris bookstore-cum-writers' hangout in the 1920s and 1930s; **Jonathan Edwards** (1703–1758), Calvinist theologian who initiated a religious revival; **George Gallup** (1908–1984), statistician and pioneer in market research; **John O'Hara** (1905–1970), popular novelist and short story writer of the mid-twentieth century; **Paul Tulane** (1801–1887), founder of Tulane University; and **Henry Van Dyke** (1852–1933), minister, English professor, author of religious works and songs, among them "Joyful, Joyful, We Adore Thee" (sung to the tune of Beethoven's "Ode to Joy"). *Witherspoon and Wiggins Streets, Princeton. Tel. (609) 924-1369. Grounds open from dawn to dusk.*

AARON BURR
1756–1836

Burr, a Newark native, came of prominent stock: His father, **Aaron Burr, Sr.** (1716–1757), also buried here, was an educator; his maternal grandfather was theologian **Jonathan Edwards** (here too). Precocious Aaron entered Princeton University as a sophomore at age thirteen and graduated with honors at sixteen. In the Revolutionary War he served under, respectively, Benedict Arnold, George Washington, and Israel Putnam. In 1782 he was admitted to the New York bar and became involved in politics, founding the Tammany Society, which became a major political machine by the late nineteenth century. In 1800 he became Thomas Jefferson's vice president, though Jefferson didn't trust him. In 1804 Burr ran for governor of New York, but Alexander Hamilton's opposition contributed to Burr's defeat. Acri-

mony between the two men led to a duel and Hamilton's death. From then on, Burr's activities belong in the category of "believe him or not," shrouded (uh-oh) in secrecy and confusion. He was accused of plotting to conquer Mexico and establish an empire in the west and south. Subsequently acquitted in three treason trials, he was by then so discredited, burr-ned out, and in debt, he left for Europe. In 1812 he returned to New York and practiced law in relative obscurity for the rest of his life.

GROVER CLEVELAND
1837–1908

Cleveland, both the twenty-second and twenty-fourth president of the U.S., was born in New Jersey, but spent most of his early career in New York State. Following the usual path of a lawyer with political ambitions (assistant district attorney, sheriff, mayor, governor), Democrat Cleveland ran for president over Tammany Hall opposition. His reputation as an honest, incorruptible administrator helped him win, but it was an ugly campaign. Cleveland, a bachelor, was accused of fathering a child out of wedlock. His opponents marched behind baby buggies, shouting, "Ma, Ma, where's my pa?" Cleveland supporters retorted, "Gone to the White House, ha, ha, ha." During his first term, the forty-eight-year-old Cleveland married twenty-two-year-old Frances Filsom. For all the age difference, theirs was a happy marriage, producing five children. Their firstborn, Ruth, became a national darling, so popular that a candy bar was named after her: Baby Ruth. Cleveland was defeated for a second term, despite winning the popular vote (sound familiar?), but came back resoundingly four years later, the first president ever to have terms that weren't consecutive.

Edison National Historic Site

WEST ORANGE

The site consists of the Edison home, Glenmont, and the Edison laboratories, both managed by the National Park Service. When Thomas Alva Edison and his wife, **Mina Miller Edison** (1865–1947), died, they were buried in Rosedale Cemetery. In 1963 their surviving children requested that the bodies be removed to Glenmont. After a considerable local flap, they were. There they rest today, under white marble headstones flat to the earth, scarcely noticeable to visitors to the house because of a low hedge screening them. Just above the name and dates on Edison's stone is incised a shell, and within it a round object resembling a baseball. This is supposed to represent a monad, which Edison believed to be an indivisible essence of life. *Main Street and Lakeside Avenue, West Orange. Tel. (973) 736–5050. House, laboratory, and grounds open Wednesday–Sunday only; call for tour hours, tours are limited and by ticket only, tickets (fee for adults) obtainable at the site on the day of the visit. The Historic Site will be closed for two years beginning October 2002.*

THOMAS ALVA EDISON

1847–1931

Edison had almost no formal schooling (three months tops, after which his mother taught him at home). His teachers called him "addled" and "inadaptable" and said he had no mathematical ability, but this didn't slow him down. At age ten he was addicted to chemistry and made his own laboratory. As a teenage telegraph operator, he saved enough money to build an "invention factory," where he experimented endlessly. Over time his tinkering led to notable breakthroughs. Although he may not have invented the incandescent lamp, his improvements made it cheap to produce and use. His "Edison effect" was the basis for the vacuum tube, which was essential in developing modern radiotelephony. From the

Edison laboratories countless new products emerged; over the years he owned more than 1,300 patents. There is no question he was one of the most creative geniuses of all time.

Quirkily, for a man of science, he became interested in ESP (extra sensory perception) and actually tried producing a machine that could speak with the dead. He won't need it now.

North Carolina

Riverside Cemetery

ASHEVILLE

A lovely old (1885) hillside burial ground in the shadows of the Great Smoky Mountains, Riverside resides on an undulating landscape of eighty-seven acres, punctuated with mature oaks and pines, holly, and other shrubs and over 9,000 fulltime residents. They include Civil War generals, governors, congressmen, educators, physicians, eighteen German prisoners of war who died of typhoid while interned during World War I, and artisans who worked on Asheville's great Biltmore estate. Among colorful local residents are **Solomon Lipinsky**, founder of the Bon Marche department store chain; **George Masa** (1881–1933), born in Japan as Masahara Iisuka, who laid out and measured Great Smoky National Park and the Appalachian Trail; and composer **William John Robjohn** (1843–1920), aka Caryl Florio. *Birch Street, Asheville (Montford exit off I-240). Tel. (828) 258-8480. Grounds open 8:00 A.M.–6:00 P.M. November–March, 8:00 A.M.–8:00 P.M. April–October. Office hours: 8:00 A.M.–4:30 P.M. Monday–Friday; map, excellent biographic pamphlet, video, rest room.*

WILLIAM "O. HENRY" PORTER
1862–1910

O. Henry, as Porter signed himself in his hundreds of short stories, was born in Greensboro, North Carolina, but moved to Texas at age twenty, where he tried a number of jobs, which later provided lots of grist for his writing mill. In Austin he worked as a bank teller, then moved to Houston, where he wrote a daily column for the *Houston Daily Post*. While in Houston, he was summoned back to Austin for embezzling about $1,000 from his former employer. Rather than try to prove his innocence, he skipped town for Honduras, via New Orleans. Learning that his wife was deathly ill, he returned to Austin. She died, he was arrested, tried, and sentenced to five years in prison. With good behavior he was released in three years, but the shame caused him to leave town, first for Pittsburgh, then New York. Using the pen name O.Henry, he became a master of the short story, usually with a surprise ending. What gave his stories such appeal wasn't just the twist, but the portraits of people in all walks of life: rich, poor, urban, rural. Stories like the humorous "The Ransom of Red Chief" and the poignant "Gift of the Magi" still resonate. To the left of his smooth gray granite headstone, with its rough sides, is that of his second wife, **Sara Coleman Porter** (1868–1959), a childhood friend. They lived part time in New York, part-time in Asheville, and now full-time in these scenic hills.

THOMAS WOLFE
1900–1938

Asheville's most famous native did come home again and an arrow here leads you quickly to his final address, one of the highest points in the graveyard, in a family plot illuminated by lines from his works. Wolfe is best remembered for four novels: *Look*

Homeward, Angel, Of Time and the River, The Web and the Rock, and *You Can't Go Home Again,* all of them semiautobiographical. Riverside is peopled with neighbors he wrote about, not all of them happy to recognize themselves and Asheville in print. He once wrote his mother: "I will think all the thoughts, feel all the emotions I am able, and I will write, write, write." One of his problems, critics say, was he wrote everything, and only severe pruning by his editor, Maxwell Perkins, made his work accessible. Son of a stonecutter and proprietress of a boardinghouse, Wolfe wrote and lived to the hilt, traveling back and forth to Europe and around the United States. He died much too young, of miliary tuberculosis of the brain. His speckled marble gravestone notes: "THE LAST VOYAGE, THE LONGEST, THE BEST," from *Look Homeward, Angel;* the words, "A BELOVED AMERICAN AUTHOR;" and, finally, "DEATH BENT TO TOUCH HIS CHOSEN SON WITH MERCY, LOVE AND PITY, AND PUT THE SEAL OF HONOR ON HIM WHEN HE DIED," from *The Web and the Rock.* Even here, even now, he can't stop talking.

Pennsylvania

West Laurel Hill Cemetery
BALA CYNWYD

West Laurel Hill, which replaced older Laurel Hill as the place to be seen en route to the great beyond, is just across the Schuylkill River, along the western edge of

Philadelphia. Among its illustrious inhabitants are two generations of sculptors: father **Alexander Milne Calder** (1846–1923) and son **Alexander Stirling Calder** (1870–1945), whose work can be seen in public places throughout Philadelphia; television personality **Dave Garroway** (1913–1982), host of the first *Today* show on NBC-TV; and **Anna Jarvis** (1864–1948), founder of Mother's Day. *215 Belmont Avenue, Bala Cynwyd. Tel. (610) 664-1591. Grounds open 8:00 A.M.–5:00 P.M. Monday–Saturday, 9:00 A.M.–5:00 P.M. Sunday. Office hours: 8:00 A.M.–4:30 P.M. Monday–Saturday; map, rest room.*

Christ Church Burial Ground

PHILADELPHIA

Here lies one graveyard on two sites. One is the ancient churchyard surrounding Christ Church, the founding church of the Protestant Episcopal Church in America. This is a pleasure to visit, with brick flooring, a petite garden of roses, hydrangeas, hosta, flowering trees, and wooden benches—a quiet, meditative place. Its brick walls shelter such people as **Charles Lee** (1731–1782), a colorful and controversial character in the Revolutionary era, and **James Wilson** (1742–1798), signer of the Declaration of Independence and justice of the U.S. Supreme Court. The second site, called Christ Church Burial Ground, is three blocks away. It is home to

Ben Franklin and four other signers of the Declaration, the largest such group in a single graveyard: **Joseph Hewes** (1730–1779), **Francis Hopkinson** (1737–1791), **George Ross** (1730–1779), and Robert Morris. **Benjamin Rush** (1745–1813), the "father of American psychiatry," is also buried here. *Churchyard: 2nd and Market Streets, Philadelphia. Tel. (215) 922-1695 . Grounds open 9:00 A.M.–5:00 P.M. Monday–Saturday, 1:00 P.M.–5:00 P.M. Sunday. Office (and shop) hours: 9:00 A.M–5:00 P.M.; map, pamphlets, postcards, tours available. Christ Church Burial Ground: 5th and Arch Streets, Philadelphia. Gates open only by appointment. Tel. (215) 922-1695.*

BENJAMIN FRANKLIN
1706–1790

Reminders of Ben Franklin are everywhere in Philadelphia, his adopted city, and rightly so. After his move from his hometown of Boston in 1723, he was as busy and industrious as his *Poor Richard's Almanack* suggests. Author, printer, inventor, statesman, diplomat, he did it all, and in his "free" time he established a hospital, philosophical society, subscription library, and fire company. That was for starters. He also invented the lightning rod, the Franklin stove, and bifocal lenses. Oh, yes, then there was his role in the American Revolution, his signing of the Declaration of Independence (which he helped write), and—late in life—his stint as American ambassador to France, where he was the French people's favorite American until Jerry Lewis came along. Franklin's *Autobiography* is a model of memoir writing in its commonsense approach to life and problem solving. His long rectangular stone is near the wrought-iron fence, at the corner of Fifth and Arch Streets, clearly visible from outside. That's the way most people see it, because the gates are locked much of the time.

ROBERT MORRIS
1734–1806

Follow the money, the saying goes, and during the American Revolution, much of the money to finance the armies was raised by Morris, who had amassed a fortune as a merchant in the import trade. John Adams wrote of him: "I think he has a masterly understanding, an open temper and an honest heart." Morris first voted against the Declaration of Independence in July 1776, thinking it premature, but he signed it in August, and from then on worked fast and furiously to raise money to help win the war. He was offered, but declined, the job of treasury secretary in Washington's first cabinet. Instead he became one of Pennsylvania's first senators, serving from 1789 to 1795. The large, rectangular, white marble Morris family headstone—bearing the names Morris and White—lies in the rear of the churchyard, beneath a pine tree. Morris's wife, Mary, was the sister of William White, a bishop of the Episcopal Church for fifty years. The vault contains members of both families.

Laurel Hill Cemetery

PHILADELPHIA

Laurel Hill began life (so to speak) as a rural graveyard in 1836, located three and a half miles north of the city center. Its seventy-eight acres made it the second largest rural cemetery in America, and it was the first designed by an architect. But the city has crept up. Now the surrounding north Philadelphia neighborhood is blighted by urban decay. Yet in its heyday, Laurel Hill was the place fashionable Philadelphians chose as their last address. Its magnificent sarcophagi, artistic sculptures, and ornate mausoleums (visible from along the Schuylkill River below) are reminders of its former status. Proof of its popularity is its register of all-stars: **Charles E. Bohlen** (1904–1974), diplomat and ambassador to Russia during the Cold War; **Henry Deringer, Jr.** (1786–1868), manufacturer of the derringer, the type of gun used by John Wilkes Booth to kill President Lincoln; **Louis A. Godey** (1804–1878), publisher, and **Sarah Josepa Hale** (1788–1879), editor, of *Godey's Lady's Book*, the bible of tastemaking for nineteenth-century American women; **Commodore Isaac Hull** (1773–1843), hero of the War of 1812; **George H. Lorimer** (1868–1937), editor of the *Saturday Evening Post* magazine; **George G. Meade** (1815–1872), Civil War general credited with the Union victory at Gettysburg; **Thomas Sully** (1783–1872), artist; and **Peter Widener** (1834–1915), financier who endowed Widener University. *3822 Ridge Avenue, Philadelphia. Tel. (215) 228-8200. Grounds open: 8:00 A.M.–4:00 P.M. Monday–Friday. Office hours: 9:30 A.M.–1:30 P.M. Saturday; map, rest rooms.*

Old Pine Cemetery

PHILADELPHIA

A modest place, Old Pine surrounds on three sides the Old Pine Street Presbyterian Church. Incorporated into the brick rear wall are ancient tombstones, whose names are largely obliterated by time. *412 Pine Street, Philadelphia. Tel. (215) 925-8051. Grounds open 6:00 A.M.–sunset.*

EUGENE ORMANDY
1899–1985

This twentieth-century cultural icon lies surrounded by an ornate wrought-iron fence. The rectangular gray granite headstone bears a circular insignia of the Philadelphia Orchestra Association with a harp etched in the center. Ormandy raised his baton at the Philadelphia Orchestra for forty-two years and established the orchestra as a major musical force. Born into a musical family in Budapest, Hungary, he was, at age five, the youngest person ever admitted to the Royal Academy of Music. As a young man, he was lured to the United States in 1921 by the promise of $30,000 for a concert tour of the country, but the bubble burst and he was stranded in New York. Short stints followed: as violinist, concertmaster, and conductor at movie theaters, radio programs, summer concerts, and five years as conductor of the Minneapolis Symphony. This led him to the Philadelphia Orchestra, and the rest, as they say, became musical history. Known for an infallible ear and tremendous memory, Ormandy rarely used a score in conducting the music he favored: mostly late romantic and early twentieth-century works. Among his many awards were the Presidential Medal of Freedom, the Kennedy Center Honors, *officier* of the French Legion of Honor, Knight Commander of the Order of the British Empire, and several knighthoods. A long life, eighty-six years, and a melodic one.

St. Peter's Cemetery

PHILADELPHIA

Lying to the left and in the rear of St. Peter's Church (vintage 1761), the burial ground is tiny, with a brick walk down the center, wooden benches for contemplation, and an abundance of magnolias and orange sage trees. At the Fourth Street entrance is posted a story of Indian chieftains from the Midwest who were invited to Philadelphia in 1793 by President George Washington (when Philadelphia was the capital) to a peace council to resolve boundary disputes in the Northwest Territory. Between January and April eight were stricken with smallpox and died; they are buried here in unmarked graves. Also here is financier **Nicholas Biddle** (1786–1844). *Third and Pine Streets, Philadelphia. Tel. (215) 925-5968. Churchyard open from dawn to sunset daily. Church open: 9:00 A.M.–4:00 P.M. daily; map posted outside on the right side of the church.*

STEPHEN DECATUR
1779–1820

The tallest obelisk here belongs to this naval commodore, with his accomplishments cited on all four sides and a bronze eagle soaring at the top (see following page). Decatur lived a short life but an honorable one. He was known as courageous, fair minded, genial, and intelligent, best remembered for his fearlessness in the Tripolitan War and the War of 1812. In 1815, on a voyage to Algeria to negotiate a treaty to end the paying of tribute to the Barbary powers, he said the words that have been abbreviated to a bumper sticker mantra ever since: "Our country! In her intercourse with foreign nations may she always be in the right; but our country, right or wrong." Gallant to the end, he was determined to aim low in a duel with a disgruntled fellow officer; his opponent wasn't as generous. He survived with a thigh wound; Decatur was mortally wounded. He was forty-one. The **Stephen Decatur House**, his handsome Federal home in Washington, D.C. (Lafayette Square; 202–842–0920), was designed by Benjamin H. Latrobe and is open to view.

CHARLES WILLSON PEALE
1741–1827

Most museum collections of early American art have at least one Peale portrait. The words on his gravestone don't say it all, but do provide a précis of his busy life: "He participated in the Revolutionary struggle for our Independence. As an artist he contributed to the history of his country. He was an energetic citizen and patriot, and in private life beloved by all who knew him." This isn't bloviating. He seems to have been a remarkable man, a fine portrait painter, naturalist, and member of the American Philosophical Society. He served in the American Revolution and was the author of a lengthy autobiography, which recounted in rich detail his life (and that of the young republic) from the 1760s to the late 1820s. Very ap-Peale-ing.

The Woodlands Cemetery

PHILADELPHIA

Incorporated in 1840, Woodlands is a, yes, woodsy enclave near the University of Pennsylvania and the Schuylkill River. Large mausoleums, giant headstones, and imposing tombs dot the verdant landscape. Among a scattering of Civil War heroes are **S. Weir Mitchell** (1829–1914), physician and novelist; and **Frank R. Stockton** (1834–1902), author of that classic puzzle story, "The Lady or the Tiger." *40th Street and Woodland Avenue, Philadelphia. Tel. (215) 386–2181. Grounds open 9:00 A.M.–5:00 P.M. daily. Office hours: 10:00 A.M.–3:00 P.M. Monday–Thursday, other times by appointment; map, rest rooms.*

THOMAS EAKINS
1844–1916

The most famous resident of Woodlands, Eakins has grown in reputation from a favorite local artist to one of national stature, whose works are in many museum collections. As a young man, he studied in Paris for four years. In addition to painting, he was also an accomplished photographer and sculptor. In 1876 he began teaching art at the Pennsylvania Academy of Fine Arts, but he ran into trouble for what were viewed as his radical ideas. When he introduced nude male models in a class of mixed students, Eakins was forced to resign. Two of his works on a heroic scale, *The Gross Clinic* and *The Agnew Clinic,* depicting a class of medical students observing an operation, were highly controversial when new but have little shock value today. Times do change.

Allegheny Cemetery

PITTSBURGH

This is Pittsburgh's oldest burial ground—and it's a beauty. The 300-acre site is a pastoral landscape, with two ponds, plantings, and a cornucopia of monuments, anchored by Romanesque Revival and Gothic Revival towers at each end. Many prominent Pennsylvanians are here. Among them: **Josh Gibson** (1911–1947), National Negro League batting champion and Hall of Famer; **William "Gus" Greenlee** (1893–1952), African American businessman, founder of the Pittsburgh Crawfords, one of the best teams in the Negro League; **George Shiras, Jr.** (1832–1924), justice of the U.S. Supreme Court; **Harry Thaw** (1871–1947), killer of architect Stanford White, because of White's affair with Thaw's wife (showgirl Evelyn Nesbit); and **Stanley "Sugar Man" Turrentine** (1934-2000), musician, known for his "soul jazz." *4734 Butler Street, Pittsburgh. Tel. (412) 682–1624. Grounds open 7:00 A.M.–7:00 P.M. April–August, 7:00 A.M.–5:30 P.M. September–March. Office hours: 8:30 A.M.–5:00 P.M. Monday–Saturday; map, tour booklets, tours available on request.*

STEPHEN FOSTER
1826–1864

There's irony in the fact that some of the most folkloric and nostalgic American songs about the South were composed by a Pittsburgh native who may have been below the Mason-Dixon line only once. "Massa's in the Cold Cold Ground," "My Old Kentucky Home," "O Susanna," "Away Down South," and "The Old Folks at Home" are Foster's best-known works. His inspiration was drawn from the popularity of Negro minstrel shows.Trained as a bookkeeper, young Foster soon realized that some of the ballads he wrote for fun were moneymakers, so he decided to devote full time to writing music. His output was enviable, forty-eight songs

in one year, but the results were often repetitous and banal. His last years were impoverished and dissolute, his death obscure—in a hospital charity ward. A dead end, yes, but not for the songs, which go on and on, as part of our national musical heritage.

LILLIAN RUSSELL MOORE
1861–1922

Born in Clinton, Iowa, as Helen Louise Leonard, this beautiful young woman made her singing debut in New York as Lillian Russell, an "English ballad singer." Her early ambition was to sing opera, but comic opera proved to be her real forte. Three failed marriages (one of which turned out to be bigamous, though no fault of hers) were secondary to her much-vaunted affair with "Diamond Jim" Brady, even more of a publicity-seeker than she was. So how did this belle of Broadway end up in Pittsburgh? In 1912 she married (her fourth try) **Alexander Pollock Moore**, a Pittsburgh publisher, and in her last ten years, she busied herself with civic activities and an occasional vaudeville appearance. It was a great life while it lasted. Her (and her husband's) narrow-sided, colonnaded Grecophile mausoleum has this inscription above its metal doors (monogramed with his-and-her initials): "THE WORLD IS BETTER FOR HER HAVING LIVED." And without a doubt more interesting.

Homewood Cemetery

PITTSBURGH

From its beginnings in 1878, Homewood's landscaped acres (200 of them) have been home to many success stories: **Earl Garner** (1921–1977), jazz musician and songwriter; **Henry John Heinz** (1844–1916), the "57 varieties" ketchup-and-pickles inventor-founder; **Henry John Heinz III** (1938–1991), heir to the pickle business and U.S. senator; **George Mesta** (1862–1925), owner of the world's largest machine shop under one roof, and his wife, **Pearl Mesta** (1889–1975), Washington's premier party giver, basking in the glory that her husband's money provided; **"Jock" Sutherland** (1889–1948), college football coach (University of Pittsburgh) and Hall of Famer; and **Harold "Pie" Traynor** (1899–1972), Pittsburgh Pirate Hall of Famer, considered among the best third basemen of all time. *Dallas and Aylesboro Avenues, Pittsburgh. Tel. (412) 421–1822. Grounds open 7:00 A.M.–5:00 P.M. October–April, 7:00 A.M.–9:00 P.M. May–September. Office hours: 8:30 A.M.–5:00 P.M. Monday–Friday, 8:30 A.M.–4:00 P.M. Saturday; map, rest room.*

HENRY CLAY FRICK
1849–1919

Born in West Overton, Pennsylvania, Frick was the fourth generation of his family, on both sides, a rarity in that era. Although his formal education ended at age seventeen, he showed entrepreneurial spirit early. While working as a bookkeeper in his grandfather's distillery, he joined several others in building and operating coke ovens in the surrounding coal district of Connellsville. By the time he was thirty, he had fulfilled his first goal: to make $1 million. At forty-one, Frick was in charge of the Carnegie Steel Company, employing 30,000 men. One of the worst labor strikes of all time took place at Homestead, Pennsylvania, in 1892. Frick was shot and stabbed by Alexander Berkman, a Russian anarchist, but survived. Despite a reputation for ruthlessness in business, Frick's art collecting revealed a more sensitive spirit than the public usually saw. Clayton, Frick's Pittsburgh home (7227 Reynolds Street; 412–371–0600), is part of the **Frick Art and Historical Center**. The house is a grand example of a late-Victorian mansion, decorated by Mrs. Frick herself.

St. John Chrysostom Byzantine Catholic Church Cemetery

PITTSBURGH

This modest place is not the world stage you might expect Andy Warhol to choose as his last address. It hugs a hillside that overlooks a highway. The headstones read like a telephone book in eastern Europe and speak of the immigrant experience, with Polish, Ukrainian, Lithuanian, and Czech names. Many stones bear photographs of the persons beneath. *Route 88 and Connor Road, Pittsburgh. Grounds open from dawn to dusk.*

ANDY WARHOL
1928–1987

It seems only natural that this pop artist's grave is embellished from time to time with Campbell's soup cans (full), Brillo boxes, and photocopies of some of his best-known art works: portraits of Marilyn Monroe, Elizabeth Taylor, and Jackie Onassis. The grave is easy to find—a polished black granite headstone, located in front of his parents' headstone. As a kid named Warhola, he would never have made anyone's list of "most likely to succeed." His Slovakian immigrant family was grindingly poor. But Andy had several things going for him: artistic talent and a flair for the outrageous that drew attention. From childhood he loved popular culture (Hollywood movies, comic books, celebrity autographs, and memorabilia) and was shrewd enough to capitalize on it. He began his career as a commercial artist in the 1950s in New York, after getting a B.F.A. degree at Carnegie Institute, and was soon making $100,000 a year, turning pop culture and kitsch into fine art. Not the first pop artist, he was the most successful and moved into compatible fields: film, magazines, books, rock music. His ultracool, deadpan persona under a moppish silver wig made him a familiar figure on the club scene. Everything he touched turned into gold, or at least gold plate, until 1986. He was hospitalized for routine gall bladder surgery but unexpectedly died of cardiac arrest, in what many consider a botched operation. His most famous quip—"In the future everyone will be world-famous for fifteen minutes"—doesn't apply to him. One of the most influential artists of the late twentieth century, he left a fortune of more than $220 million and an art legacy worth even more.

South Carolina

St. Philip's Churchyard

CHARLESTON

In the heart of Charleston's historic center, the graveyard is located on three sides of stately St. Philip's Church and extends to larger "digs" across the street. Hidden by magnolias and live oak festooned with Spanish moss, this is a restful place, graced with brick walkways and heavy wrought-iron gates. Buried here, along with numerous high-profile Charlestonians, are **Charles Pinckney** (1757–1824), governor, senator, and signer of the U.S. Constitution; **Colonial William Rhett** (1666–1722), who captured the notorious pirate Stede Bonnet; and **Edward Rutledge** (1749–1800), signer of the Declaration of Independence, governor, and plantation owner. *142 Church Street, Charleston. Tel. (843) 722-7734. Grounds open 9:00 A.M.–4:30 P.M.*

JOHN CALDWELL CALHOUN
1782–1850

Calhoun's curriculum vitae is impressive: congressman from South Carolina (1811–1817), secretary of war (1817–1825), vice president of the United States (1825–1832), and U.S. senator (1832–1843, 1845–1850). History remembers him as a states' rights advocate, fiery orator, and defender of slavery, praised in the South, villified in the North. He was one of the first Southerners to urge secession. His imposing gray granite sarcophagus (right), located under an aged magnolia tree with gnarled trunk, to the right of the brick walk near the entrance

gates across the street from the church, is inscribed on one side with the words: "ERECTED BY THE STATE OF SOUTH CAROLINA A.D. 1884." During the Civil War sextons at the church feared that Yankee forces might dig up their hero or desecrate his grave, so in the stealth of night, they excavated and reburied him under the church itself. Later, after danger had passed, he was returned to his original grave. Last word is that he is lying low at last.

EDWIN DUBOSE HEYWARD
1 8 8 5 – 1 9 4 0

If the name on DuBose Heyward's modest gravestone doesn't ring an instant bell, start humming "Bess, you is my woman now" or "Summertime," and you might make the connection. Heyward, born into an impoverished branch of a prominent old Charleston family, was the author of *Porgy*, a 1925 novel, which Heyward and his wife, Dorothy, then converted to *Porgy: A Play in Four Acts*. This in turn morphed into the opera *Porgy and Bess*, with music by George and Ira Gershwin, lyrics and libretto by the Heywards. It became, and still is, a worldwide favorite. Heyward's success as a young man in the insurance business gave him time and the means to pursue his real interest: poetry and fiction writing. He wrote essays, magazine articles, and a screenplay of Eugene O'Neill's play *Emperor Jones*. But Porgy was his first and favorite work—a breakthrough of sorts: the first American novel by a white to treat African American culture with understanding. Heyward's gray granite headstone is located near, but overshadowed by, Calhoun's.

Woodlawn Memorial Park

GREENVILLE

On 120-acre Woodlawn, which opened in 1938, all graves are denoted by their bronze-on-granite markers, even that of the cemetery's most famous full-timer, "Shoeless Joe" Jackson. *1901 Wade Hampton Boulevard, Greenville. Tel. (864) 244-4622. Grounds open all the time. Office hours: 9:00 A.M.–5:00 P.M. Monday-Friday, 9:00 A.M.–4:00 P.M. Saturday, 1:30 P.M.–4:30 P.M. Sunday; map, rest room.*

JOSEPH "SHOELESS JOE" JACKSON
1 8 8 8 – 1 9 5 1

Bats and baseballs still accumulate as belated tribute at the flat gravestone of this once-surefire, but-not-to-be Hall of Fame baseball player. The nickname "Shoeless Joe," which Jackson hated, came from a single incident that occurred when he was in the minor leagues. His new spike shoes wore blisters on his feet, so he played the next game in stocking feet. Some fan yelled, "You shoeless son-of-a-gun," and the name stuck. In a career that spanned twelve years, he was possibly the greatest natural hitter ever. A few stats: His career .356 batting average was the third best of all time; he led the league in triples eight times, batted over .340 eight times, hit .408 in the 1911 season. All of this went for naught because some players on the 1919 Chicago White Sox team colluded with gam-

blers to throw the World Series. As the movie *Eight Men Out* makes clear, Jackson was probably among the least culpable. In fact, in that ignominious series, he had the most hits (twelve) and didn't make an error. But he was banished forever from baseball, along with seven others, by Judge Kenesaw Landis, the commissioner. So far, moves to rescind the ban have failed. Joe remains benched.

Virginia

Arlington National Cemetery

ARLINGTON

Our national pantheon of fallen heroes is located on land that was once owned by the Washington and Lee families. The property was seized for back taxes by the U.S. government during the Civil War and converted to a burial ground. The Lees were later compensated. The cemetery overlooks the Potomac River, its rows and rows of servicemen markers, more than 19,000 Union soldiers alone, spread like an army over the land. Here are the likes of **Henry "Hap" Arnold** (1886–1950), World War II five-star general of the U.S. Air Force; **Omar Bradley** (1893–1981), U.S. Army general; **Ira Hayes** (1923–1955), Native American marine, among servicemen who raised the flag at Iwo Jima; **Kara Spears Hultgreen** (1965–1994), first woman fighter pilot; **General John "Blackjack" Pershing** (1860–1948), hero of World War I; and **Philip Henry Sheridan, Jr.** (1831–1888), a Union general and hero in the Civil War.

A surprise is to find so many civilians here. To claim this prestigious final address, they must have served in or have some ties to the military (father, mother, son, daughter, spouse). These include **Julius Ochs Adler** (1893–1955), major-general in the U.S. Army and publisher of the *New York Times*; **Fay Bainter** (1893–1968), navy wife and character actress of the 1940s; **Floyd Bennett** (1890–1928), arctic explorer; **Hiram Bingham** (1875–1956), U.S. senator from Connecticut, credited with discovering Machu Picchu; and **Hugo Black** (1886–1971), **Harry A. Blackmun** (1908–1999), and **William Brennan** (1906–1997), justices of the U.S. Supreme Court. Also here are **Claire Chennault** (1890–1958), organizer of the Flying Tigers in China in World War II and of the Civil Air Transport (CAT), a commercial carrier connected to the CIA and a key supplier in the Korean War; **George Washington Parke Custis** (1781–1853), adopted son of George Washington; **Medgar Evers** (1925–1963), civil rights leader killed by white racists; **Oliver Wendell Holmes, Jr.** (1841–1935), prominent jurist, major voice on the U.S. Supreme Court for more than thirty-three years; **Pierre L'Enfant** (1754–1825), architect of Washington, D.C.; **Joe Louis** (1914–1981), one of the greatest prizefighters of all time, who defended his heavyweight boxing title twenty-five times and reigned for twelve years; **Francis Gary Powers** (1929–1977), U-2 spy pilot; and **Walter Reed** (1851–1902), who tamed yellow fever. Every hour on the hour (every half-hour May–September) the changing of the guard takes place at the Tomb of the Unknown Soldier, an impressive sight. *Directly west of Memorial Bridge, Arlington. Tel: (703) 697-2131. Grounds open 8:00 A.M.–7:00 P.M. daily April–September, 9:00 A.M.–5:00 P.M. daily October–March. Map, rest rooms.*

ABNER DOUBLEDAY
1819–1893

Some myths have a life of their own. Abner Doubleday invented baseball on the fields of Cooperstown, New York, in 1839, right? Not! This Yankee military man was born in Ballston Spa, New York, and attended schools in Auburn and Cooperstown, but he was nowhere near Cooperstown in 1839. A graduate of West Point in 1842, he received a commission in the artillery, fought in the Mexican War and in a campaign against the Seminole Indians in Florida, and was a captain in Charleston Harbor when the first shot in the Civil War was fired at Fort Sumter. Loyal to the Union and to Lincoln, he viewed the South Carolinians as traitors. Doubleday ended his service in 1873 as a colonel, retiring to Mendham, New Jersey. Now about that baseball stuff: There's no evidence he ever played or talked about the game, nor was it mentioned in his *New York Times* obituary. Sorry. Out on strikes!

JOHN FOSTER DULLES
1888–1959

Dulles earned his final home in Arlington as a World War I veteran in the intelligence service. A Presbyterian minister's son, Dulles inherited his fascination with foreign affairs from his maternal grandfather, John Foster, secretary of state under Benjamin Harrison, who helped negotiate the 1895 treaty that ended the Sino-Japanese War. One of Dulles's own achievements was negotiating, at President Truman's request, the peace treaty with Japan at the end of World War II. He was best known as Dwight D. Eisenhower's secretary of state,

stern moralizer, and Cold Warrior supreme. He was the first of a series of globe-trotting secretaries of state, logging hundreds of thousands of miles on trips to London, Berlin, Paris, Caracas, Bonn, Manila, Tokyo, and points beyond. Other credentials included degrees from Princeton University and Georgetown University law school, membership on various economic and diplomatic commissions, service as a U.S. senator, representative to the United Nations, and chairman of the Carnegie Endowment for International Peace. Dulles navigated his way through treacherous Cold War waters, but sometimes alienated nonaligned nations like India by chiding them for their neutrality in a world, in his view, of good versus evil. His wife, **Janet Avery Dulles** (1891–1969), lies with him in an imposing sarcophagus with a cross carved into the top.

SAMUEL DASHIELL HAMMETT
1894–1961

Creator of Sam Spade, the tough but idealistic prototype of fictional detectives, Dashiell Hammett invented the modern detective story. He earned his credentials the hard way: working for the Pinkerton National Detective Agency. As a private operative he was involved in some headline-making cases of the day: the hunt for accused securities thief Nick Arnstein and the Hollywood trial of Fatty Arbuckle for rape and murder. When tuberculosis (a World War I legacy) flared, he gave up sleuthing and began writing about it. Huge successes followed, especially when *The Thin Man* became a popular movie series. Readers of *Red Harvest*, *The Dain*

Curse, The Maltese Falcon (considered his finest work), *The Glass Key,* and *The Thin Man* respect Hammett for his inventive plots, memorable characters, and realistic style. He didn't publish a book after 1934. What followed reads like fiction itself: great wealth in royalties, high living, stints as a Hollywood screenwriter, five months in jail for refusing to testify to a congressional committee during the Joe McCarthy era, alcoholism, a thirty-year attachment to playwright Lillian Hellman, unpaid taxes to the IRS, lung cancer, and death. Enough already!

JOHN FITZGERALD KENNEDY
1917–1963

From his birth in Brookline, Massachusetts, JFK, possessor of wit, wealth, and intelligence, seemed to lead a charmed life, until his assassination that awful day in Dallas. The Harvard years; the narrow escape from his PT boat in World War II; a Pulitzer Prize–winning book, *Profiles in Courage*; his marriage to a beautiful socialite; a short career as a U.S. senator; his quick rise to the U.S. presidency as the youngest elected to that office, all were part of a story that mesmerized the public. There were serious issues: the Bay of Pigs disaster, the Berlin Wall, the Cuban Missile Crisis, the struggle for civil rights, the germination of the Vietnam War. Mostly, the Kennedy presidency will be remembered not for what was but for what might have been. His gravesite encompasses more than three acres, dotted with magnolia, hawthorn, crab apple, holly, and cherry trees, with a good view of Arlington House, the former Lee Mansion (open to the public). The area leading to the grave is paved with irregular-shaped Cape Cod granite stone, quarried near the site of the Kennedy family home. A plaza edged by a low wall with quotations from JFK's inaugural address and other speeches, overlooks the flat, five-foot-round granite gravestone, in the center of which burns an eternal flame. Camelot it's not, but moving nonetheless.

ROBERT KENNEDY
1925–1968

Bobby Kennedy's grave is near his brother's, but it is marked simply by a white wooden cross. Nearby is a reflecting pool, with a wall on which are etched quotations from some of his speeches. During JFK's presidential campaign, detractors viewed younger brother Bobby as both ruthless and an intellectual lightweight. That perception changed when he became attorney general of the United States. A commitment to civil rights and an idealistic streak signaled the emergence of the new Bobby. His brother's death, a single term as a U.S. senator from New York, opposition to the Vietnam War, an emotion-charged run for the presidency, ending in his assassination in Los Angeles—these are the bare bones reminders of his short life. There are loyalists who believe he was "the best of the Kennedys," the most committed to social justice. Too late to know for sure.

GEORGE CATLETT MARSHALL
1880–1959

Too modest and self-effacing to be a popular hero, Pennsylvania-born Marshall may have been the finest American military officer of the twentieth century, serving in World Wars I and II and as secretary of defense dur-

ing the Korean War. He is the only man ever to be both a secretary of defense and secretary of state. In 1939 President Roosevelt passed over thirty-three more senior officers to choose Marshall as chief of staff of the U.S. Army. His talents as an administrator and global strategist were so great they cost him the job he really wanted, command of Overlord, the Allied invasion of France (it went to Dwight Eisenhower), because, said Roosevelt, "I didn't feel I could sleep at ease with you out of Washington." FDR wasn't the only one impressed. Winston Churchill cabled that "he is the true 'organizer of victory.'" Later, as Harry Truman's secretary of state, he developed the Marshall Plan to help Europe recover from the war. For this he won the Nobel Peace Prize in 1953.

THURGOOD MARSHALL
1908–1993

The milestones on Marshall's march to the U.S. Supreme Court, as its first African American justice, were many: graduation from Howard University magna cum laude; twenty-seven years with the National Association for the Advancement of Colored People (NAACP), advocating justice for minorities; twenty-nine victories arguing cases in the U.S. Supreme Court, including the landmark case of *Brown v. Board of Education of Topeka*, which demolished the legal basis for segregation in America; appointment as circuit judge (1961), whose 112 rulings were all upheld by the Supreme Court; U.S. solicitor general, appointed by Lyndon Johnson, winning fourteen of his nineteen cases. In appointing Marshall a justice to the Supreme Court, Johnson said it was "the right thing to do, the right

time to do it, the right man and the right place." His twenty-four years on the country's top bench proved Johnson right. Age (eighty-two) and poor health led to retirement in 1991; he died two years later.

JACQUELINE BOUVIER KENNEDY ONASSIS
1929–1994

Future generations might wonder what all the fuss was about: a pretty woman with a little-girl voice, widow of two powerful men, one a U.S. president, the other a self-made Greek mogul/millionaire. But for anyone alive between the 1960s and the beginning of the twenty-first century, Jackie Kennedy Onassis—or Jackie O or just plain Jackie—seemed larger-than-life. She was born in Southampton, New York; attended Vassar College; married a glamorous Washington bachelor; and in 1961 became the mistress of the city's best address, 1600 Pennsylvania Avenue. French speaking, fashion conscious, smart, and well read, she lured the best and brightest in the arts to her White House dinners. That's the happy part of the story. What brought her mythic status were the tragedies: a miscarriage, loss of a second baby through stillbirth, assassination of her husband and his brother, her own cancer, and the way she coped with them, with dignity and—unusual in this confessional age—silence. R.I.P. Jackie. You deserve it.

EARL WARREN
1891–1974

Few chief justices of the U.S. Supreme Court in the twentieth century aroused such admiration and such ire. Warren's long precourt career gave few clues that he would later preside over a

court famous as a respecter of civil rights and individual liberty. A brief stint in the U.S. Army in World War I was followed by three terms as the Alameda County (California) district attorney, California attorney general, and then three-term governor of the state. While governor, Warren supported the relocation of the state's Japanese Americans during World War II, a mistake he acknowledged only in his posthumously published memoirs. In 1948 he ran for vice president on the Republican ticket with Thomas E. Dewey. In 1954 Warren was appointed by Dwight Eisenhower as chief justice of the U.S. Supreme Court. This was believed by many to be a quid pro quo, a payback for Warren's having supported Ike in his race for the Republican nomination for president in 1952. For the next fifteen years, the Warren Court took on one controversial issue after another, presiding over the desegregation of American society; one-man, one-vote apportionment; and *Miranda v. Arizona*, which recognized that even the accused had rights. It was a tumultuous time; in the South billboards called for Warren's impeachment. His critics charged that his was an activist court, but activism cuts two ways (note the court's role in the presidential election of 2000). Warren retired in 1969 but lived only another five years.

Lee Chapel

LEXINGTON

The chapel, located on the Washington and Lee University campus, houses the Lee family crypt, the family art collection, and Robert E. Lee's office, which is a virtual time capsule from the late nineteenth century. There is no tomb; Lee's body is in the crypt in the lower level of the museum. *West Washington Street, Lexington. Tel. (540) 463-8400. Open: 9:00 A.M.–5:00 P.M. Monday–Saturday, 2:00 P.M.–5:00 P.M. Sunday April–October; 9:00 A.M.–4:00 P.M. Monday–Saturday, 2:00 P.M.–4:00 P.M. Sunday November–May; closed Thanksgiving, December 24, 25, 31; and January 1.*

ROBERT E. LEE
1807–1870

As the son of Henry "Light Horse Harry" Lee, a cavalry hero of the American Revolution, it was probably a "given" that Robert E. Lee would gravitate to a military career. Bright and capable, he studied at West Point and eventually became its superintendent. Loyal to the army and the Union but to his state of Virginia as well, he feared secession. But once Virginia seceded, Lee resigned his commission as colonel of the First U.S. Cavalry. He hoped to avoid fighting against the Union, but Jefferson Davis soon turned to him to command the Confederate Army in Virginia. When Lee took over, he was fifty-five years old and in excellent health, but he had never led troops in battle before. Throughout the war, his forces were always outnumbered three to two or three to one. Yet he knew the terrain

and used his strategic and organizational skills to outmaneuver the enemy for over three years. He had an uncanny ability to put himself in the enemy's place and outthink him. After the surrender at Appomattox Court House, Lee was treated with respect by the Union army. That September he accepted the presidency of Washington College in Lexington, where he remained until his death. He left a rare legacy: Respected as a man of peace who rose to the challenge of war, in defeat he resumed the role of an educator of men. Here he lies, in the university where he last lived, and which changed its name to Washington and Lee in his honor. With him among many in the Lee crypt are his eldest son, **George Washington Custis Lee** (1832–1913), and **Traveller** (1857–1870), his much loved horse.

Stonewall Jackson Memorial Cemetery

LEXINGTON

In this small revered spot, hundreds of Confederate soldiers are buried. Among them is **Elisha "Bull" Paxton** (1828–1863), brigadier general in the Confederate Army on Jackson's staff; he fought at the first Battle of Manassas and died at Chancellorsville. *East side of South Main Street, Lexington. Tel. (703) 463-3777. Grounds open from dawn to dusk.*

THOMAS "STONEWALL" JACKSON
1824–1863

Born in Clarksburg, West Virginia, Jackson took the usual route to a military career, starting at West Point (where he was seventeenth in a class of fifty-nine), then serving in the Mexican War. Later he resigned from the army to teach at the Virginia Military Institute (VMI) in Lexington, Virginia. While there, he founded a Sunday school for slaves, even though teaching slaves to read—even the Bible—was illegal. When the Civil War began, Jackson came into his own. He was put in charge of Confederate troops that became known as the "Stonewall Brigade," after his brilliant campaign in the first Battle of Manassas. A fellow soldier said, "Look, there stands Jackson like a stone wall"—and his nickname was born. Victories followed all across Virginia: Front Royal, Winchester, Cross Keys, Port Republic, Cedar Mountain, Second Manassas, Antietam, as "Stonewall" demonstrated his bravery and skills at military maneuvers. In October 1862, he was given command of half of Lee's Army of Northern Virginia. At Chancellorsville, on May 2, 1863, Jackson was the victim of "friendly fire," and his left arm had to be amputated. Eight days later, after uttering his famous last words about crossing over the river to "rest under the shade of the trees," he died.

Hollywood Cemetery

In 1848 two local citizens who had seen and admired Mount Auburn in Cambridge, Massachusetts, developed Hollywood. High above the James River, over a terrain of forty-two acres graced with ravines, hills, gorges, plateaus, and holly trees (hence the name), it is the quintessential nineteenth-century burial ground, ornamented with Gothic tombs, romantic statuary, towering obelisks, and a Gothic chapel at the entrance. Ensconced here, along with twenty-five Civil War generals and 18,000 Confederate soldiers, are **James Branch Cabell** (1879–1958), novelist; **Ellen Glasgow** (1874–1945), novelist and Pulitzer Prize winner; **Matthew Fontaine Maury** (1806–1873), naval officer, considered the father of modern oceanography for his charts of the Atlantic Ocean; **George Pickett** (1825–1875), Confederate general of "Pickett's Charge" fame; and **Lewis F. Powell, Jr.** (1907–1998), justice of the U.S. Supreme Court. In driving, the blue line in the road takes you on the historic route past most of the famous graves. *412 South Cherry Street at Albemarle Street, Richmond. Tel. (804) 648-8501. Grounds open 8:00 A.M.–5:00 P.M. daily. Office hours: 8:30 A.M.–4:30 P.M. Monday–Friday; map (fee), rest rooms. At the rear of the parking lot is a monument with a map engraved on it.*

JEFFERSON DAVIS
1808–1889

In Civil War histories, Davis, president of the Confederacy, rarely holds the spotlight. Yet this Kentucky-born Mississippi planter-soldier-politician lived a long and complex life. A post as secretary of war under Franklin Pierce was followed by a second term in the U.S. Senate, from which he withdrew in 1861 when Mississippi seceded from the Union. He wanted to be commander in chief of the rebel army but ended up as the compromise president of the Confederacy. Convinced the South would win the war, he was stunned when Richmond fell in 1865. Two months later he still urged resistance, promising that Richmond would be retaken. Wearing his wife's clothes to escape (with a reward of $100,000 on his head), Davis was captured within a month by Union cavalry. He was accused of treason and spent two years in prison. When released, he was just fifty-nine, but a man without a country. With twenty-two years left to live, he spent some of it writing a revisionist history, *The Rise and Fall of the Confederate Government*. When he died, he was interred in a splendid tomb in New Orleans, but his body was claimed by several Southern locales. Richmond won, and here he is. It wasn't until 1978 that another Southerner, President Jimmy Carter, restored Davis's U.S. citizenship. After that, the words on his pedestal, below his statue, seem especially appropriate: "AT REST." At last.

JAMES MONROE
1758–1831

The Monroe Doctrine has been a cornerstone of U.S. foreign policy (summed up succinctly as: "Don't mess with us on our turf—leave the Americas alone") since Monroe, the fifth U.S. president, decreed it. It was the peak of a long career that began as a soldier fighting at White Plains, Brandywine, Monmouth, and Trenton (where he was wounded). Then came politics: He studied law with Thomas Jefferson, served in the Virginia House of Delegates and Congress, opposed ratification of the U.S. Constitution until the Bill of Rights was added, and was a U.S. senator and twice governor of Virginia. Jefferson sent him to France, where he helped negotiate the Louisiana Purchase in 1803. Elected president in 1816, he was reelected four years later with all but one electoral college vote. His presidency was known as the "era of good feeling," during which he settled boundaries with Canada, obtained Florida from Spain, and supported the antislavery position that led to the Missouri Compromise. In retirement he had to sell his estate, Oak Hill, to pay debts. His wife **Elizabeth Kortright Monroe** (1768–1830), died a year before he did. He then went to live in New York with a daughter, died, and was buried there. But one hundred years after his birth he returned to Virginia to be reunited with his wife. His beautiful tomb (below), designed by Richmond architect Albert Lybrock, resembles a Gothic chapel in openwork cast iron, with his sarcophagus visible inside.

JAMES EWELL BROWN "J.E.B." STUART
1 8 3 3 – 1 8 6 4

One of the most dashing figures in the Confederate Army, Major General J.E.B. Stuart—in a gray cape lined in red, plumed hat tilted to one side, a flower in his jacket lapel, galloping on a magnificent stallion—was considered a master at outpost duty (stealthily riding at the enemy's rear to gather intelligence) and scouting. Robert E. Lee called him the "eyes of the army" who "never brought me a piece of false information." Like many Confederate officers, Stuart received his military training at West Point. When the Civil War broke out, Virginia-born Stuart resigned his U.S. Army commission and joined Lee's command. After swashbuckling performances in the two battles of Manassas and at Fredericksburg, his disappearing act at Gettysburg, seeming to disregard Lee's orders, is still a mystery. In any case, when his forces met Sheridan's, Stuart was wounded and died the next day. Now, joined by his wife, **Flora**, he rests under his obelisk on a high hill overlooking a sunken meadow.

JOHN TYLER
1 7 9 0 – 1 8 6 2

The tenth U.S. president (1841–1845), Tyler earned his presidency the easy way: He inherited it—by succeeding William Henry Harrison, who died a month after his inauguration. Vice President Tyler stepped in immediately. No neophyte, he came from a political family and had served in the Virginia House of Delegates, the U.S. Congress, as governor of Virginia, and U.S. senator. As a Virginian he supported states' rights, but later chaired a Washington conference that tried to avoid civil war. The conference failed, the war began, and Tyler became a member of the Confederate House, though he died before that body met. He resides here in great splendor, with his bust on a pedestal in front of an obelisk topped by two bronze eagles holding aloft a Greek urn, along with his second wife, **Julia Gardiner** (1820–1889), and a number of his sixteen children. It all seems so peaceful now, but when widower Tyler (his first wife, Letitia, died during the second year of his presidency) secretly married a socialite thirty years his junior, it shocked the public and the seven Tyler children, some of whom were older than the bride. But the beautiful Julia brought the high style of New York society to the capital: She introduced dancing to the White House and insisted that the presidential band play "Hail to the Chief" the moment Tyler entered the ballroom. Tyler doted on her every whim. This was one May–December marriage that really worked.

Woodland Cemetery

R I C H M O N D

Woodland, situated above the river, is not easy to find, and when you do, it is a disappointment. Although Arthur Ashe's grave is well kept, enclosed behind an iron fence, the rest of the burial ground is a bit overgrown, with many headstones overturned. But it was Ashe's express desire to be here, and only here, where his mother also lies at rest within the same iron fence. *2300 Magnolia Road,*

Virginia **121**

ARTHUR ASHE

1943–1993

In a sport usually associated with the first-person pronoun, Ashe was an exception: a gracious tennis player, respected and admired for his gentlemanly demeanor, sense of privacy, and exemplary behavior on and off the court. Perhaps it stemmed from learning as a kid to cope with a segregated sport, when he was barred from some courts on the tour and excluded from team invitations to exclusive private clubs. But he was helped in his hometown of Richmond by an African American doctor, Robert Walter Johnson, who mentored young black tennis players. Ashe was the first black to win at Wimbleton and the first to be inducted into the International Tennis Hall of Fame. He was the first African American champion of the U.S. Open and Australian Open. He was a member nine times and then captain (1981–1985) of the U.S. Davis Cup team. He was ranked number one in the world twice (1968 and 1975). Ashe was also a writer (*A Hard Road to Glory: A History of the African-American Athlete, Off the Court,* and *Days of Grace: A Memoir,* among other books), lecturer, and spokesman for civil rights. A tainted blood transfusion administered after heart surgery in 1983 gave him Acquired Immune Deficiency Syndrome (AIDS), which led to his death ten years later—a loss to tennis, sports in general, and a world in sore need of his brand of grace under pressure. His headstone lists many achievements, along with the words "DISTINGUISHED ATHLETE, SCHOLAR AND HUMANITARIAN—A HARD ROAD TO GLORY." True words, indeed.

The Midwest and South

Dividing the United States into regions for the purpose of a book's chapters is an art, not a science and often, even as in this case, creates artificial borders. So be it. I have drawn an invisible line from the north—Minnesota, Iowa, Michigan—straight south as far as Alabama, Mississippi, and Louisiana, from east (Ohio) to west (Missouri).

Some states in this region have settlements, and thus burial grounds, that predate the country's founding; others go back to the early nineteenth century. Many of the nineteenth-century cemeteries were created in the so-called rural or garden style, which spread west from New England and flourished in urban areas, especially cities like Cleveland, St. Louis, Chicago, and Minneapolis. Shade trees dominate such tranquil places, and many boast as residents Civil War soldiers and veterans, prominent local industrialists, and a hardy crop of political leaders.

Alabama

Tuskegee Institute National Historic Site

TUSKEGEE

The large 5,000-acre campus of Tuskegee University includes "The Oaks," Booker T. Washington's home, the George Washington Carver Museum, and the chapel, next to which are the graves of Tuskegee's two most famous personages. *Tel. (334) 727–6390. Open daily, except Thanksgiving, Christmas, and January 1.*

GEORGE WASHINGTON CARVER
1861–1943

From ignominious beginnings, Carver rose to become a teacher, botanist, and agricultural chemist. Eventually, through odd jobs and homesteading, he left his Missouri home and moved to Iowa, where a friendly white family encouraged him to attend college. He subsequently earned B.S. and M.S. degrees at Iowa State College of Agriculture at Ames. Invited by Booker T. Washington to Tuskegee as director of agricultural work, he began the studies that would make him famous, developing peanuts and sweet potatoes from noncommercial crops into major ones. His studies brought him major honors both in the United States and worldwide. The Thomas A. Edison research laboratories wanted him, but he refused to leave Tuskegee. Segregation took its toll on Carver's research, for he couldn't attend scientific meetings, and facilities were restricted. He lived to be eighty-two and is in repose next to his friend and mentor, Booker T. Washington.

BOOKER T. WASHINGTON
1856–1915

Horatio Alger had nothing on Washington, whose best-known work, *Up from Slavery* (1901), was an inspiring saga of his rise from a Virginia childhood as the son of a white father and African American mother to a position as the leading black spokesperson of his era. He led the transformation of Tuskegee Institute from a one-room schoolhouse with fifty students to a respected center of African American education. Washington's modus operandi of working with the white establishment was criticized by more militant blacks like W.E.B. DuBois, but in its time it worked, and he was a role model and inspiration for many.

Graceland Cemetery

CHICAGO

One of America's great nineteenth-century cemeteries, Graceland opened its doors, er, grounds, in 1861. On 119 spacious acres the rectangular terrain epitomizes the emphasis Victorians put on surroundings vis-à-vis funerals. Verdant parklike grounds, speckled with magnificent mausoleums, reflect the day-in-the-country ambience the affluent of the era craved. Landscape architect Ossian Simonds created a naturalistic landscape, using native plantings and trees, keeping the buildings—the chapel, waiting room, office, and crematorium—low slung and compatible with the land. Graceland's permanent occupants reflect Chicago's importance in industrial America. Their memorials were designed by leading architects of the period, one more reason that Graceland is such a treat to visit. Here you'll encounter: meat-packing magnate **Philip D. Armour** (1832–1901); architect and city planner **Daniel Burnham** (1846–1912), whose irregular-shaped, glacial granite grave boulder is on an island reached by a footbridge; department store mogul **Marshall Field** (1834–1906), richest man in Chicago in his day, as demonstrated by his massive monument of a bronze seated figure (by Daniel Chester French and Henry Bacon) reflected in a sunken pool; piano manufacturer **William Kimball** (1828–1904), whose roofless Greek monument (designed by McKim, Mead & White), with its four enormous Corinthian columns, is one of Graceland's largest memorials; **Cyrus McCormick** (1809–1884), inventor and manufacturer of the labor-saving McCormick reaper; **Ludwig Mies van der Rohe** (1886–1969), modern architect, exponent of the Bauhaus style, whose sleek, flush-with-the-grass gravestone reflects his philosophy of austere elegance; and **Martin Ryerson** (1818–1887), lumber and real estate magnate, whose Egyptian-style, pyramid-topped mausoleum was designed by Louis Sullivan. Most of the high-profile potentates lie around or near Lake Willomere, at the north end of Graceland, near Montrose Avenue. *4100 North Clark Street, Chicago. Tel. (773) 525-1105. www.graveyards.com/graceland. Grounds open 8:00 A.M.–4:30 P.M. Office hours: 8:00 A.M.–4:30 P.M. Monday–Saturday; map, tours available through Chicago Architecture Foundation tours (312) 922-3432 (fee).*

JACK JOHNSON
1878–1946

Heavyweight fighter Johnson is probably best known today because of James Earl Jones's portrayal of him, as a fictionalized character, in the play and movie *The Great White Hope*. Johnson was, in some experts' views, the greatest boxer of all time, one of the first to be chosen for the Boxing Hall of Fame. He had a classic style: swift, nimble, with quick reflexes and the skill to score a knockout with either hand. He was only knocked out three times in forty-seven years of fighting. Johnson's main problem was timing. He had the bad luck to be a black fighter in an age of prejudice when boxing was a white man's sport, and white fans did not take to a black defeating their white "hopes." On top of that he was "uppity," a flamboyant personality who loved the spotlight, fast cars, and women, especially white ones, in equal proportions. His independent style enraged the public and the boxing establishment, which finally persuaded James Jeffries, the former heavyweight champion—the "great white hope"—to come out of retirement to trounce Johnson. It didn't happen: Johnson beat Jeffries handily in the fifteenth round, having floored him three times. Johnson's troubles didn't stop. Convicted of violating the federal Mann Act by an all-white jury and sentenced to a year in prison, he jumped bail and fled to Europe. After a seven-year exile, Johnson returned home, served his term, then cobbled together a living giving lectures and exhibition matches. His lifelong addiction to speed finally caught up with him on a highway in North Carolina: He hit a light pole and died in a hospital in Raleigh. He lies in a grave unmarked (to protect it from defacement) next to the small granite stone of **Etta Duryea Johnson**, his second wife.

ALLAN PINKERTON
1819–1884

The first notable thing that happened to Pinkerton on his way from Glasgow, Scotland, to his new home in Chicago was that he discovered a counterfeiting ring and helped capture the members—a symbolic start to his new career. He settled in Chicago, and, after a stint in the Chicago police department, opened

his own detective agency in 1852, with the logo of an all-seeing eye (leading to the phrase "private eye"). When he uncovered a plot to kill newly elected president Abraham Lincoln in 1861, Lincoln asked him to organize the U.S. Secret Service. Subsequently a double agent helped the new service uncover a plot to free 8,000 Confederate prisoners of war in Camp Douglas, Chicago. Buried near Pinkerton's large obelisk (see opposite page) are several Pinkerton aces: **Kate Warn**, first woman detective; **Timothy Webster**, a Lincoln bodyguard hanged by the Confederates as a Union spy; and **Joseph Whichler**, killed while hunting down Jesse James.

GEORGE PULLMAN
1 8 3 1 – 1 8 9 7

The idea of a sleeping car on trains really took off after one was attached to the funeral cortege that brought Abraham Lincoln's body from Washington home to Illinois. Pullman, the inventor, was a ruthless businessman, clearly not a warm and cuddly type. In 1880–1884, as a way of controlling his employees, he created a "model town" owned and operated by the company, where all Pullman workers were expected to live, like it or not. When the company fell on hard times, Pullman cut wages by 25 percent but refused to lower rents or grocery prices in the town. A worker delegation protested, so he fired them. This led to a brutal strike. Railway workers refused to handle any train with Pullman cars attached. Things got so bad that federal troops had to break the strike, and Pullman workers had to pledge never to join a union. Pullman was so despised by his employees that when he died, his family feared his workers might steal the body and hold

it for ransom. To prevent this they covered his coffin in tar paper and asphalt and kept it in a huge concrete block, reinforced with railroad ties. Writer Ambrose Bierce commented that the family "was making sure the sonofabitch wasn't going to get up and come back." His permanent quarters here are substantial enough to prevent that: A towering Corinthian tower rises above a platform flanked by curved stone benches, designed by Solon Beman. Beman also designed the town of **Pullman** (614 East 113th Street, Chicago; 773–785–8181), which can be toured today. Its original buildings are intact.

LOUIS SULLIVAN
1 8 5 6 – 1 9 2 4

Boston born, educated at the Massachusetts Institute of Technology and Ecole des Beaux-Arts in Paris, Sullivan came along at the right time. After the Chicago fire of 1871, the burgeoning city required a makeover. Sullivan and his partner, Dankmar Adler, recognized that the invention of the elevator and fireproof steel frames made it possible to build up instead of out. The early skyscrapers took hold quickly in Chicago, and Sullivan, an architectural visionary (and mentor of Frank Lloyd Wright), was a pioneer. After the Columbian Exposition brought a revival of the Beaux Arts style, the modern look went into decline—and so did Sullivan's practice. But he continued to write. A great theorist as well as practitioner of architecture, he authored numerous books, three in his final year. He died penniless in a cheap boardinghouse—a, ahem, dead end. He had no headstone, until fans of his work contributed a final fitting tribute. Sullivan's headstone really suits the man: the artistry of the irregular rock itself; the elegance of the six-pointed plaque (a Sullivan design), with his profile in the center, attached to its front; and the heads-on directness of his full name engraved into the rock. Sullivan's masterpiece still exists: **Carson Pirie Scott** department store in the Loop (State and Madison Streets, Chicago; 312–641–7000), a gem.

Oak Woods Cemetery

CHICAGO

Located in the Woodlawn area, this is one of the city's oldest burial grounds, dating back to 1853. In the nineteenth-century garden tradition, Oak Woods is a natural-looking parkland with hills, trees (lots of oaks, of course), lakes, and gently serpentine roadways, with an English Gothic chapel. Ensconced here are many luminaries, including **Solon Beman** (1853–1914), architect of the town of Pullman; **Judge Kenesaw Mountain Landis** (1866–1944), Major League Baseball's first commissioner; **Jesse Owens** (1913–1980), great track-and-field star, four-gold-medal winner in the 1936 Berlin Olympics; **William "Big Bill" Thompson** (1867–1944), crooked mayor of Chicago during the Al Capone era, with the tallest obelisk here; **Harold Washington** (1922–1987), Chicago's first African American mayor, elected twice, but died in office; and **Ida B. Wells** (1862–1931), African American reformer, crusader for black suffrage, and leader of protest marches against lynching. *1035 East 67th Street, Chicago. Tel. (773) 288-3800. Grounds open 8:30 A.M.–4:15 P.M. daily. Office hours: 8:30 A.M.–4:15 P.M. Monday–Friday, 9:00 A.M.–3:00 P.M. Saturday; map, rest room; Chicago Architecture Foundation tours (fee).*

ENRICO FERMI
1901–1954

A plain granite rectangular headstone states only the occupant's name, dates, and the word *physicist*, but that's enough. Fermi, an Italian immigrant, received the Nobel Prize in physics in 1938, recognition of his work on artificial radioactivity. But it was his creation, while working at the University of Chicago, of the first self-sustaining nuclear chain reaction that is his strongest claim to posterity's recognition. From Chicago he went to Los Alamos, New Mexico, as one of a group of scientists who worked on the development of an atomic bomb. He contributed to the hydrogen bomb as well but ended up opposing it on ethical grounds. Here he is, back in Chicago and very near the university where he was most at home.

Rosehill Cemetery

CHICAGO

Rosehill sometimes plays second fiddle to Graceland, but it too is an impressive old burial ground, full of massive monuments. Note the castellated Gothic main gate, made of Joliet limestone; the soldiers and sailors memorial facing the main gate; the Gothic-cum-Romanesque chapel, and a neoclassical mausoleum; Egyptian tombs; statuary that includes stone bucks and greyhounds; a mother-and-daughter sculpture reclining under glass on a stone slab; and the small-scale, granite rendition of a railway mail car, marking the grave of **George S. Bangs** (1826–1877), designer of the first such full-size mail car. Rosehill is the largest nonsectarian cemetery in the city, dating back to 1859. It has a formidable clientele; the names read like a list of the corporate elite. Residents include **Avery Brundage** (1887–1975), industrialist and sports czar; **Charles Dawes** (1865–1951), thirteenth U.S. vice president (under Coolidge) and recipient of a Nobel Peace Prize; **Bobbie Franks** (1910–1924), teenager victimized and murdered "for kicks" by Leopold and Loeb in the most notorious criminal case of the 1920s; **Charles J. Hull** (1820–1889), real estate developer, whose mansion, which he leased to social reformer Jane Addams, became famous as Hull House; **Oscar Mayer** (1859–1955), meat-packing magnate; **Richard Warren Sears** (1863–1914), founder of a mail-order empire; and **Montgomery Ward** (1843–1913), creator of the world's first mail-order business. *5800 Ravenswood Avenue, Chicago. Tel. (773) 561-5940. Grounds open: Ravenswood gate 8:00 A.M.–5:00 P.M. daily, Peterson and Western gates 9:00 A.M.–4:00 P.M. daily. Office (in main building on the right side) hours: 8:00 A.M.–5:00 P.M. Monday–Saturday; map, rest rooms; Chicago Architecture Foundation tours (fee).*

Carl Sandburg State Historic Site

GALESBURG

This consists of a museum and Sandburg's restored white frame birth cottage (with many family belongings), a typical dwelling of a late nineteenth-century working-class family. Behind the house is Remembrance Rock (named after his novel), marked by evergreen shrubs on two sides. Under the rounded rock are Sandburg's ashes, mixed with soil he collected from places he lived and from his parents' birthplaces in Sweden—as he requested. The rock (see next page) rests in the grass between a brick walkway and a quiet area with two stone benches near the back fence. *331 East 3rd Street, Galesburg. Tel. (309) 342-2361. Open 9:00 A.M.–5:00 P.M. daily, except for major holidays; donation suggested, bookshop.*

CARL SANDBURG
1 8 7 8 – 1 9 6 7

Born of immigrant Swedish parents, Sandburg became a wanderer early in life, traveling west from Illinois at age seventeen, doing odd jobs, ending up in the army in San Juan, Puerto Rico, during the Spanish-American War. In 1902 he was back home, getting a college degree at local Lombard College. He served a stint as secretary to the mayor of Milwaukee and in 1914 won *Poetry* magazine's Levinson Prize for his poem "Chicago." His book of poems, *Chicago Poems,* written in 1916 in a vibrant, free verse style, full of rich and raw images, made him famous and was followed by *Cornhuskers, Smoke and Steel,* and *The People, Yes.* In the Whitman tradition, he was a poet of the people who loved life in its splendor and squalor. Sandburg called modern poetry "a series of ear wigglings." Though primarily a poet, his writing talents took many forms: columnist for the *Chicago Times* syndicate, compiler and anthologist of American folk songs, author of children's books and one historical novel, *Remembrance Rock.* With his widely praised *Abraham Lincoln: The Prairie Years,* he earned serious credentials as a biographer-historian, and the second volume, *Abraham Lincoln: The War Years,* brought him a Pulitzer. A second Pulitzer came for *The Complete Poems.* Although he called himself a hobo and loved to travel, this amiable, unassuming man died at his Flat Rock, North Carolina, home. But true prairie lad that he was, he ended up here in his old family home in Galesburg, a wanderer no more. The inscription at the base of Remembrance Rock is from the novel of the same name: "FOR IT COULD BE A PLACE TO COME AND REMEMBER." And it is.

Mount Carmel Cemetery

HILLSIDE

Connoisseurs of cemeteries will delight in this one, located in a Chicago suburb. Mount Carmel is a Catholic burial ground, with the bishops' mausoleum topped by a sculpture of the angel Gabriel blowing a trumpet. Three Chicago cardinals rest within, including the much-revered **Joseph Cardinal Bernardin** (1928–1996), along with several archbishops. What gives Mount Carmel its uniqueness are two factors. First, many of the grave occupants are Italians, and their mausoleums are highly personal, fanciful, and unique "dwelling" places, chiseled by experienced stonecutters, with sentimental statuary and inscriptions. You'll find the **Di Vito** family mausoleum, for instance, with busts of Mr. and Mrs. Di Vito carved into niches between Ionic columns covered with vines—the entire work in carved rough-cut gray granite. There is also the **Di Salvo** mausoleum, with a large marble sculpture of five family members in a grouping with the mother in the center. Second, of interest to anyone on the trail of mafiosi, Mount Carmel offers one-stop tracking. There are so many gangsters lying low here that I'm tempted to say, "There goes the neighborhood." Here, deep-sixed, are **Sam Giancana** (1908–1975), Mafia boss of the 1960s, who was killed in his kitchen while cooking Italian sausage; **"Machine Gun Jack" McGurn** (1904–1936), a killer in the St. Valentine's Day Massacre of 1929; **Dion Charles "Deanie" O'Bannion** (1892–1924), Irish American bootlegger and gangland boss of the 1920s; and **Roger "The Terrible" Touhy** (1898–1959), head of a dangerous 1930s Chicago gang. *1400 South Wolf Road (corner of Roosevelt), Hillside. Tel. (708) 449-2340.*

ALPHONSE "AL" CAPONE
1899–1947

This master crime boss, mobster, and bootlegger of the 1920s and 1930s was first buried elsewhere, but the grave was so besieged by visitors, he was moved here. Finding the marker is a grave matter, as it lies behind a big bush, near the right side of the Roosevelt entrance. The family memorial is more commanding: a tall marble cross between two towers with the name Capone at the base. Capone was one of nine children born to Neapolitan immigrants to Brooklyn.

As a young man, Capone insulted another young punk, who slashed him, leaving him with three scars on the left side of his face and the nickname "Scarface," which he loathed. Capone followed Johnny Torrio, another Brooklyn gangster, to Chicago as his right-hand man, eventually taking over control of his mob. Capone's name and that of Eliot Ness are linked through time. It was Ness, the Treasury Department man, who realized the best way to get Capone was through his wallet. So Ness and colleagues went after Capone's illegal breweries, figuring the less money Capone took in, the less power he had to buy protection from crooked cops. In time Ness and company seized and shut down nineteen distilleries and six main breweries, costing Capone $1 million in revenue. Although this hurt Capone financially, the government still couldn't get him

legally. He was finally brought down on income tax evasion. In 1931, Capone was found guilty and served eleven years in federal prison. His simple stone in the ground reads, below his name and dates: "MY JESUS MERCY." Al, it may be too late for that.

Joseph Smith Historic Center

The center contains the log cabin that Joseph Smith, founder of the Mormons, occupied when he and his followers first arrived in Nauvoo in 1839; Smith's Federal-style frame house, where he lived in 1843–1844; his redbrick store; and his grave. *149 Water Street, Nauvoo. Tel. (217) 453-2246. Open 9:00 A.M.–5:00 P.M. Monday–Saturday, 1:00 P.M.–5:00 P.M. Sunday; free tours, eighteen-minute tape.*

JOSEPH SMITH
1805–1844

From humble Vermont beginnings—born to a poor family that moved ten times in nineteen years—Smith spent much of his youth in Palmyra, New York. At age twenty-two, while a day laborer, he claimed that, following a vision, he had found the golden plates of the *Book of Mormon* on a hill nearby. He supposedly translated the plates from a form of Egyptian hieroglyphics. In 1830 the *Book of Mormon* was published as the sacred scripture of the new religion, officially called the Church of the Latter-day Saints, with Smith as the Prophet. Smith led his followers first to Ohio, then Missouri, where he hoped his "Saints," as they called themselves, would settle. But conflicts with non-Mormons led to a virtual civil war, and the state's governor ordered Smith and his followers to leave. Their next stop

was Nauvoo. In five years the town grew to about 10,000 people. Again they aroused the enmity of neighbors, partly because of their religious practices, their power, and immunity from outside interference and also because of Smith's announcement that he would run for president of the United States. When a local newspaper was about to expose Mormon polygamy, Smith tried to destroy the paper's press and a riot followed. The prophet and his brother Hyrum were put in a nearby jail. Some sources say it was protective custody, others because the Smiths had started the riot. One thing is clear: An angry mob descended on the jail and killed them both. A rift then developed within the Mormon community. Brigham Young, claiming to be Smith's successor, led most members west to Utah, but another faction, calling themselves the Reorganized Latter-day Saints, claimed to be the true church and rejected polygamy. Tucked behind Smith's original log cabin are the markers of Smith, his wife, Emma, and Hyrum.

Oakridge Cemetery

S P R I N G F I E L D

As befits a burial ground in the capital of the state, Oakridge has more than its share of imposing monuments, obelisks, and the kind of graceful sculpture that warmed the hearts of Victorian visitors. Its permanent residents include **William H. Herndon** (1819–1891), Lincoln's law partner; **Nellie Grant Jones** (1855–1922), daughter of president Ulysses S. Grant; **John L. Lewis** (1880–1969), powerful labor leader, head of the United Mine Workers of America; and **Vachel Lindsay** (1879–1931), the "prairie troubadour" whose most famous poem was "The Congo." *1441 Monument Avenue, Springfield. Tel. (217) 789-2340. Grounds open 7:00 A.M.–5:00 P.M. daily in winter, 7:00 A.M.–8:00 P.M. daily in summer. Office hours: 8:00 A.M.–5:00 P.M. Monday–Friday winter, same hours plus 9:00 A.M.–12:00 P.M. Saturday in summer; map, rest rooms, tape tours. Once a year in late September, the Springfield Historical Society three-hour cemetery walk is held 12:00 P.M.–3:00 P.M., with actors portraying the famous residents of the place. Call cemetery for date.*

ABRAHAM LINCOLN
1 8 0 9 – 1 8 6 5

The born-in-a-Kentucky-log-cabin image of our sixteenth president is, still, of a kindly, raw-boned man of the people, intelligent but not cerebral. Although some of this is true, "Honest Abe" was much more shrewdly political than he usually let on. "I don't know much about how things are done in politics," he once said. Uh-huh! As a lawyer in rural Illinois, he worked his way up from grassroots politics, as a member of the General Assembly, then U.S. congressman, and learned from an early age how things are done in politics. Even so, he was remarkably principled: He opposed the Mexican War and the pro-slavery Kansas-Nebraska Act and ran for president on an antislavery platform. His Emancipation Proclamation lives on as one of the noblest documents of the nineteenth century. His speeches, the Gettysburg Address and inaugural address among them, still read as eloquently now as they did when written. After he was shot in Washington on April 14, 1865, he lived on for less than one day and has been mourned ever since. Ironically, this man who was so proud of his humble origins remains now inside a domed interior in a grandiose memorial that includes four-foot-high statues in niches, honoring periods in his life. The shrine's exterior is a 117-foot granite obelisk, with a ten-foot-high bronze statue of Lincoln himself. Four heroic Civil War scenes in bronze surround the base of the monument. Lincoln's large sarcophagus is empty; he is ten feet below (to thwart grave robbers who made attempts to steal the corpse). Buried in the wall opposite the sarcophagus are Mary Todd Lincoln and three of their four sons: **Tad** (1853–1871), **Edward** (1846–1850), **William "Willie"** (1850–1862), as well as Lincoln's father, **Thomas Lincoln** (1778–1851), and stepmother, **Sarah Bush Lincoln** (1788–1869).

MARY TODD LINCOLN
1818–1882

Probably no First Lady has been as maligned (until recently) as Mrs. Lincoln. She was not what she looked: a short, plain frontier housewife. The Todds were a respected old Kentucky family with the Southern tradition of genteel hospitality. Mary knew what was expected of a president's wife, but she was rarely able to demonstrate it to a skeptical capital. For one thing, one of her brothers fought for the Confederacy, so she was accused of being a Southern spy. Some of her

problems were her own doing: She spent huge sums renovating the White House; too much on clothes, in an attempt to prove her style; and way, way too much on lavish soirees and receptions, all of which were considered unseemly during wartime. But she suffered great personal trials, first the death of a beloved son, Willie, then her husband's assassination before her eyes. The latter tipped her over the edge into a nervous breakdown. As a last straw, she was accused of stripping the White House of many possessions when she left. (The truth, many believe now, is probably that while she remained upstairs wracked with grief, "well-wishers" and others were free to roam the public areas and made off with "souvenirs.") The fact that she outlived three of her four sons only adds to the sad tale of her life. The Federal-style **Lincoln Home National Historic Site** (426 South 7th Street; 217–492–4241) looks as it did during the last year of the Lincolns' seventeen-year domicile there and contains family and period artifacts.

Rose Hill Cemetery

BLOOMINGTON

City-owned Rose Hill, which opened in 1876, spreads over twelve acres of grass, hills, and greenery. In repose on its gentle grounds are **Alfred C. Kinsey** (1894– 1956), biology professor, researcher, and author of the controversial *Sexual Behavior in the Human Male* and a follow-up, *Sexual Behavior in the Human Female;* and **Ross Lockridge** (1914-1948), author of *Raintree County* and other novels. *Corner of Elm and West Fourth Streets, Bloomington. Tel. (812) 349-3498. Grounds open all the time. Office hours: 8:00 A.M.–4:30 P.M. Monday–Friday; map, rest room.*

HOAGY CARMICHAEL
1899–1981

"Hoagland Howard Carmichael" reads the full name on the flat gravestone of the songwriter-composer who will forever be remembered as Hoagy, a nickname given him by a college girlfriend. Hoagland is not the name of a folksy fellow, which Hoagy was. Remembered mostly for romantic, nostalgic tunes like "Georgia," "Stardust," "Two Sleepy People," "Small Fry," and "Up a Lazy River," Hoagy also wrote for the movies, collaborated with Johnny Mercer on "Skylark" and with Frank Loesser on "Heart and Soul," and appeared in a number of movies himself, beginning with *To Have and to Have Not.* Hoagy had a B.A. and law degree from Indiana University, had his own jazz band, met and became buddies with Bix Beiderbecke (for whom he wrote his first recorded song, "Riverboat Shuffle"), and practiced law briefly in Florida. He later said, "I wasn't a good lawyer. A note to me was something that belonged on a musical staff." Pennies scattered over his simple grave stone are reminders that he also composed "Pennies from Heaven."

Park Cemetery

FAIRMOUNT

Even though this is a large rambling graveyard, markers easily direct visitors to the last known address of its most famous resident, James Dean, in the north addition. Caretaker Phyllis Seward speaks of "Jimmy" familiarly, as the country boy most Fairmount folks knew him to be, scooting along on his motorcycle past the cemetery from his home just north of it. *150 East (extension of North Main Street), 1/2 mile north of State Road 26. Tel. (765) 948-4040. Grounds open 8:00 A.M.–5:00 P.M. daily. Office hours: 8:00 A.M.–5:00 P.M. Monday–Friday.*

JAMES DEAN
1931–1955

This short-lived, long-gone movie actor was like a meteorite flaring across the sky and quickly vanishing. But in Jimmy Dean's case, the memory lingers on. He made just seven films, after a brief New York success in a play, *The Immoralist*, but his impact in them was of an inherently good bad boy, whose "badness" was merely restlessness and nonconformity. No wonder so many young men—and women—identified with his screen roles and have kept the flame alive. His movies, especially *East of Eden*, *Rebel Without a Cause*, and *Giant*, had instant impact, as did the news of Dean's death at age twenty-four in a head-on car accident. The tragedy of such a life, just on the cusp of fame and fortune, has kept him a cult hero of the eternally young. Hollywood couldn't have scripted it any better. His plain upright granite headstone is a replica—the original was stolen—and is usually covered with lipstick kisses and surrounded by cigarette stubs, beer cans, and bouquets of fresh flowers.

Crown Hill Cemetery

INDIANAPOLIS

A classic garden-style burial ground, which opened for business in 1864, Crown Hill is now listed on the Register of Historic Places. It is the third-largest nongovernment cemetery in America. Among its assets are 555 acres of woodland, enclosed by brick and wrought-iron fencing, in which are 25 miles of paved roads, leading past splendid Greek temple-mausoleums and a Gothic chapel. On these spacious grounds deer, possums, foxes, rabbits, and groundhogs frolic among rare specimen-tagged trees (like weeping European beech, sweet gum, catalpa, black walnut, gingko, and cucumbertree magnolia) and flowering shrubs. The illustrious here include numerous senators and governors, Indianapolis 500 drivers and personnel, as well as **August Duesenberg** (1879–1955), auto magnate; **Charles Warren Fairbanks** (1852–1918), twenty-sixth vice president of the United States (1905–1909); **William "Willie" Gardner** (1934–2000), basketball Hall of Famer, member of Harlem Globetrotters; **Richard Jordan Gatling** (1818–1903), inventor of the Gatling machine gun; **J. J. Johnson** (1924–2001), legendary jazz trombonist who bebopped with Dizzy Gillespie and Charlie Parker; **Eli Lilly** (1839–1898), pharmaceutical expert and manufacturer; **Minnie F. Ransom** (1913-2001), famed jazz pianist and music teacher; **James Whitcomb Riley** (1853–1916), popular Hoosier poet of his era, who wrote "Little Orphant Annie," and now lies within a Pantheon-type Greek "temple"; **Booth Tarkington** (1869–1946), playwright and novelist, author of *Alice Adams* and *Seventeen;* and some 600 Confederate prisoners of war. *700 West 38th Street, Indianapolis. Tel. (317) 925-8231. Web site: www.crownhillcemetery.com. Grounds open 8:00 A.M.–5:00 P.M. October–March, 8:00 A.M.–6:00 P.M. April–September daily. Office hours: 8:30 A.M.–5:00 P.M. Monday–Friday, 8:30 A.M.–2:00 P.M. Saturday; free map, free tree map with scientific and common names of over one hundred labeled trees, book on the cemetery (fee) and other books for sale, ten themed tours (authors, burial customs, Civil War, African Americans, for example) available (fee for adults).*

JOHN DILLINGER
1903–1934

His was a short life but a violent one. What caused a local boy, who at age twelve joined the Disciples of Christ Church, worked in a machine shop at seventeen, and lived on a farm for two years hunting, fishing, and playing baseball to turn to crime at age twenty-one? There must have been something percolating underneath, for after a year in the navy he received a dishonorable discharge. What followed was a series of bank and factory robberies all across the Midwest—Indiana, Illinois, Ohio, Wisconsin, and Minnesota—committed with a gang he recruited in jail. By 1933 Dillinger was the FBI's "Public Enemy Number One." He was shrewd, breaking out of jail twice, and audacious, twice raiding police stations. But eventually one of the women accompanying the gang (dubbed the "Lady in Red" by the tabloids of the day) betrayed him, and he was shot and killed as he left a Chicago movie theater. No Robin Hood he—he stole a lot of money and spent it on himself and cronies. He nonetheless captured the public imag-

ination and remains a major figure of interest in crime annals. His original small gravestone was stolen in 1976 but has been replicated and lies beside the simple but handsome family headstone. As for Dillinger himself, he's still—or again—in the underworld.

BENJAMIN HARRISON

1833–1901

Ohio-born, like so many U.S. presidents, he studied law at Miami University in Oxford, Ohio, then practiced it in Indianapolis, Indiana. During the Civil War he fought at Kennesaw Mountain, Peachtree Creek, Nashville, and in the Atlanta campaign, ending up a brevet brigadier general. But it was politics that captured his postwar attention. No surprise. After all, his grandfather was "Old Tippecanoe," William Henry Harrison, who died within a month of his inauguration. Failing in his bid to be governor, Benjamin did win a U.S. senate seat, going on to defeat Grover Cleveland for president in 1888, even though he won with fewer popular votes. "Dull" and "stodgy" best describe his brief four years in the White House. In a replay the next time around, Cleveland won the election (in 1892). Harrison died nine years later. His wife, **Caroline Scott Harrison** (1832–1892), died in the White House during the last year they lived there and is buried here with him, as is his second wife, **Mary Lloyd Harrison** (1858–1948). Their solid, cabinetlike, elevated granite tomb has a decorative incised band along the top and ornate "feet." "Lawyer and publicist" his stone reads just below his name, words as low-key as the man.

Mount Hope Cemetery

PERU

Founded in 1854, Mount Hope encompasses sixty-eight acres of rolling grounds, trees, and interesting tombs and is a favorite place for walkers and hikers. Peru was a onetime center for the Great Wallace Show, a circus, so many performers are at rest here under colorful tombstones, including one that sports a big top. Mount Hope doesn't have restrictions about plantings, so at Christmas time, relatives of many permanent residents bring in Christmas trees and decorate and light them, a rare, colorful, and festive sight in a cemetery, not bare bones at all. *411 North Grant Street, Peru. Tel. (765) 472-2493. Grounds open all the time. Office hours: 9:00 A.M.–4:00 P.M. daily, except 9:00 A.M.–12:00 P.M. Wednesday and Saturday; map, rest room.*

COLE PORTER
1891–1964

"It was just one of those things" that a big city sophisticate like Cole Porter should owe his origins to a little town in Indiana. But Porter's life had other anomalies. His mother, daughter of a wealthy landowner named Cole, pampered her only child, while his middle-class father faded into the background. Cole went to preparatory school in Massachusetts, then on to Yale, but opted out of Harvard Law School for a career as a composer for the musical theater. Though believed to be homosexual, Porter married a woman eight years older than he. One thing is for sure: He was one of the great popular songwriters of the twentieth century, unique for the wit and grace of his lyrics and melodies. Many of his songs have outlived the shows he wrote them for, like "Love for Sale," "You

Do Something to Me," and "What Is This Thing Called Love?" but some musicals, like *Anything Goes, Gay Divorcée, Panama Hattie,* and *Kiss Me, Kate,* all packed with Porter songs, are frequently revived. Porter wrote songs for movies as well and even had a movie made about his life (though not very accurately), *Night and Day,* starring the elegant Cary Grant playing the elegant Mr. P. He lived as stylishly as he wrote, but a horseback accident in 1937 injured his legs so badly that there was the possibility of amputation. To avoid it, Porter underwent numerous painful operations but needed braces and a cane to walk. Constant pain didn't keep him from composing a series of wonderful songs, but in 1958 his right leg had to be amputated. Then there were no more songs. His health steadily declined and so did he.

Iowa

Oakdale Memorial Garden

DAVENPORT

This tranquil space, opened in 1856, comprises eighty-seven acres, with trees, shrubs, and a pond. *2501 Eastern Avenue, Davenport. Tel. (563) 324–5121. Grounds open from sunrise to sunset. Office hours: 10:00 A.M.–3:00 P.M. Monday–Friday; map, rest room.*

BIX BEIDERBECKE

1903–1931

An icon to jazz fans, Leon Bismark Beiderbecke lived a short, troubled life. But while he was alive, he made great music as a cornetist, influenced by Louis Armstrong and influencing scores of musicians who came after him, especially Hoagy Carmichael, Bunny Berrigan, Red Nichols, and Rex Stewart. Beiderbecke was the son of hardworking German immigrants who disapproved of his career choice, his unsteady income, drinking, and lifestyle. "Bix" was hampered by his inability to read music, but that didn't stop him from being an inspired soloist and improvisor. At various times he played with Jean Goldkette's band, "Pee Wee" Russell, Tommy Dorsey, and the Paul Whiteman band. He died from complications from lobar pneumonia at age twenty-eight. But his recordings live on, and his life has been fictionalized in the book and movie *Young Man with a Horn*. Every July in Davenport there's a **Bix Beiderbecke Memorial Jazz Festival** (Riverfront at LeClaire Park; 563–324–7170).

Herbert Hoover Historic Site

WEST BRANCH

A 187-acre park encompasses Hoover's restored, modest childhood home, the presidential library-museum, the Quaker meetinghouse where the family worshipped, and the graves of the president and his wife. *110 Parkside Drive, West Branch, 1/2 mile north of exit 254, off I-80. Tel. (319) 643-2541. Open 9:00 A.M.–5:00 P.M. daily, except Thanksgiving, Christmas, January 1; no fee to graves, fee to house and library-museum.*

HERBERT HOOVER
1874–1964

The thirtieth president of the United States, Hoover was born in West Branch and returned there for the hereafter. In between he grew up in Indian Territory (now Oklahoma) and Oregon, earned an engineering degree from Stanford University, and then set forth as a mining engineer in Australia, Asia, Europe, Africa, and the United States—undoubtedly the most traveled of any president up to his time (even beyond). While in China, he directed food relief for victims of the Boxer Rebellion in 1900. Later his relief work in Belgium, Russia, and other nations catapulted him into a job as secretary of commerce from 1921 to 1928, when he ran successfully for president. His seemed like a charmed life, but in the first year of his presidency, the stock market crashed and the Great Depression began. Hoover, for all his efficiency, seemed unable to cope with the armies of unemployed and opposed federal aid. He was defeated for a second term, but then went on to a sedate and service-oriented rest-of-his-life, as coordinator for Harry Truman of a European food program in 1947 and head of a Commission for the Reorganization of the Executive Branch (1947–1949). Hoover is buried in a simple granite tomb on a quiet knoll behind and overlooking the library-museum. His wife, **Lou Henry Hoover** (1874–1944), who preceded him in death by twenty years, has been reinterred by his side.

Frankfort Cemetery

FRANKFORT

Large and old (1844), this burial ground sprawls over one hundred acres. Finding the gravesite of its most celebrated resident is easy: Just follow the markers and yellow line in the road to the hillside where Daniel Boone's stately monument overlooks both the State Capitol and the Kentucky River. Dan'l would have liked that. *215 East Main Street, Frankfort. Tel. (502) 227-2403. Grounds open 7:00 A.M.–sundown. Office hours: 8:00 A.M.–4:00 P.M. Monday–Friday; map, rest room.*

DANIEL BOONE
1734–1820

Hunter, surveyor, Indian fighter, Boone looms large in America's cultural history and legends. Although many of the claims made for him were inaccurate— he did not discover Kentucky, nor was he the "first white man of the West"— he was a good man, loyal, honest, modest, and, crucial in the West, courageous. He came from Quaker stock, born near Reading, Pennsylvania; had little real schooling; and was almost illiterate, but at age twelve he was a good hunter and trapper. Stimulated by stories about Kentucky (considered west at that time), in 1775 he led a group to found a settlement that later became known as Boonesborough. Indian fights, time in the militia, stints as a sheriff, legislator, and deputy surveyor followed. In the end he lost all the land tracts he claimed in Kentucky because of improper filings. In 1788 he left Kentucky in debt, moved to West Virginia, and later to what is now Missouri. In 1810 he returned to Kentucky and paid off his debts, which left him with 50 cents. From then on, especially after his wife died, he lived mostly at his son Nathan's Missouri home. His wife, **Rebecca Bryan Boone** (–1813), is with him now as in life. Note the well-executed bas reliefs on the sides of his handsome monument (see opposite), erected when the bodies were reinterred here, brought in 1845 by steamboat to this then-new cemetery.

Riverside Cemetery

HOPKINSVILLE

Riverside is in the nineteenth-century garden mode, with lovely trees, Greek-style mausoleums, rolling hillsides, and iron gates. 530 North Main Street, Hopkinsville. Tel. (270) 887–4071. Grounds open from dawn to dusk. Office hours: 7:00 A.M.–4:00 P.M. Monday–Friday.

EDGAR CAYCE
1877–1945

In his heyday Cayce (pronounced "kay-see") was a name to be reckoned with. As a clairvoyant and faith healer, he had a remarkable success rating when it came to medical analysis and recommended cures. He actually backed into faith healing. Although as a boy he had visions and trances, it wasn't until he was a young man that his "gift" became apparent. He lost his voice to laryngitis, and a friend hypnotized him. While under hypnosis, Cayce gave his own diagnosis, which cured the laryngitis. The friend was intrigued and persuaded him to diagnose his ailment, a stomach problem. This diagnosis too was a success. Little by little Cayce was drawn into medical readings and advice. Before long people wanted "life readings" on all kinds of matters, and his spirit was willing to provide them. Skeptics came to scoff and ended up converts. Much of Cayce's advice would today fall into the category of holistic healing. **The Edgar Cayce Foundation** still exists as a center for alternative medicine and spirituality. Faker or legitimate pre-New Age guru? Your call. His grave is near the chapel, well signed at the cemetery entrance.

Lexington Cemetery

LEXINGTON

This is a garden spot, with 170 acres of plantings, lily ponds, two lakes, sunken gardens, a four-acre flower garden, flowering trees, and shrubs. Some forty-two labeled trees are real specimens—like the 200-year-old American linden, a gingko, weeping mulberry and cherry, northern catalpa, royal paulowina, and European hornbeam—and a tree walk notes them. Lexington's resident celebrities include **John C. Breckinridge** (1821–1875), vice president (under James Buchanan), and secretary of war of the Confederacy; **Adolph Rupp** (1901–1977), a great basketball coach who led the Kentucky team to the NCAA championship four times; **Robert S. Todd** (1790–1849), senator, father of Mary Todd Lincoln; and scores of Union and Confederate soldiers. *833 West Main Street, Lexington. Tel. (859) 255-5522. Grounds open 8:00 A.M.–5:00 P.M. daily. Office hours: 8:00 A.M.–4:00 P.M. Monday– Friday, 8:00 A.M.–12:00 P.M. Saturday; map, brochures, including checklist for birders, rest room; walks, including tree walk and children's tour.*

HENRY CLAY
1777–1852

Humble beginnings in Virginia led— thanks to a mentor who urged him to study law—to a career in politics. For forty-three years Clay was a Kentucky political star, spending most of that time in the U.S. Senate. While there he made three unsuccessful runs for the presidency. His accomplishments were many, helping the U.S. acquire Alabama and Florida, statehood for Missouri, and the annexation of Texas. "The Great Compromiser," as he was known, can rest easy now: no more straddling the line between North and South. Now, in full statue-form, he stands proud, atop his own ornate Corinthian column, overlooking the parkland.

Zachary Taylor National Cemetery

LOUISVILLE

In the northeast corner of a sixteen-plus-acre veterans' cemetery are the mausoleum and memorial shaft honoring the twelfth U.S. president. Taylor's remains and those of his wife were transferred here in 1926 from a vault on the Taylor property. The towering granite column with a marble statue of Taylor on top rests just thirty feet from the neoclassical, colonnaded limestone mausoleum of the Taylors, with its glass-paneled bronze doors. Soldiers from seven wars repose nearby, including two Congressional Medal of Honor winners from World Wars I and II. *4701 Brownsboro Road, Louisville. Tel. (502) 893-3852. Grounds open all the time. Office hours: 8:00 A.M.–4:30 P.M. Monday-Friday; map, rest rooms.*

ZACHARY TAYLOR
1784–1850

"Old Rough and Ready" was Taylor's nickname, for his closeness to his soldiers in the field and his willingness to do battle. He was first and foremost a soldier, a brilliant commander whose skills and determination helped open up vast sections of the country to development. Although distinguishing himself in battle in the War of 1812, Black Hawk War, and Seminole conflict, he really catapulted to national prominence in the battle of Buena Vista against General Santa Ana during the Mexican War. That battle led to his nomination for president and over-whelming victory in 1849. It was a short-lived honor. Just a year and a half later, at age sixty-six, he was dead. On a Thursday, while spending three hours in the hot sun at a dedication of the Washington Monument, he drank ice water and ate a basket of ripe cherries and was then stricken with what was believed to be typhoid fever. That Sunday he said, "In two days I shall be a dead man." He was right. Not far from his childhood home, Taylor, his wife, **Margaret Smith Taylor** (1788–1852), his mother, and sixty-six Taylor family members now lie in rest on this little half-acre plot. Hail, hail, the Taylor gang's all here.

State House

BATON ROUGE

The Huey Long monument is visible in front of the State House, in a sunken garden area. *North 3rd Street and Boyd Avenue, Baton Rouge. Grounds open day and night.*

HUEY LONG
1893–1935

Larger than life in his heyday, Long is a Louisiana legend, hated and loved with equal fervency. Robert Penn Warren is believed to have modeled Willie Stark, the fascinating protagonist of *All the King's Men*, on Long. But Long, known as "the Kingfish," was more colorful (and cruder) than any fictional version. He began his long political career as a populist. Early on, as chairman of the Public Service Commission, he regulated public utilities and turned this state agency into a true, independent watchdog of the public interest. As governor (1928–1932), he brought the state into the twentieth century with a number of social welfare, public works, and education programs. While still governor, he ran for the U.S. Senate and won (1932–1935), but he wouldn't let his lieutenant governor take his place because he feared the man, an enemy, would demolish Long's potent politi-

cal machine. It meant calling out the National Guard and a seventeen-month siege before Long was able to finagle his own man into the job to finish out Long's term. Dictator? Who, Huey? As senator, he led a "Share the Wealth" campaign that competed with F. D. Roosevelt's New Deal and blocked federal New Deal dollars and influence. Fiercely loved as a populist and loathed as a fascist, he was shot and killed by a young local doctor, Carl Weiss, possibly for personal and political reasons. Weiss was immediately killed by Long's bodyguards, so we'll never know the real motive for sure. Long's last words were, "God, don't let me die. I have so much to do." His grave is beneath a double-life-size obelisk with his many achievements delineated on its sides. A bronze statue of him, arms outstretched, faces the State Capitol, where he held court so decisively.

Metairie Cemetery

Like so many New Orleans graveyards, Metairie has its resting places mostly above ground, doubtless as insurance against flooding of the semiswampy land. The largest of the city's graveyards (150 acres), Metairie dates back to 1872 and was built on the site of a former racecourse. It still retains a racetrack configuration. Here are tombs that resemble Egyptian pyramids, Greek temples, English abbeys, among other imaginative edifices, housing Civil War generals, governors, mayors, and Mardi Gras carnival kings. Metairie's most famous tenant had a short lease: **Jefferson Davis** (1808–1889), president of the Confederacy, died in New Orleans and, after a funeral cortege of more than 50,000 followers, was laid to rest in a tomb, in a dramatic circular site honoring the Army of Northern Virginia. Davis was removed in 1893 and reburied in Richmond, Virginia, but his crypt was sealed and his thirty-eight-foot-high granite statue remains on guard, perhaps protecting the 2,500 Confederate soldiers buried in the tomb's fifty-seven vaults. **Josie Arlington** (–1914), proprietor of one of New Orleans's most opulent bordellos, had a $15,000 ornate pink marble mausoleum (from which, neighbors swore, emanated a mysterious red light at night), but it was sold out from over her by ghoulish relatives, leaving poor Josie to find cheaper final digs. Also in Metairie: **Pierre Beauregard** (1818–1893), Confederate general known for bravery and skills in fortification; **Alois "Al" Hirt** (1922–1999), jazz trumpeter who toured with the Dorsey brothers and Benny Goodman, and whose own band was a New Orleans favorite; **Louis Prima** (1910–1978), bouncy jazz cornet player; **John A. Stevenson**, builder of the ironclad ship *Manassas,* used in New Orleans's defense in 1862; and **Richard Taylor** (1826–1879), general and son of president Zachary Taylor. *5100 Pontchartrain Boulevard, New Orleans. Tel. (504) 486-6331. Grounds open 8:00 A.M.–5:30 P.M. daily. Office hours: 8:00 A.M.–5:00 P.M. daily; map, rest rooms.*

MELVIN OTT

1909–1958

Mel Ott's twenty-two-year career as a rightfielder with the New York Giants baseball team was and remains a modern major league record, unimaginable in this era of player hopscotch. Ott was a natural who leapfrogged from semi pro ball to the major leagues without passing "go" or any minor league stop in between. At age sixteen, with a one-way ticket from his home in Gretna, Louisiana, he traveled to New York and the "big leagues," every schoolboy's fantasy. He ended his career in 1947 with 511 home runs, third only to Babe Ruth and Jimmy Foxx at the time; a lifetime batting average of .304; and participation in eleven All-Star games. Ott was known for his modesty and likeability, prompting brash Leo Durocher to taunt him with the line, "nice guys finish last." Ott had a brief stint managing the Giants. In 1951 he was elected to the Baseball Hall of Fame. In mid–1958 he and his wife, Mildred, were injured in a car accident in Mississippi. Rushed to a New Orleans hospital for surgery when his kidneys began to fail, he died on the operating table. Ott-a-there, so to speak—now here for good.

St. Louis Cemetery No. 1

NEW ORLEANS

Probably the city's most famous burial ground, St. Louis is a magnet for tourists, intrigued by all the aboveground mausoleums and oven-shaped tombs, some built on top of one another. No wonder it, and other local cemeteries like it, is called a "city of the dead." Most of the old mausoleums are made of soft red brick, whitewashed. Many bear old French and Spanish names, relics of the city's past, and are embellished with delicate bas reliefs. Unfortunately, tombs have been overturned, left to vandals, and many are in a sad state of decay. Furthermore, in recent years robbers and muggers have skulked behind the big "houses," ready to pounce on purses and wallets. For this reason it is advisable to visit in a group and always in full daylight. Tucked among the many close-together avenues of mausoleums are **Stanislaus Fornier** (1814–1883), French-born clockmaker; **Benjamin Henry Latrobe** (1764–1820), the most accomplished resident, an architect and engineer with a penchant for Greek classicism whose work changed the look of Washington, D.C., and Philadelphia and led to the Greek Revival period of American architecture; **Marie Laveau**, a voodoo queen; and **Paul Morphy** (1837–1884), considered the best chess player of his era. *Basin and St. Louis Streets, New Orleans. Grounds open all the time.*

Oak Hill Cemetery-Crematory

BATTLE CREEK

As its name implies, Oak Hill has hillside views and plenty of oak trees on its fifty-three acres. The burial ground, which celebrated its 150th year in 1994, has pretty white gates front and back and is home to **John Harvey Kellogg** (1852–1943), surgeon, health food advocate, and corn flakes inventor; **Will Keith Kellogg** (1860–1951), manufacturer of cereals; and **Charles William Post** (1854–1914), inventor of Grape-Nuts, manufacturer of breakfast cereals and Postum. *255 South Avenue (corner of Oak Hill Drive) Battle Creek. Tel. (616) 964-7321. Grounds open from dawn to dusk. Office hours: 9:00 A.M.–5:00 P.M. Monday-Friday; map, rest room.*

SOJOURNER TRUTH
1797–1883

Heroine of the civil rights movement, this ambitious woman was born a slave but taught herself to read and write. She was born as Isabella Baumtree in upstate New York and was first sold at age nine to an Englishman. She was sold twice more, married and had five children, and ran away when her last master wouldn't free her (even though New York State abolished slavery). She gained her freedom in the 1820s, changed her name to Sojourner Truth, and set forth to abolish slavery and spread the word of God. Both goals would last her lifetime. Her independent spirit led to controversies and at least two lawsuits. She won them both and achieved two "firsts": the first African American to win a slander suit against establishment whites and the first to challenge segregation in Washington, D.C., streetcars. Throughout the Civil War she helped fugitive slaves escape. She died in a sanatorium here, fighting for civil justice and God's word to the end. Her simple upright vertical monument is located between Oak and Summit, not far below the office at the northwest entrance. Note her sad quote: "Is God dead?"

Lakewood Cemetery

MINNEAPOLIS

With its motto "Celebrating life for over 125 years," Lakewood has the right idea, certainly one to which its most optimistic resident (Hubert Humphrey) would subscribe. It is a favorite final home to many prominent Minneapolitans, with its beautiful pines and oak trees and its handsome Byzantine-style domed chapel. Here lie **Ossie Bluege** (1900–1985), Major League Baseball player, manager, and scout; **Dick Enroth** (1918–1999), sports announcer for the Minneapolis Lakers; **Bill Goldsworthy** (1944–1996), hockey player, original member of the Minnesota North Stars; **Theodore Hamm** (1825–1903), founder of Hamm Brewing Company; **Rudy Perpich** (1928–1995), longest-serving governor of the state; and **Lyle Z. Wright** (1898–1963), member of the U.S. Hockey Hall of Fame. Here also is **Herbert Khaury** (1932–1996), whose "fifteen minutes of fame" came in the late 1960s when, as "Tiny Tim," he appeared on many television shows, warbling falsetto and plucking a banjo with retro 1920s and 1930s songs such as "Tiptoe through the Tulips." *3600 Hennepin Avenue, Minneapolis. Tel. (612) 822-2171. Grounds open 8:00 A.M.–5:00 P.M. daily. Office hours: 8:00 A.M.–4:30 P.M. Monday–Friday, 8:00 A.M.–12:00 P.M. Saturday; map, rest rooms.*

HUBERT HORATIO HUMPHREY
1911–1978

This bouncy, ebullient man epitomized the optimist who sees the glass half full instead of half empty. From a boyhood of lower-middle-class, Depression-era hard times, he rose to graduate magna cum laude from the University of Minnesota; become mayor of Minneapolis, a U.S. senator, and vice president under Lyndon Johnson; and to come within a hair's breadth of the presidency. Along the way he never forgot his humble roots and built his career on helping other people. While mayor, he oversaw the passage of the nation's first municipal fair employment practices act, and as senator he proposed health care for the aged (which eventually became a medicare bill) and helped push through the Nuclear Test Ban Treaty of 1963 and the Civil Rights Act of 1964. A proud liberal, he got bogged

down with the Johnson administration in the Vietnam War, which alienated many of his natural supporters. After his defeat for the presidency in 1968, he did the usual upbeat Humphrey thing: He ran for senate again in 1970 and won two terms but died from cancer during his second term. Then, as the saying goes, they broke the mold. His wife, **Muriel** (1912–1998), who is here with him, was appointed to fill out his second term.

Greenwood Cemetery

SAUK CENTRE

A small Protestant burial ground, just south of two Catholic ones, Greenwood is home to the entire Sinclair Lewis family. He is buried in the family plot, between the stones of his mother and father. *County Road 17, Sauk Centre. Grounds open all the time.*

SINCLAIR LEWIS
1 8 8 5 – 1 9 5 1

Sauk Centre is the "Gopher Prairie" of author Lewis's first and most famous novel, *Main Street*, in which the town and its natives are objects of satire and occasional derision. The 1920 novel catapulted Lewis, the son of a local doctor, to fame, but infuriated Lewis's fellow townspeople. They eventually got over it and may have had the last laugh: by turning the town into a permanent Lewis shrine.

After *Main Street*, Lewis, a Yale student (though he didn't graduate), journalist, and editor, turned full time to novel writing. *Babbitt* (1922) followed, then *Arrowsmith* (1925), which won a Pulitzer Prize in fiction—a prize he refused because he didn't feel the book fulfilled the award's requirements of representing "the wholesome atmosphere of American life." These three books are still considered his major works, though of his twenty-three novels,

Dodsworth and *It Can't Happen Here* were his most successful. In 1930 Lewis received the Nobel Prize in literature, the first American to be so honored. Argumentive, short tempered, sometimes crass, with a major inferiority complex (caused mostly by his looks—a pitted acne complexion, gawky appearance, untamed red hair), Lewis wasn't always a barrel of laughs to be around, as his two ex-wives and many literary acquaintances attested. Yet this lonely man, who called himself a "scold" because of the critical content of his novels, could be charming. But he died alone in Rome at a clinic for nervous disorders, convulsed from advanced alcoholism and possibly drug withdrawal. According to local lore, the day Lewis's ashes were brought to Greenwood was cold and windy, and the ashes, so they say, were dumped from an urn into the ground, but because of the wind, they didn't all make it. Dust to dust. The **Sinclair Lewis boyhood home** (812 Sinclair Lewis Avenue; 320–352–5201) is open, with its original furnishings.

Mississippi

St. Peter's Cemetery

OXFORD

This old, city-maintained burial ground, located near the town square, is sizable, shadowed by drooping trees, ghostly quiet, and unattended; a visitor might easily (or uneasily) believe it to be haunted. In short, it's everything you'd expect of a cemetery in Faulkner's Yoknapatawpha County. A marker at the Jefferson Avenue entrance tells the way to the Faulkner grave. *Off Jefferson Avenue, Oxford. Grounds open all the time.*

WILLIAM FAULKNER
1 8 9 7 – 1 9 6 2

This is Yoknapatawpha County, and if you hang around long enough, you'll see landmarks from the novelist's many books. Although some readers may find his run-on sentences difficult, this Oxford-born writer is generally acknowledged as one of the best, if not the best, American novelists of the twentieth century. He created a world within one small Mississippi county. Jefferson, its county seat, was based on Oxford, Faulkner's hometown, where he spent most of his life. Although he sometimes worked elsewhere—in Europe, where he joined the expatriate writers of the 1920s, in New York, and later in Hollywood writing movie scripts—he didn't stay away long. He seemed to recognize early on that the world he could best write about was right in Oxford and its environs. *Flags in the Dust* was the first of his Yoknapatawpha County novels. *Sanctuary* in 1931 was the first to grab the public's attention, perhaps because of its violent and shocking nature. In the 1930s and 1940s, he wrote what are considered his best novels: *Light in August, Absalom, Absalom!, The Wild Palms, The Hamlet,* and *Go Down, Moses.* In 1949 Faulkner won the Nobel Prize in literature and twice won both the Pulitzer and the National Book Award, among many other awards for his novels and short stories. **Rowan Oak** (Old Taylor Road; 662–234–3284), Faulkner's home from 1930 onward, is open and free to view.

Missouri

Harry S. Truman Library and Museum

INDEPENDENCE

In the courtyard of this library-museum complex are the graves of Harry Truman and his wife, **Bess Wallace Truman** (1885–1982). *US 24 and Delaware Street, Independence. Tel. (816) 833-1400 (library) or (816) 833-1225 (museum). Open daily, except major holidays; courtyard free.*

HARRY S. TRUMAN
1884–1972

Anecdotes abound about the most no-nonsense "common man" U.S. president. Yet in so many ways he was very uncommon: in his honesty, frankness, disdain for pretense and phoniness, his endless interest in history. Much has been written about his early life as a haberdashery salesman and a product of the Prendergast political machine in Kansas City. When U.S. Senator Truman was chosen to run as vice president with Franklin Roosevelt for his (FDR's) fourth term, there were those who said, "Harry who?" But when Roosevelt died early in his term, Truman soon demonstrated his potential for growth as president,

faced with decisions about dropping the atom bomb and reconstructing postwar Europe and Japan. His devotion to his wife, Bess, who is with him now as throughout life, is the stuff of true romance. Truman, a farm boy, married above his station, and his mother-in-law never let him forget it, even when she was living in and enjoying the perks of the Truman White House. It is one more example of Harry's character that he didn't complain about her numerous put-downs. If you have any doubts about the unpretentious simplicity of his and Bess's lives, visit their home, now the **Harry S. Truman Historic Site** (219 North Delaware Street; 816–254–9929) nearby.

Lincoln Cemetery

KANSAS CITY

This old burial ground, located behind Mount Washington Cemetery, is now full, thus unattended. *24 Highway and Blue Ridge, Kansas City. Grounds open all the time.*

CHARLIE "BIRD" PARKER
1 9 2 0 – 1 9 5 5

"Bird"—short for "yardbird," country slang for "chicken," derived from a childhood anecdote—played the alto saxophone like there was no tomorrow, and for him there wasn't. His fire burned bright and hot, but for jazz lovers much too briefly. His childhood in Kansas City, a place alive with blues and jazz, led him in his early teens to the sax, an instrument made for his kind of innovating. With "Dizzy" Gillespie, his frequent collaborator, he created a new vocabulary for music. Fame was a "given" for someone with such talent, but there were too many distractions: booze, women (married the first time at age sixteen), marijuana and heroin (which hooked him permanently at seventeen). When he flamed out at thirty-four, pneumonia was listed as the official cause. His grave is located next to his mother's.

Mount Olivet Cemetery

KEARNEY

The old Baptist Church once stood on what is now the burial ground and the property is still church owned. There is no signage leading to the current home of the most famous (or infamous) resident, Jesse James, but if you enter at the gate next to the railroad tracks, the grave is easy to find, about 100 feet forward and on the right. The tombstone has been replaced three times (having been chipped at for souvenirs), the last time to dig up the remains for DNA testing. Yes, skeptics, it was/is Jesse, up close and personal. Other members of the large James clan are also buried in Mount Olivet. *State Road 92. Tel. (816) 628–7392 (caretaker). Grounds open from sunrise to sunset.*

JESSE JAMES
1 8 4 7 – 1 8 8 2

Jesse Woodson James was the third son in a family of four children, who lived on a 257-acre farm in Kearney. The oldest son, Frank, joined the Confederate army in 1861 at age eighteen. Jesse, age sixteen, joined "Bloody" Bill Anderson's guerrilla forces in 1863, and the next year he killed Union Major A. V. Johnson at the Centralia massacre, in which unarmed Union soldiers were kidnapped from a train and slaughtered by Anderson's gang. In the aftermath of the Civil War, lawlessness was rampant, with bank, train, and stagecoach robberies. The James-Younger gang was blamed or credited (take your choice) for many, some of which they didn't commit. A crime spree of major league proportions savaged the South and West, from Missouri, Iowa, and Nebraska, to Virginia, Alabama, and Arkansas. It lasted for seventeen years, between 1865 and 1882, when Jesse James was finally killed for the reward money, shot in a house he had rented under an alias in St. Joseph, Missouri. The **Jesse James Farm** (Jesse James Farm Road; 816–628–6065), 2 miles away, is the house where the James brothers were born; it has family artifacts, furnishings, and a museum.

Bellefontaine Cemetery

S T . L O U I S

It seems only natural that with St. Louis as the "Gateway to the West" in the mid-nineteenth century, Bellefontaine, founded in 1849, would be the final meeting place for many of those coming and going. This silent city covers some 327 acres of curving roads and hillocks and epitomizes the elaborate burial styles of the period, with a plethora of Egyptian- and Greek-style mausoleums, cenotaphs, and funereal sculptures. The Wainwright mausoleum is of major interest. Commissioned by brewing magnate **Ellis Wainright** (1850–1924) for his wife, **Charlotte** (1867–1891), and designed by Louis Sullivan, this domed limestone tomb, with its great ornamentation, is a certified national landmark. Other permanent residents of Bellefontaine include brewing magnate **Eberhardt Anheuser** (1805–1880); **Dr. William Beaumont** (1785–1853), a medical revolutionary noted for his studies of digestion; **Thomas Hart Benton** (1782–1858), Missouri's first U.S. senator, highly esteemed and principled; **Peter Blow** (1777–1832), who owned the slave Dred Scott, and his brother **Taylor Blow** (1820–1869), who freed him; **William S. Burroughs** (1855–1898), inventor of the mechanical calculator; **Roswell Martin Field** (1807–1869), Dred Scott's lawyer and father of poet Eugene Field; **Major Albert B. Lambert** (1875–1946), aviation enthusiast who was taught to fly by Orville Wright, bought a plane from Wilbur, and then backed Lindbergh on his trans-Atlantic flight; **Irma Rombauer** (1877–1982), author of the evergreen *Joy of Cooking;* and poet **Sara Teasdale** (1884–1933), winner of the first Pulitzer Prize in poetry. Note the **Lemp** family tomb. The German immigrant Lemps were wealthy brewers and art collectors, whose ranks were thinned by suicides, heart attacks, and madness. During prohibition, their brewery was closed and liquidated, their fancy mansion and its elaborate furnishings all gone; like it or Lemp it, the tomb is all that's left. *4947 West Florissant Avenue (at Kings Highway), St. Louis. Tel. (314) 381-0750. Grounds open daily. Office hours: 8:00 A.M.–4:00 P.M. Monday–Friday, but two gatekeepers are available at the office Saturday, Sunday, and holidays to assist visitors; map and detailed biographies of residents, rest rooms.*

ADOLPHUS BUSCH
1 8 3 8 – 1 9 1 3

You might think that the occupant of the splendid churchlike Gothic-style mausoleum, made of Missouri red granite with a roof of gray-green slate, was a high-ranking minister of means. But the hop vines on the ornate gates are the tip-off. German-born Busch was the youngest of twenty-one children of a supplier of wine and brewery goods. During a mid–nineteenth-century German exodus to the United States, he followed relatives to St. Louis, and there married the daughter of brewer Eberhard

Anheuser. No beer expert, Busch joined Anheuser as a partner, and with great organizational and sales skills helped create the largest brewing empire in the world, Anheuser-Busch. At the time Busch joined the company, there were forty breweries in St. Louis. In the mid–1870s a new beer, called Budweiser, was added to the, ah, brew, and became Busch's special bailiwick. The A-B empire made Busch one of the wealthiest men in the country. While maintaining four homes—three in the United States, one in Germany—he was a generous patron of the arts, especially theater and opera, and a contributor to many worthy causes. Of his fourteen childen, nine lived to maturity, and many Busch offspring are major players in St. Louis's public life to this day.

WILLIAM CLARK
1770–1838

The obelisk, bronze bust, and history of Clark engraved on all sides of a marble platform form a fitting testament to one member of a great American can-do team, Lewis and Clark. Together, Meriwether Lewis, President Thomas Jefferson's secretary, and Clark, an army officer, led an expedition to find and explore a land route to the Pacific Ocean. They began in Illinois in 1804, and journeyed by horseback, foot, and boat to the headwaters of the Columbia River. They had intended to return by sea, but with no ships available until spring, they had to retrace their route by land and ended up in St. Louis two years and four months after they started out. Lewis was the head honcho, but mapmaker Clark had more frontier experience and was more resourceful and daring. They worked beautifully in

tandem, and at the end, in 1806, reported to Jefferson in Washington. Clark then returned to St. Louis as superintendent of Indian affairs for the Missouri Territory (Lewis was named governor of Louisiana), later became governor of the Missouri Territory (in 1813); surveyor general for Missouri, Illinois, and Arkansas; and laid out the town of Paducah, Kentucky. He was a spokesman for Indian causes in Washington and provided hospitality to men of both races who passed through town. He is buried here with his second wife and three of his children.

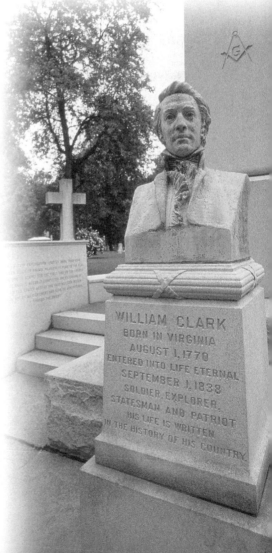

Calvary Cemetery

Near Bellefontaine, Calvary (1857) is an expansive 477-acre Catholic burying ground, overlooking the Mississippi River. Calvary has many illustrious permanent residents, often with monuments to match. Among them: **Auguste Chouteau** (1749–1829), cofounder of St. Louis, reburied here; medical missionary **Dr. Thomas Dooley III** (1927–1961), founder of Medico; **Charles Eames** (1907–1978), St. Louis native, successful designer, architect, and filmmaker; **Dred Scott** (ca. 1800–1858), the slave whose 1857 lawsuit for freedom was a factor that led to the Civil War; and **Antoine Soulard**, last surveyor-general of Upper Louisiana under Spanish rule. *5239 West Florissant Avenue (at Calvary Avenue), St. Louis. Tel. (314) 381-1313. Grounds open 8:00 A.M.–5:00 P.M. daily. Office hours: 8:30 A.M.–4:30 P.M. Monday-Friday, 8:30 A.M.–12:30 P.M. Saturday, closed holy days and major holidays; map and printed historical/biographical tour, rest rooms.*

KATE CHOPIN
1 8 5 1 – 1 9 0 4

Catherine "Kate" O'Flaherty was a St. Louis belle when she met and married Oscar Chopin, a Creole cotton broker, and they soon moved to New Orleans. She took happily to the city's social life and soon bore six children. Then in a relatively short time her world fell apart: Oscar's business failed, three years later he died, and two years after that, Kate's beloved mother died. It is unclear when Kate began writing, but by 1889 she had authored several short stories, much influenced by Guy de Maupassant, and in 1890 published her first novel, *At Fault*. What really caused a stir, and ultimately, posthumously, made her reputation, was *The Awakening* (1899), her second novel, which dealt with themes a proper young Southern lady of her time did not discuss, let alone write about: a boring marriage, a woman's lust and need for emotional and sexual fulfillment, infidelity, and

suicide. Wow! Not exactly eye-poppers now, but think 1899. Today she is admired by feminists and others for her courage in writing about taboo subjects. The outpourings of abuse and vituperation against the book seemed to snuff out Chopin's creative impulses. She never wrote again and died in 1904 from a brain hemorrhage, after a long day spent at the St. Louis World's Fair. Her grave is in the plot of C. F. Benoit, a family of early St. Louis bankers; Oscar Chopin was a Benoit nephew.

WILLIAM TECUMSEH SHERMAN
1 8 2 0 – 1 8 9 1

Sherman's flag-draped monument is a modest one for one of the most successful Union generals of the Civil War. Ohio-born Sherman was a close ally, friend, and supporter of Ulysses S. Grant. Together they fought at Shiloh and supported each other in later battles. It was Sherman who "marched through Georgia" to the sea, incurring the wrath of generations of Southerners for his troops' burning of Atlanta. The point of the march was to break the South's resistance by cutting off supplies, and Georgia was the last major source of supplies. Orders were to live off the land but maintain discipline. This proved impossible to do with an army in a celebratory, reckless mood. Though Sherman's "war is . . . hell" statement was heartfelt, he also wrote in his memoirs that "to be at the head of a strong column of troops, in the execution of some task that requires brains is the highest pleasure of war—a grim one and terrible, but one which leaves on the mind and memory the strongest mark." His life was undistinguished before the war, but afterward he continued to serve, from St. Louis, as commander of the Division of the Mississippi and was helpful in mollifying Indian opposition to the new transcontinental railroad. He repeatedly rebuffed Republican Party pleas to run for office. (Maybe war wasn't the only thing he thought was hell.) Interred with Sherman are his wife, daughter, and two sons; the epitaph to one reads, "Our little sergent Willie."

TENNESSEE WILLIAMS
1911–1983

Tennessee, the name that Thomas Williams chose when beginning his writing career (as a poet), sounds more like a country-western singer than one of America's best playwrights. Author of more than twenty-four plays and winner of two Pulitzer Prizes, he changed the nature of theater in America, bringing a new level of poetic naturalism and introducing subject matter—homosexuality, incest, drug addiction, madness, and cannibalism—never dealt with on stage before. Actually, he was thirty-five years old before success as a playwright struck. Plays like *The Glass Managerie*, *A Streetcar Named Desire*, *Cat on a Hot Tin Roof*, *Sweet Bird of Youth*, *The Rose Tattoo*, *Orpheus Descending*, and *Summer and Smoke* are now part of the theater lexicon. That he could produce so many exceptional plays in just a few years is all the more remarkable because as a human being he was a bit of an emotional basket case: temperamentally fragile, depressive, drug dependent, and in and out of mental institutions. In fact his own dysfunctional family life fed his genius. He wrote in his memoirs that at death he wanted his body dropped in the sea "12 hours north of Havana, so that my bones may rest not too far from those of Hart Crane." Instead, his brother Dakin, his frequent nemesis, buried him here, far from Key West, which he loved and where he spent much of his time (when not in New York). His pink marble upright gravestone bears the inscription, " 'The violets in the mountains have broken the rocks'—*Camino Real.*" Nearby, in death as rarely in life, is his mother, **Edwina Dakin Williams**.

Ohio

Spring Grove Cemetery

CINCINNATI

Created in the garden or rural style in 1845, Spring Grove is a tranquil spot, a National Historic Landmark with Gothic and Greek-style mausoleums, woodland, lakes, and waterfall. Its beautiful trees—twenty-three designated Ohio Champion specimens, all more than one hundred years old—make it a magnet for birders and nature lovers. In spring the terrain is a festival of tulips, daffodils, pansies, and azaleas; in summer roses and lilies dominate; and in fall it's a field of chrysanthemums. Spirited residents include **Levi Coffin** (1789–1877), abolitionist and president of the Underground Railroad; **Charles L. Fleischmann** (1835–1897), yeast manufacturer, whose Parthenon mausoleum overlooking Geyser Lake is one of Spring Grove's masterpieces; **Jesse R. Grant** (1794–1873) and his wife, **Hannah**, parents of Ulysses S. Grant; **Miller Huggins** (1878–1929), manager of the New York Yankees baseball team 1918–1929, leading the team to six pennants and three World Series; **Alexander H. McGuffey** (1816–1896), publisher of children's textbooks; and **Kate Chase Sprague** (1840–1899), socialite daughter of Lincoln's secretary of treasury. *4521 Spring Grove Avenue, Cincinnati. Tel (513) 681-7526. Grounds open 8:00 A.M.–6:00 P.M. daily. Office hours: 8:00 A.M.–5:00 P.M. Monday–Friday, 8:00 A.M.–4:00 P.M. Saturday, 12:00 P.M.–4:00 P.M. Sunday; map, rest rooms.*

SALMON CHASE
1808–1873

New Hampshire–born Chase graduated Phi Beta Kappa from Dartmouth College in 1826, then moved to Washington to study and practice law. Three years later he opened a law practice in Cincinnati. One of his early cases was defending James Birney, an abolitionist editor who had harbored a runaway slave. The case was an epiphany for Chase, who became convinced slavery was wrong and African Americans deserved equal rights. When he began defending slaves themselves, he was dubbed the "attorney general of fugitive slaves." He organized two independent political parties, and was elected to the U.S. Senate, but only served one term. He then organized the Anti-Nebraska Party, which morphed into the Republican Party of Ohio. In 1855 he became governor. His goal was to be president of the United States and he tried three times, 1856, 1860, 1864, but never won the nomination. Instead he returned to the Senate in 1861 but only served two days before newly elected President Lincoln chose him as secretary of treasury. It was a job Chase was good at: He created a national banking system and organized an internal revenue division. Busy as he was, he found time to carp at Lincoln and in a snit offered four times to resign. The fifth time, in late 1864, Lincoln accepted, but two months later appointed Chase chief justice of the U.S. Supreme Court, where he served until his death. Being on the court didn't stop Chase from yet another "go" at a presidential nomination, this time, 1868, in the Democratic Party. But Chase's commitment to voting rights for African Americans destroyed his chance. He seemed to change his party loyalties as often as his clothes, but his core principles never.

JAMES GAMBLE
1836–1932
WILLIAM C. PROCTER
1862–1934

It's one of life's jokes that a man named Gamble owed his fortune to chance. Irishman Gamble, an apprentice soapmaker, and Procter, an English candlemaker, were on their way west independently, when they met by chance in Cincinnati and married sisters. Their new father-in-law, Alexander Norris, persuaded them to become business partners, manufacturing soap and candles. The business began in 1837 and prospered with government contracts during the Civil War. Later, Gamble's son, James Norris, a trained chemist, came up with a cheap white soap similar to imported, high quality castiles. It was named "Ivory," because of a Bible passage, "out of ivory palaces," and it made P & G a household word. Electricity pretty much extinguished the candle business, but by then it was upward and onward for Procter and Gamble. So-ap be it.

JOSEPH HOOKER
1815–1879

After reading in so many history books about Civil War officers who seemed like noble Boy Scouts, trustworthy and brave, it is refreshing to encounter Hooker, an irascible rapscallion, notorious for quarreling with his superiors. Massachusetts-born and West Point–educated, Hooker capped his service in the Mexican War by testifying against fellow officer Winfield Scott before a military board of inquiry. Later, as a civilian who witnessed the first Battle of

Bull Run, he wrote to President Lincoln on how mismanaged the Union effort was, yet volunteered to serve again. Lincoln agreed and Hooker joined McClellan's army. Despite a reputation for heavy drinking, Hooker eventually was appointed commander of the Army of the Potomac. His headquarters quickly became known as a brothel and a bar. In one battle, after a brilliant maneuver around General Lee's flank, Hooker lost his nerve. Dazed by a shell hitting his headquarters in Stonewall Jackson's surprise attack, Hooker ordered a full retreat. By 1864 he asked to be relieved and ended the war far from the action. It has been suggested that the word hooker stems from his attempt to round up and confine prostitutes in one area of Washington.

Lake View Cemetery

CLEVELAND

This beautiful parklike place with steep and rolling hills, flower beds, myrtle, and trailing ivy remains the city's best address for the hereafter. Magnificent mausoleums, obelisks, angelic statuary, and the Wade Chapel with its opalescent Tiffany window, all reflect Cleveland's long-time prosperity and home base of many distinguished doers of both the nineteenth and twentieth centuries. Resting here are **Helene Britton** (1856–1928), first woman owner of a baseball team (the St. Louis Cardinals 1911–1916); **Charles Brush** (1849–1929), inventor of the arc lamp; **Ray Chapman** (1891–1920), Cleveland Indian shortstop, the only major league player to die from a game-related injury; **Mark Hanna** (1837–1904), national leader of the Republican party, known as the "president maker"; **Adella Prentiss Hughes** (1869–1950), founder of the Cleveland Orchestra and manager for fifteen years; **Garret Morgan, Sr.** (1877–1963), inventor of the gas mask and three-color traffic light; **Eliot Ness** (1903–1957), U.S. Treasury official, immortalized by the television series, *The Untouchables;* **Gloria Hershey Pressman** (1923–1991), child actress, who appeared in the original *Little Rascals* and in the first talking movie, *The Jazz Singer;* **Rufus Spalding** (1798–1886), politician, justice of the Ohio Supreme Court; and **Carl B. Stokes** (1927–1996), politician, judge, broadcaster, two-term African American mayor of Cleveland. *12316 Euclid Avenue at East 123rd Street, Cleveland. Tel. (216) 421-2665. Web site: www. lakeviewcemetery.com. Grounds open 7:30 A.M.–5:30 P.M. daily. Office hours: 8:30 A.M.–5:00 P.M. Monday–Friday, 8:30 A.M.–12:30 P.M. Saturday, closed Sunday; map, bookshop, rest rooms. "Stones and Bones" tour available through Trolley Tours of Cleveland (fee).*

JAMES GARFIELD
1 8 3 1 – 1 8 8 1

Intellectually intense, our twentieth U.S. president was a self-made man who propelled himself, through study and hard work, to the professorship of ancient languages and literature at Hiram College and later became its president. Serious and religious, he might not seem a likely candidate for president, but he marched from college life to major general in the army during the Civil War and then on to the U.S. Congress and the Senate before being elected president. After all this overachieving, he had just a few months to enjoy the White House: on July 2, 1881, a disgruntled office seeker confronted Garfield in the Washington train station and shot him. Two months later the well-liked president died from his gunshot wounds. His wife, **Lucretia Garfield**, who shared all his cerebral interests, shares this final home as well. Their bronze caskets are in repose in the crypt just below the Memorial Hall of the Garfield monument (see above). With

its peaked roof, this is one of the prides of Lake View, staffed with its own guide, and open 9:00 a.m. to 4:00 p.m. daily, April through mid-November.

JOHN D. ROCKEFELLER, SR.
1 8 3 9 – 1 9 3 7

Patriarch of an American dynasty that has been known for philanthropy and public service, John Davison Rockefeller began his career as an assistant bookkeeper for a Cleveland commission merchant. In 1863 he stuck his toe, as it were, in the oil business and two years later immersed himself full time. By organizing Standard Oil Company with himself as its largest stockholder, his fortune was assured. Later, to counter his image as a monopolist and ruthless operator, he began giving dimes away promiscuously. Rockefeller's towering memorial, reminiscent of the Washington Monument, is a reminder of the man's monumental fortune; he was worth over $1 billion at the time of his death. No wonder he could afford a few thousand dimes.

Woodland Cemetery and Arboretum

DAYTON

When Woodland opened in 1843, it was indeed in the woods, at the highest point in town, with magnificent views and, of course, beautiful trees. Now the city surrounds its 200 acres, as is the case with many once-rural burial grounds. The arboretum part of Woodland's name isn't accidental: There are some 3,000 trees, many more than one hundred years old, on the rolling hillsides. Add to the natural beauty a Romanesque gateway, office, and chapel, which boasts a magnificent Tiffany window, and a listing on the National Register of Historic Places. Monuments range from rugged boulders to Greek temples and Victorian and Hellenic statuary. Resident "names" include **James M. Cox** (1845–1932), newspaper publisher and presidential candidate in 1920; **Paul Laurence Dunbar** (1872–1906), African American poet; **Charles F. Kettering** (1876–1958), inventor of an all-electric ignition system for starting a car, eliminating the need to hand-crank it; and **Major David Ziegler** (1748–1811), Revolutionary War veteran, commander of troops in early Indian wars, and Cincinnati's first mayor. *118 North Woodland Avenue, Dayton. Tel. (937) 222-1431. Web site: www.woodlandcemetery.org. Woodland gate open 8:00 A.M.–6:00 P.M. winter, 8:00 A.M.–7:00 P.M. summer; Waldo Street gate 8:00 A.M.–5:00 P.M. winter, 8:00 A.M.–6:00 P.M. summer. Office hours: 8:00 A.M.–4:30 P.M. Monday–Friday, 8:00 A.M.–12:00 P.M. Saturday; map, rest rooms.*

ERMA BOMBECK
1927–1996

The wit and wisdom of humorist Bombeck were dispensed in a syndicated newspaper column that appeared in more than 800 newspapers. A journalist since her high school days in Dayton, she later wrote six best-selling books, collections of her columns. Her column was the first thing people all over the country turned to in their morning newspaper, as she related her adventures with her three children, husband, and daily life, always in an original way. Her funny lines always had a homey dimension, such as, "Never go to a doctor whose office plants have died." Personally, I always liked "Seize the moment. Remember all those women on the *Titantic* who waved off the dessert cart." Her grave marker here is a 29,000-pound boulder, lugged by flatbed truck from near her former home in Arizona (who says you can't take it with you?). Her husband, Bill, wanted her to have "a piece of Arizona" at her grave, commemorating the twenty-five years they spent together there. She would have made an amusing column out of this.

ORVILLE WRIGHT
1871–1948
WILBUR WRIGHT
1867–1912

They weren't really peas in a pod, the Wright brothers, but born four years apart, in Dayton, Ohio. Yet their inquisitive natures seemed bred in the bones. When their father brought home a self-propelling toy, the brothers became fascinated and began reading everything they could find on flight and machines. Serious readers and questioners, they wanted to know how things worked and tested theories by making mechanical toys. This later led to a large printing press, on which they published a newspaper. They then moved on to a bicycle repair shop, where they experimented with wheels, tires, air pumps, and other mechanical equipment. Determined to find ways to fly, they tested the effect of air pressure on some 200 wing surfaces. In 1903 they built and put into the air the first power-driven, person carrying controllable airplane. Traveling to the windiest place they could find, they tested their 750-pound machine in Kitty Hawk, North Carolina, and kept the machine in the air for fifty-nine seconds. That was the start. They went on to set new distance and altitude flight records. But in 1912 the partnership ended: Wilbur died of typhoid fever. Orville lived on another thirty-six years. The family graves are all together.

Tennessee

Meriwether Lewis Park

H O H E N W A L D

Located about 70 miles south of Nashville, the park consists of greenland, a museum, and picnic area. Meriwether Lewis's grave is marked by a broken column, easy to spot. *Natchez Trace Parkway, 7 miles east of town on Route 20. Tel. (931) 796–2675.*

MERIWETHER LEWIS
1774–1809

Soldier and explorer, Lewis was a native of the Charlottesville area of Virginia and a neighbor of Thomas Jefferson. At age twenty, Lewis, a member of a local militia, answered the call to put down the Whiskey Rebellion. He later attended the treaty signing in Greenville, Ohio, that ended the Indian wars in the Northwest Territory. Lewis subsequently served in various outposts and at one point, because of his honesty and work ethic, was appointed paymaster for his regiment. When Jefferson was elected president, he asked his young neighbor to be his private secretary. This was a rare opportunity to work in the White House and be privy to Jefferson's plans and programs. Since at least 1792 Jefferson had considered the idea of an expedition to find a land route to the Pacific Ocean, a prospect that fired the youthful Lewis's imagination. President Jefferson persuaded Congress to appropriate the money, and Lewis was put in charge of the expedition. (See earlier entry, William Clark, St. Louis.) When the expedition ended successfully, Jefferson appointed Lewis governor of Louisiana, based in St. Louis. In less than two years, he took charge of codifying the laws and organizing a militia for the new U.S. possession. In mid-summer, 1809, he started back to Washington to settle a dispute. He never got there. He died in an isolated country inn in Tennessee, supposedly a suicide (he was subject to depression). But the evidence pointed to murder—his money was missing and his watch later turned up in New Orleans. The crime still remains shrouded in mystery. He was buried near the inn in a coffin made of rough-hewn oak planks. In 1848 the state of Tennessee erected a memorial over the gravesite; the broken column signifies that he was cut down in his prime.

Graceland Estate

MEMPHIS

This isn't just where Elvis lived, but where he died and where he now lives on, in memory at least. Whether you take just the mansion tour or the so-called platinum tour that includes house, automobile museum, and other sights, you'll be able to see the grassy gravesite, which is on the mansion grounds. The raised granite rectangular gravestones, with their bronze facing, of Elvis and his relatives—located around a circular pool with fountains—are, like everything at this star-spangled property, in tiptop shape. *3734 Elvis Presley Boulevard, Memphis. Tel. (901) 332-3322, (800) 238-2000. Hours: 10:00 A.M.–4:00 P.M. daily except Tuesday, October–February; 9:00 A.M.–5:00 P.M. Monday–Saturday, 10:00 A.M.–4:00 P.M. Sunday, March–September; closed Thanksgiving and Christmas; fee (call for details and reservations).*

ELVIS PRESLEY
1935–1977
There have been more sightings of Elvis over the years than of UFOs, proof that fans, a diehard lot (oops), refuse to believe what they don't want to believe. In life Elvis showed enormous talent, breaking through as a white boy who could sing black, melding country music and rhythm and blues in an appealing, Memphis-accented voice and a delivery that grooved right into the changing lifestyles of the late 1950s. His sweet face, bad-boy body language that teenagers loved and their parents

✝

ELVIS
AARON
PRESLEY

JANUARY 8, 1935
AUGUST 16, 1977

SON OF
VERNON ELVIS PRESLEY
AND
GLADYS LOVE PRESLEY
FATHER OF
LISA MARIE PRESLEY

HE WAS A PRECIOUS GIFT FROM GOD
WE CHERISHED AND LOVED DEARLY.

HE HAD A GOD-GIVEN TALENT THAT HE SHARED
WITH THE WORLD. AND WITHOUT A DOUBT,
HE BECAME MOST WIDELY ACCLAIMED;
CAPTURING THE HEARTS OF YOUNG AND OLD ALIKE.

HE WAS ADMIRED NOT ONLY AS AN ENTERTAINER,
BUT AS THE GREAT HUMANITARIAN THAT HE WAS;
FOR HIS GENEROSITY, AND HIS KIND FEELINGS
FOR HIS FELLOW MAN.

HE REVOLUTIONIZED THE FIELD OF MUSIC AND
RECEIVED ITS HIGHEST AWARDS.

HE BECAME A LIVING LEGEND IN HIS OWN TIME;
EARNING THE RESPECT AND LOVE OF MILLIONS.

GOD SAW THAT HE NEEDED SOME REST AND
CALLED HIM HOME TO BE WITH HIM.

WE MISS YOU, SON AND DADDY. I THANK GOD
THAT HE GAVE US YOU AS OUR SON.

BY VERNON PRESLEY

loathed, exuberant voice and show-manship spelled instant stardom and the birth of rock 'n' roll. His records were huge hits, his TV performances and special live shows instant sellouts. But this blue-collar former truck driv-er was sabotaged (not intentionally) by a manager who lacked discrimina-tion and committed him to a series of humdrum movies that misused his tal-ent. After the "king" returned from a two-year army stint, things changed. He divorced his wife, Priscilla Beaulieu, whom he had met in the army in Germany when she was four-teen. Binge eating, binge consumption of prescription drugs, and an entou-rage of women and hangers-on became a lifestyle. It was a sad spectacle, and then suddenly the "king" was dead, out on a sour note, from heart failure and cumulative drug abuse. But the Elvis industry that thrived when he was alive continues undiminished. His grave is a shrine; his legend is fed by a voluminous production of kitschy memorabilia. The king is dead, long live the king.

The Hermitage

NASHVILLE

This impressive property consists of Andrew Jackson's mansion, a museum, smokehouse, slave cabins, and Jackson's grave. The Greek temple-style monu-ment marking Jackson's and his wife's graves is in the garden, a few steps from the mansion. *Twelve miles east off I-40, exit 221A. Tel. (615) 889-2941. Open 9:00 A.M.–5:00 P.M. daily; closed Thanksgiving, Christmas, and last week of January; fee.*

ANDREW JACKSON
1767–1845

"Old Hickory," as Jackson was called, was proud of being a man of the peo-ple, though his enemies called him "King Andrew" for his expensive tastes while in the White House. The popular view of him was as the leader of backwoodsmen in battles against the Creek Indians, against the British in the War of 1812, and against the Seminoles in 1818. He rode these pop-ular victories to the presidency, which he won in the popular vote in 1824, but lost to John Quincy Adams in the House of Representatives. Four years later the same candidates competed, and this time Jackson won, carrying the South and West. Despite his slo-gan, "Let the people rule," he some-times opposed westward expansion, and he introduced the "spoils system" to government, which meant winners-take-all appointments to various cabi-net positions and federal offices. His frontiersman image is strangely out of synch with his splendid Greek Revival residence, as is his elaborate grave, which he actually had built for his beloved wife, **Rachel Donelson Robards Jackson** (1767–1828). She was much maligned while she lived and died just months before Jackson became president, but now she shares this sizable space with him. Alone together at last.

Forest Home Cemetery

MILWAUKEE

Comprising some 200 green acres in the city center, this garden parkland is fraught with history and even includes an impressive Hall of History, offering information about its many notable residents. Among them, along with governors, mayors, and the city's many beer barons at repose in their sepulchral mausoleums, are **Edward P. Allis** (1824–1889), founder of Allis Chalmers; **Mathilde Anneke** (1817–1884), founder and publisher of the first women's suffrage newspaper; **Victor Berger** (1860–1929), father of the Socialist Party in the United States; **William "Billy" Mitchell** (1879–1936), pilot, aviation expert, and advocate of air power; and **Fred Pabst** (1836–1904), president of what was once the world's largest brewery. *2405 West Forest Home Avenue, Milwaukee. Tel. (414) 645-2632. Grounds open from dawn to dusk daily. Office hours: 8:00 A.M.– 4:30 P.M. Monday–Friday, 8:30 A.M.–12:00 P.M. Saturday, closed Sunday; map, rest rooms, walking and driving tour booklets.*

LYNN FONTANNE
1887–1983
ALFRED LUNT
1892–1977

Lunt and Fontanne were a team, though they hated the term, throughout a long Broadway career. She, London born, student of actress Ellen Terry, and he, a local Wisconsin lad, trained as an architect, developed a sophisticated style that was as custom-made as the clothes in their stylish drawing room comedies. They were acting, with mild success, before they met and married in 1922, but as a couple their careers soared skyward, and for the next thirty years, they acted exclusively as a, yes, team and almost exclusively for the Theatre Guild.

Although the Lunts played in everything from *The Brothers Karamazov* to *Volpone* and *Pygmalion*, their forte was light comedy, like *The Guardsman* and Noël Coward's *Design for Living*. The list of plays they appeared in reads like a précis of theater history. A major triumph, late in their careers in 1957, was in the U.S. premiere of Friedrich Durrenmatt's somber study of vengeance, *The Visit*. Between engagements they came to their Wisconsin home for some restorative rest and relaxation. It seemed to work. They bounced back with exuberance to play after play, season after season, winning all kinds of awards and honorary degrees in the process. It's fitting that their final getaway is here.

Central and Southwest

Drawing an invisible line from southwest states Texas, Arizona, and New Mexico, straight north to Montana and North Dakota, west to Idaho, and east as far as Nebraska, Kansas, and Oklahoma provides the geographical boundaries of this chapter. Note how the demographics change in this region. With a few exceptions many occupants of the cemeteries are local figures, politicians, an unusual number of outlaws and colorful western types, and just a scattering of Civil War veterans. Graveyards for the most part are simpler, too, more straightforward with fewer flourishes.

Arizona

Christ Church of the Ascension

PARADISE VALLEY

In the brick-floored, dazzling white Memorial Garden of this imposing Episcopal church, the ashes of U. S. Senator Barry Goldwater reside, as do those of his wife **Peggy J. Goldwater** (1909–1985), in a marble wall vault with copper markers. The peaceful, fenced-in garden, with its tiled fountain and white flower boxes is to the left of the church itself. *4015 East Lincoln, Paradise Valley. Tel. (602) 840–8210. Grounds open all the time.*

BARRY MORRIS GOLDWATER
1 9 0 9 – 1 9 9 8

When this U.S. senator, the scion of a mercantile family in Phoenix, burst on the national political scene, he was perceived as a radical right-wing fanatic at the Republican Convention of 1964. His acceptance speech as the GOP's candidate for the presidency raised hackles with the lines: "I would remind you that extremism in the defense of liberty is no vice! And . . . that moderation in the pursuit of justice is no virtue!" Goldwater's quixotic campaign may have been doomed anyhow in the Lyndon B. Johnson landslide, but these lines helped seal the senator's fate. But a funny thing happened on Goldwater's march through life: Either the country became more conservative or he became more mellow. Probably a little of both. It is generally acknowledged that the Goldwater activists of that campaign helped reshape the Republican Party. By the time Goldwater retired from the U.S. Senate in 1987, after five terms and with the status of elder statesman, many of his party colleagues were far more extremist than he had ever been. As a westerner and outdoorsman, Goldwater was an environmentalist and supporter of women's rights. He wrote a number of books, including *Barry Goldwater and the Southwest* and *With No Apologies,* but the one that launched him nationally was *The Conscience of a Conservative* in 1960.

Boothill Cemetery

TOMBSTONE

As touristy as the town seems to many, there's something evocative of the Old West in sparse, cactus-dotted Boothill Cemetery, with its dirt path, stone mounds, and white metal signs on posts. Although there's nobody "rich or famous" tucked into this turf, there is considerable history and a reminder of the frontier justice and lawlessness that prevailed in the Arizona Territory in the late nineteenth century. Sun City it wasn't. For example, the large wooden pallet of a former Wells Fargo agent reads: "Here lies **Lester Moore.** Four slugs from a 44. No Les, no more." Here also is **Stinging Lizard**, "shot by Cherokee Hill," as well as **Seymore Dye**, "82, killed by Indians." Outlaw brothers **Frank McLaury** (1848–1881) and **Tom McLaury** (1853–1881) are also here, as is fellow bandit **Billy Clanton** (1862–1881). Note also **George Johnson,** who was "hanged by mistake 1882. He was right, we was wrong, but we strung him up and now he's gone." Also buried here, more respectably, was **Emmett Crook Nunnelley** (1884–1946), who helped restore Boothill and whose final request was to stay. Ironically, with his middle name he fits right in with the outlaws and cattle rustlers who call this sparse burial ground home. Boothill is now a registered National Monument. *U.S. Highway 82, Boothill, Tombstone. Tel. (520) 457-9344. Grounds open 7:30 A.M. to dark. Entrance free through Boothill Gift Shop. Map (fee).*

Colorado

Crown Hill Cemetery

DENVER

Established in 1907, Crown Hill is a place where local residents have been dying to get in ever since. Prominent among the enduring guests are members of the Coors family. A five-foot-high evergreen hedge surrounds the family plot, inside of which, in the shade of a cluster of conifers, is a twenty-five-foot-high obelisk. Note the floral designs at the base of this mini-Washington Monument, repeated on the sarcophogi of Adolph Coors and his wife, **Louise Coors** (1847–1941), as well as on the smaller stones of their children and other family members. *7777 West 29th Avenue, Denver. Tel. (303) 233-4611. Grounds open 8:00 A.M.–8:00 P.M. daily. Office hours: 8:00 A.M.–4:30 P.M. daily; map, rest room.*

ADOLPH COORS
1847–1929

Adolph Herrman Kohrs, aka Adolph Coors, is the classic rags-to-riches story. Coors had a sturdy apprenticeship in brewing in his native Germany, but during a period of unrest, he joined the massive German migration of the 1860s. As a twenty-one-year-old stowaway on a ship from Hamburg, he headed for the United States. Doing odd jobs, he worked his way west with a single dream: to brew the world's best beer. In Golden, Colorado, in the foothills of the Rocky Mountains (about 20 miles west of Denver)—after testing the pure spring waters—he knew he had found the spot. He hunkered down, borrowed money to convert an old tannery, and in 1873 opened Coors Brewery. The company grew slowly, but when Prohibition wiped out half the breweries in America, Coors stayed alive by producing a near-beer, malted milk, cement, and chemical products. Today, long after the founder's death, Coors ranks number three among U.S. brewers, with some two dozen varieties of beer, a far cry from the 3,500 barrels a year produced in the late 1870s—proof that old Adolph had the Coor-age of his convictions.

Buffalo Bill Memorial Museum and Grave

GOLDEN

Just thirty minutes from downtown Denver, above the winding curves of Lookout Mountain, lies William F. "Buffalo Bill" Cody. His homey, stone-encrusted grave, inside a cast-iron fence, overlooks the Rockies and Great Plains, just as he requested. A nearby museum displays extensive artifacts relating to his life and times. *987 ½ Lookout Mountain Road, Golden. Tel. (303) 526-0744. Grave site is open from dawn to dusk.*

WILLIAM "BUFFALO BILL" CODY
1846–1917

The Iowa-born, Kansas-bred Cody left home at age eleven, signing on as an ox-team driver westward bound. Wagon master, trapper, Pony Express rider, and, during the Civil War, Union ranger and scout, all formed his youthful resume. He earned his sobriquet "Buffalo Bill" as a buffalo hunter for a railroad; in one eight-month foray, he is said to have killed 4,280 buffalo. (And we wondered where they all went!) His bona fides as a soldier, Indian fighter, and man of courage were genuine, but he is just as well known for his later career as showman, self-promoter, and entrepreneur. For years he traveled America and Europe with his Wild West Show, an extravaganza of western hoakum that at times featured Sitting Bull and "Little Sureshot," Annie Oakley. In 1896 he founded the town of Cody, Wyoming. Eventually, bad investments and his extravagances ruined him. But by the time he was buried here on Lookout Mountain, he'd had one heck of a (horseback) ride.

Ketchum Cemetery

KETCHUM

This old burial ground, which shelters some residents from the 1800s, is located just north of town on five acres. The most famous guest is Ernest Hemingway, buried here along with his fourth and last wife, **Mary Hemingway** (1908–1961), a journalist who shot herself as her husband had, and his granddaughter

Margaux Hemingway (1954–1996), actress and also a suicide. *U.S. Highway 75, Ketchum. Tel. (208) 726-9201. Grounds open all the time. Office hours: erratic, best to call ahead, rest room.*

ERNEST HEMINGWAY
1899–1961

How to explain the fact that in a comfortable middle-class Oak Park, Illinois, family, a father, three children, and, years later, a granddaughter, all committed suicide? "Something in the genes" is the glib psychobabble answer. Recent research indicates that Grace Hemingway, Ernest's mother, was the incubus: a dominating, ego-hungry woman with unfulfilled artistic ambitions. But all this after-the-fact, blame-the-mom theorizing can't negate the fact that her son Ernest was a highly successful, world-renowned author, whose work is still read and widely admired. He was an early practitioner, in fact the prototype, of clean, sparse, understated, minimalist prose. This is evident in the short stories about his boyhood summers in upper Michigan and in his best novels, *A Farewell to Arms, The Sun Also Rises, For Whom the Bell Tolls,* and, written in his later years, *The Old Man and the Sea.* His sharp prose also sparkles in *Death in the Afternoon,* his classic primer on bullfighting. However, Hemingway's life was anything but crisp and simple. He seemed to revel in a macho image: drinking, fighting, and womanizing as an expatriate in Paris in the 1920s; fishing in Cuba; hunting in Idaho. In 1953 he won the Pulitzer Prize in fiction and the following year was awarded the Nobel Prize in literature. But in the end he faced the loneliness of a cabin in Ketchum, despair, the sense that his muse had deserted him, and a shotgun.

Kansas

Eisenhower Center

ABILENE

Situated on twenty-one acres, the Eisenhower Center encompasses his family home (where he grew up), a museum, library, and visitors center. The thirty-fourth U.S. president rests in peace in the floor of a small chapel (see opposite), the Place of Meditation, alongside his wife, **Mamie Doud Eisenhower** (1896–1979), and their four-year-old son, **Doud Dwight Eisenhower** (1917–1921). Ike's parents, **David J. Eisenhower** (1863–1942) and **Ida Stover Eisenhower** (1862–1946), can

be found elsewhere in Abilene. *200 Southeast 4th Street, Abilene. Tel. (785) 263-4751 or (877) RING-IKE. Hours: 9:00 A.M.–4:45 P.M. daily mid-August to Memorial Day; 8:00 A.M.–5:45 P.M. daily after Memorial Day to mid-August. Fee for museum, chapel free, rest rooms.*

DWIGHT D. EISENHOWER
1890–1969

Unlikely as it seems, the road from a little farmhouse in Kansas lead to the White House for Dwight David "Ike" Eisenhower. The Texas-born, Kansas-bred Ike—as he was universally known—was the only career military man in the twentieth century to become president of the United States. Using his West Point education, Ike built a distinguished army career, culminating in his role as a five-star general and supreme Allied commander in Europe during World War II, in charge of the invasion of Normandy, June 6, 1944. A year later, by then a full general, he accepted the surrender of the German army at Rheims, France. Later his war memoirs, *Crusade in Europe,* became an instant best-seller. Five years as president of Columbia University followed, broken by a brief stint as commander of NATO forces. Besieged to run for office by both parties, Ike resigned from the army and in 1952 won the Republican nomination for president. His two terms were marked by moderation, and he retired as popular as when he arrived. His later years were spent golfing and at his Gettysburg, Pennsylvania, farm and giving advice to his three successors in office, Kennedy, Johnson, and Nixon.

Little Bighorn Battlefield National Monument

HARDIN

This memorial (located within the Crow Indian Reservation in southeastern Montana) is both the Custer National Cemetery and the battlefield where in 1876 Colonel George A. Custer and some 263 soldiers of the seventh Cavalry were vastly outnumbered and mowed down by a much larger number of Plains Indians (Lakota and Cheyenne), who lost only about one hundred warriors. Bodies of the cavalrymen were gathered and buried in a mass grave nearby, marked by a large granite obelisk. Note especially the grave of Major Marcus A. Reno, Custer's second-in-command (see the following). Custer is buried at West Point, New York. (See New York chapter.) *Entrance 1 mile east of I-90 on U.S. Highway 212, Hardin. Tel. (406) 638-2621. Hours: 8:00 A.M.–4:30 P.M. winter, 8:00 A.M.–6:00 P.M. spring and fall, 8:00 A.M.–9:00 P.M. summer; guided tours, fee (per vehicle).*

MAJOR MARCUS A. RENO
1834–1889

One of the casualties of this infamous battle was the career of Custer's second-in-command. Reno, born in Carrollton, Illinois, was admitted to West Point at age seventeen, but showed certain character traits that would damage him later in life: argumentiveness and indifference to regulations and discipline. Suspended and reinstated twice, Reno graduated in 1857. In the Civil War he was viewed as a brave and competent officer earning quick promotions for "gallant and meritorious service." Later, serving in Spartanburg, South Carolina, he and his troops were commended for their handling of the area's Ku Klux Klan. While in South Carolina, his wife died and he was refused permission to attend her funeral and settle her affairs. This seemed to alter his personality. He was assigned to George Armstrong Custer's Seventh cavalry. A loner, where Custer was a popular war hero, Reno chafed under Custer's command and proved quarrelsome and a drinker. During Custer's absence Reno undertook a scouting expedition aimed at discovering what hostile Indian tribes were up to. Exceeding orders, he was rebuked by Custer. Their relationship worsened. After the battle known as Custer's Last Stand, in which the popular commander was killed, a scapegoat was needed and Reno, who organized the army's retreat, more than filled the bill. He was accused of cowardice and disobedience at Little Big Horn. In 1879, after two years of accusations and innuendo, Reno was exonerated by a Court of Inquiry. That should have ended his troubles, but his self-destructiveness continued. Within months he faced another court-martial, this time for fighting with a junior officer and spying on another officer's daughter. For these offenses he was dismissed from the army in 1880. For the next nine years he sought reinstatement, but died of pneumonia after surgery for mouth cancer. In 1967, thanks to the efforts of a descendant, Reno was finally—rather late in the day—given an honorable discharge. That's the after life for you.

Dowd Chapel

BOYS AND GIRLS TOWN

The chapel where Father Flanagan is buried is part of what is now a large facility that provides services to some 17,000 troubled youths a year. *138th Street and West Dodge Road, Boys and Girls Town. Tel. (402) 498-1140. Open daily, no fee.*

EDWARD JOSEPH FLANAGAN
1886–1948

Merely the ghost of a name today, Father Edward Flanagan was an icon in the 1930s, immortalized on the screen by Spencer Tracy in the movie *Boys Town,* for which Tracy won an Oscar for best actor. The actual town, just outside Omaha, was founded by this Irish priest who came to the United States as a youth in 1904. He started Boys Town in 1921 as a home for rehabilitating wayward boys. By 1936 the home had expanded into an official town with a boy mayor and a

local government. Later he opened Girls Town, and eventually the towns were joined as Boys and Girls Town. Today this is a thriving community of farm; health care facility; and diagnostic, treatment, and research institute for children, with mini–Boys Town campuses around the country, pretty much governed by the youths themselves. Father Flanagan's mantra, "There's no such thing as a bad boy," might seem a bit optimistic in the current era of horrendous crimes committed by the very young, but for generations such optimism seemed to work.

New Mexico

Old Fort Sumner Cemetery

FORT SUMNER

Once a military burial ground, Old Fort Sumner Cemetery was abandoned in 1867, and the soldiers were moved and reinterred in Santa Fe. Left in peace on the four-acre plot are civilians. The most visited grave on the property—that of Billy the Kid—is easy to spot: It is the size and shape of a doll's house with peaked roof and is securely locked up (as rarely happened in life) inside a massive cagelike enclosure with padlocks and chains. The Kid's small footstone is wedged in concrete secured by steel straps. Such security measures aren't paranoia: The footstone was stolen three times, and the headstone chipped at (for souvenirs) endlessly. Inside the cage with the Kid are two of his fellow outlaws, **Charlie Bowdre** (–1880) and **Tom O'Folliard** (–1880). A large white stone monument with the word *pals* at the top memorializes the friendship of the three outlaws. *Fort Sumner. Grounds open all the time.*

WILLIAM "BILLY THE KID" BONNEY
1859–1881

Actually, this most famous of all the outlaws who raised hell in the Old West wasn't William Bonney at all. That was as much an alias as "Billy the Kid." His real name was Henry McCarty and his origins were the New York City slums, not the Wild Wild West. His widowed Irish mother went west after the Civil War and took young Billy with her, first to Indiana, then Kansas, and finally New Mexico. where she died when he was just sixteen years old. He began his short life of crime early, at age fifteen, pilfering, then graduated to stealing horses, rustling cattle, chases, and shoot-outs. Though he supposedly killed twenty-one (one for each year of his life), only four deaths can be documented. He finally met his at the hands of a sheriff named Pat Garrett, who also killed Billy's pals, Bowdre and O'Folliard, months earlier. Why this particular outlaw and cattle rustler captured the American imagination is difficult to understand—but contemporary newspaper accounts of his doings helped to make his name. It may have been his young age and the fact that when he wasn't killing folks he was good-natured enough. Some kid. At least now he's permanently lying low. **The Billy the Kid Museum** (1601 East Sumner Avenue; 505–355–2380) is 5½ miles from the cemetery and contains his artifacts, along with others of the Old West and the old fort.

Kit Carson Park and Cemetery

T A O S

In 1952 the state of New Mexico bought this minuscule, tree-shaded cemetery and nineteen extra acres to turn the entire property into Kit Carson Park and Cemetery. Many of the graves have fascinating markers with a detailed resume of the occupant's life, which often dovetailed with town history. The sum total of all the markers provides a précis of Taos in the late nineteenth century. For instance, there is **Maria Ignacia Bent**, (1815–1882), Carson's sister-in-law and wife of Charles Bent, New Mexico's first territorial governor. When Charles was killed in the 1847 Taos Rebellion, Maria escaped by tunneling out of the governor's grounds through an adobe wall. There's also **Peter Joseph De Trevis** (1814–1862), a Kit Carson friend who helped put down the 1847 Indian rebellion. **Captain Smith H. Simpson** (1832–1916), another Carson friend, helped replace the U.S. flag in Taos Plaza after invading Confederates had removed it. There is also a Soldiers' Memorial dedicated to those who quelled the Indian rebellions in Taos in 1847 and 1854. *211 Paseo del Norte, Taos. Tel. (505) 758–8234. Grounds open all the time, but closed to vehicles after 8:00 P.M. Rest rooms.*

CHRISTOPHER "KIT" CARSON
1 8 0 9 – 1 8 6 8

Many accomplishments of this legendary Indian fighter, scout, trapper, soldier, and explorer are delineated on his upright stone. His Mexican American wife, **Maria Josefa Jaramillo Carson** (1828–1868), is buried here as well. Their graves are enclosed behind a small cast-iron fence, and to their right also enclosed are **Kit Carson II** (1858–1929) and daughter-in-law **Lupie R. Carson** (1870–1957). Born in Kentucky to a family whose offspring eventually numbered fifteen, Carson grew up in a frontier area of Missouri where Indian raids were common-

place. Apprenticed to a saddlemaker, he ran away at age sixteen to Santa Fe, worked as a teamster, then became a trapper, and eventually a guide for Colonel John C. Fremont. At the outbreak of the Civil War, Carson helped organize the First New Mexican Volunteer Infantry and took part in two successful campaigns against the Apaches and Navajos. Modest, brave, and intelligent, Carson epitomized the best of a breed of legendary mountain men. He was married three times, twice to Indians, finally to a Hispanic woman. Although he could sign his name, he never adequately learned to read. With his lifestyle, he never needed to. The restored **Kit Carson Home and Museum** (1825 vintage) is nearby (Route 64; 505–758–4741) and has Carson mementos and Indian artifacts.

MABEL DODGE LUHAN
1879–1962

A small marble upright stone is a bare reminder of this wealthy woman, patron of Taos's artistic life. Her largesse helped put Taos on the cultural map. She is best known outside Taos as a sponsor and ardent supporter (shall we say sycophant?) of D. H. Lawrence. A free spirit in a post-Victorian world, she moved from Buffalo, New York, to Florence, Italy, Greenwich Village (where she had an affair with author John Reed), and finally Taos. All along the way she lived to the hilt the bohemian life as she imagined it, sometimes having a bevy of lovers at one time. In Greenwich Village she held weekly salons, frequented by New York's glitterati—artists, writers and those attracted to them—and organized and sponsored numerous cultural events. She lured Lawrence and his wife to Taos with the promise of a house where he could work. She also surrounded herself with other artists and writers, the likes of Georgia O'Keeffe, Thornton Wilder, and Robinson Jeffers. In Taos she married for the fourth and last time. Her final soulmate was Tony Lujan, a Taos Pueblo Indian, whose face she claimed had appeared in her dreams, but whose name she modified with an "h" instead of the traditional "j."

ARTHUR ROCKFORD MANBY
1859–1929

Who? Rich, infamous, and interesting, Manby is one of those serendipitous discoveries one finds on a graveyard crawl. Manby is actually in the park, just outside the cemetery proper. Fittingly so. No hallowed ground for this black sheep of an aristocratic English family, who arrived in New Mexico in the roaring 1880s. Well educated in architecture, mineralogy, and art, he made a fortune selling bogus quit-claims and numerous property deed manipulations. He once owned the land (and planted its trees) that he and the other graveyard occupants now inhabit. Manby was implicated in the shooting death of a neighbor but was acquitted. The last twenty years of his life he accumulated enemies faster even than land because of his unscrupulous wheeling and dealing. In 1929 he was found decapitated in his home. The murder was never solved. Too many suspects perhaps because of his swindling? Only he can tell—but he's not talking.

JOSE ANTONIO MARTINEZ
1798–1867

Another notorious resident of this tiny graveyard, Martinez was a priest and curate of Taos (1793–1867). The son of Severino Martinez, prominent local land owner, he was controversial and rebellious. He helped organize the New Mexico Territory, but in 1856 he was defrocked and excommunicated for his political activism and disregard of higher church authority. (Note: The bishop who excommunicated him was John Lamy, inspiration for the character Willa Cather created in her novel *Death Comes for the Archbishop.*) Martinez later started the Schismatic Church. At the **Martinez Hacienda** (708 Ranchitos Road; 505–758–1000), with its excellent depiction of upscale early New Mexican life, a placard says that Padre Martinez "retired from the pastorate due to the stress of his time." The family spin on history.

Kiowa Ranch

TAOS

The final home of the charismatic English author David Herbert Lawrence and his German-born wife, **Frieda von Richthofen Weekley**, Kiowa Ranch was a gift to the Lawrences from Mabel Dodge Luhan, but it now belongs to the University of New Mexico. The modest homesteader log cabin where the Lawrences lived was also the first place the painter Georgia O'Keeffe stayed when she came to New Mexico in 1929. She called the tree she painted, which was near the cabin, the "Lawrence tree." The twenty-one cabins on the property have eighty rooms, now used for recreation by university personnel. *Some 15 miles north of Taos on Route 522, then 5 miles east on a washboard-bumpy dirt road. Tel. (505) 776-2245. Open year-round in daytime, but difficult to reach in bad weather.*

D. H. LAWRENCE
1 8 8 5 – 1 9 3 0

Author of numerous novels, short stories, essays, poetry, and travel books, David Herbert Lawrence was most acclaimed for his sensuous novels, especially *The Rainbow, Women in Love,* and *Sons and Lovers.* The book that caused a monumental scandal and was banned in England and the United States was the sexually explicit *Lady Chatterly's Lover.* Not only was the language shocking for the time, but the story depicted a torrid affair, intimately described, between a lady and a gameskeeper, a no-no in class-conscious Britain. Lawrence was an outspoken advocate of more open sensuality, but some critics speculated he may have been impotent ("methinks he doth protest too much," some implied). Lawrence and his wife, Frieda, who had left her first husband and three young children to elope with Lawrence, came to New Mexico at the invitation of Mabel Lodge Luhan, an admirer of Lawrence's work. Lawrence loved the New Mexico mountains and was very productive at Kiowa, though he only spent eleven months here, in 1923, 1924 and 1925. Ever restless, he and Frieda then traveled in Europe, and he died of tuberculosis in Italy. The Lawrence grave, inside a chapel-like shrine, is 100 yards uphill along a long concrete walkway lined with ponderosa pine trees. At the base of the walk are roses, rabbitbrush, and Indian paintbrush. A legal paper with the seal of the U.S. consul in Marseilles, is on a wall in the shrine, stating, "I hereby certify that the box bearing the seal of this consulate and that of the Police Commissioner of Marseilles contains an urn which con-

tains only the remains after cremation of David Herbert Lawrence, which are being taken to the U.S. on board the S.S. *Conte di Savoia.* 25 March 1935." The casket, with the initials D.H.L., green leaves, and intertwined sunflowers painted on top, is inside the shrine, which is a fantasy of yellow interior walls, blue roof, and silver-painted exposed wood beams. Despite their often turbulent relationship, **Frieda** (1899–1956) created this dramatic pilgrimage site in 1934. By then she had taken a third husband, Angelo Ravagli. Her own white marble headstone, to the left of Lawrence's shrine, has her photograph in back, inscribed, "In memory of 25 years of incomparable companionship—Angie." It's too late to unscramble it all, but rest in peace David, Frieda, Mabel, Angie, and whomever.

Holy Cross Cemetery

FARGO

On thirty flat-as-a-pancake acres, this Catholic cemetery plays landlord to some notable year-round guests, who are sheltered under a variety of evergreens, apple, spruce, and maple trees. The earliest stone dates back to 1860, but more recent arrivals are **Ronald Davies** (1904–1996), the judge who ordered the integration of Central High School in Little Rock, Arkansas, in 1957; **Ken Hunt** (1934–1997), major league outfielder with the New York Yankees, Los Angeles Dodgers, and Washington Senators; and **Stan Kostka** (1912–1997), member of 1934 National Champion Minnesota Gophers football team. Although there is no map available, those seeking the most prominent resident, Roger Maris, will find it is no great undertaking. He is in block 15, easily identified by a large polished black granite, diamond-shape (as in baseball) headstone, with the inscription "61 and 61," signifying his record-breaking number of home runs and the year in which he hit them. *1502 32nd Avenue North, Fargo. Tel. (701) 237-6671. Grounds open all the time.*

ROGER MARIS
1934–1997

Maybe being born in the cold of Hibbing, Minnesota, and growing up in Fargo, North Dakota, gave Maris the stoicism that characterized his Major League Baseball career. Despite his good statistics and the Most Valuable Player (MVP) award he won in his first season as a New York Yankee (after a season as a Cleveland Indian and another as a Kansas City Athletic), he was never the fan favorite that Mickey Mantle, his more flamboyant teammate, was. So in 1961, when the two slugged their way toward Babe Ruth's record of sixty home runs in a single season, it was Mantle the fans were rooting for to break it. When the season ended and Maris had hit sixty-one homers and Mantle fifty-four, Mantle fans were outraged. To make matters worse for the ever-placid Maris, his grand achievement was, ah, spooked by the asterisk that baseball commissioner Ford Frick unfairly (in this fan's view) placed beside it in the record books, reminding fans that it took Maris 162 games to beat Ruth's record, because the baseball season's length had changed from the Ruth era's 154-game season. For his achievement Maris received a second MVP, but five years later he was traded to the St. Louis Cardinals, where he played for two years before retiring at age thirty-four.

Still, his record lasted thirty-eight years, until it was broken in 1999 by Mark McGwire—61 in '61, a number to be proud of.

Oklahoma

Will Rogers Museum

CLAREMORE

Located on twenty acres once owned by Rogers in the town where he was born (and to which he'd hoped to retire), the museum contains mementos of the cowboy-humorist's life, as well as films and tapes of him at work—a wonderful way for people to see and understand what all the fuss over him was about. At the end of a very pretty sunken garden (designed by his wife), with a stone wall above which rides a bronze Will on his bronze horse Soapsuds, is a gigantic square stone tomb with "Rogers" etched on its side and in the base the place and dates of Rogers's birth and death. With him in the underlying mausoleum, now as in life, is his wife, Betty, along with son, Fred, daughter, Mary, and daughter-in-law, Astria. *1720 West Will Rogers Boulevard, Claremore. Tel. (800) 324–WILL. Hours: 8:00 A.M.–5:00 P.M. daily, donation.*

WILL ROGERS

1879–1935

In the early 1930s there was no public figure, other than President Roosevelt, more popular or revered than the humorist born William Penn Adair Rogers. His was not a long life, but it was a fun one. Although he began his career as a cowboy in the Texas Panhandle, learning to ride well and do rope tricks with a lasso, he soon transfered these talents to show business, where his slow southwestern drawl made audiences laugh. He was quick to build on that with wry comments and homespun humor. Before long he was on the Broadway stage in musicals (such as the *Ziegfeld Follies*), then in the movies (*State Fair, A Connecticut Yankee, David Harum, Steamboat 'Round the Bend,* among others) and writing a newspaper column. His line in the *Follies,* "All I know is what I read in the papers," became a mantra he used in his later lectures and radio performances. Rogers's "aw shucks," cowboy image was only half the story. He was, as he claimed, half-Indian, son of a prosperous Irish-Cherokee Oklahoma rancher and Indian mother. (A famous Rogers line was, "My ancestors didn't come over on the *Mayflower*—they met the boat.") Will had a great down-home sense of humor, philosophical bent, and genuine naturalness that made him a friend of both regular folks and several U.S. presidents. He often said, "I never met a man I didn't like." He was a man for his season, with an upbeat personality well suited to the Depression era, which was the time of the common man. Eventually, Rogers and his family moved to southern California. An ardent flier (he flew to Europe, South America, and Asia, unusual for the late 1920s and early 1930s), he helped promote commercial aviation. He was en route to the Far East with his friend and fellow Oklahoman, Wiley Post, when their monoplane crashed off Point Barrow, Alaska, killing them both. **The Will Rogers Birthplace and Dog Iron Ranch,** about 12 miles northwest (Oklahoma Highway 88 at Oologah; 800–324–WILL), are open to the public, with many family artifacts.

South Dakota

Mount Moriah Cemetery

DEADWOOD

On a dark hillside, below the pinnacles of White Rocks, mildly spooky from the shade of a wealth of trees, Mount Moriah is a venerable old burial ground dating from around 1877, but no longer in use. It started as a Masonic cemetery but is now run by the city of Deadwood. Offering a précis of the town and the Black Hills, the grounds include a Chinese section, where immigrant railroad workers were buried; a surprising number of children's graves (over 350, many of whom died from scarlet fever and diphtheria epidemics of 1878–1880); and a potter's field with scores of unknown paupers. What really gives Mount Moriah its personality are the final "digs" of some of the Old West's most colorful characters and two of its most famous (see the following). In addition to Calamity Jane and Wild Bill Hickok, there are **Seth Bullock** (1849–1919), Deadwood's first sheriff, friend of Teddy Roosevelt, and organizer of his Rough Riders; **Blanche Colman** (1884–1978), last of the original Jewish pioneers to Deadwood and the first woman admitted to the South Dakota bar; **"Potato Creek Johnny" Perrett** (1866–1943), a Welsh prospector during Deadwood's gold rush days; and **Henry Weston "Preacher" Smith** (1827–1876), a minister killed by Indians. *Deadwood. Tel. (605) 578-2082 (City Hall). Grounds open from dawn to dusk year-round. Bus tours available in summer from downtown (fee).*

MARTHA "CALAMITY JANE" CANNARY BURKE
1852–1903

Having grown up with a romanticized image of Calamity Jane, based on Jean Arthur's portrayal in the movie *The Plainsman,* I was shocked to see a picture of the real (plain) Jane Burke and learn that the truth bore scant relation to the movie. (So what else is new?) The real Jane was born in Princeton, Missouri; orphaned early; grew up roaming the streets of mining towns in the West; and married a man named Clinton Burke, who deserted her in short order. She was addicted to men's clothing and, according to hyperbolic local lore, had as many as twelve husbands. Yes, she did know "Wild Bill" Hickok, but whether theirs was a love affair no one knows for certain. And yes, she was a sureshot. Whether she was a Pony Express rider and scout for General Custer, which she claimed, are matters of pure speculation. Like many western legends, she was a famous yarn-spinner, especially about herself. Two things are for real: She did tour in Wild West shows and, yes, she did ask to be buried next to "Wild Bill." That seemed to have been her final death wish. And so there she is, no longer spinning, both their gray granite markers and graves securely embedded in field stones, enclosed by a sturdy metal fence.

JAMES BUTLER "WILD BILL" HICKOK
1837–1876

The boy James Butler Hickok, son of strict Baptist farmers in Illinois, bore scant resemblance to the man he later became. Always fascinated with guns and the Wild West, he headed for the frontier when he turned eighteen and soon had a job as a stagecoach driver on the Santa Fe and Oregon Trails. Handsome and gutsy (think Gary Cooper), with a quick temper and quick draw, he soon was dubbed "Wild Bill" and became the stuff of which western legends are made. Though not all of his "achievements" could survive close scrutiny—he was known for stretching the truth, as when he claimed he shot fifty Confederate soldiers with fifty bullets—he was unquestionably bold and brave and a sharpshooter who could shoot equally well with either hand. During the Civil War he worked as a Union scout, known for some derring-do behind enemy lines. A U.S. marshal, then professional gambler, heavy drinker, and performer in Buffalo Bill's Wild West Show, Hickok was on a downward spiral when he was shot in the back of the head, while playing poker at Sweeney's Silver Dollar Saloon in Deadwood. His killer was Jack "Crooked Nose" McCall, who was first acquitted by a stacked jury, later retried, convicted, and hanged. In the category of trivia: The hand Hickok held when he was killed supposedly contained a pair of black aces, a pair of black eights, and a nine of diamonds, which ever after became known as a "dead man's hand."

Sitting Bull Monument

MOBRIDGE

Located about 5 miles southwest of town, the Sitting Bull Monument pays homage to one of the great Native American warriors, whose bones lie under the base. The bust was the work of sculptor Korczak Ziolkowski. The hillside site, his final resting place, offers splendid views of the Missouri River and prairie landscape. *Off U.S. Highway 12, Mobridge.*

SITTING BULL
CA. 1834–1890

Erase all the movie caricatures of this great Native American chief and the image of him late in life as part of Buffalo Bill's Wild West Show. Think instead of the great warrior that he was earlier in life: the leader who united all the Lakota Indian tribes, fought bravely and resolutely against U.S. soldiers and their encroachment on Indian lands, and remained a spiritual leader of his people throughout his life. Tatanka-Iyotake—his aptly suited tribal name, which depicted a buffalo sitting on its haunches, as intractable as he proved to be—was determined to defend Lakota lands. When gold was discovered in the Black Hills, the U.S. government first tried to buy the land, then set aside the

treaty that had given the land to the Indians. Battles followed, the biggest of which was at Little Big Horn, where Crazy Horse and his forces roundly defeated Custer's men. This prompted an onslaught by U.S. cavalry, pursuing and conquering tribe after tribe. Only Sitting Bull refused to surrender, leading his forces across the Canadian border to safety. But four years later, near-starvation forced him to return. He was, in his words, "the last man of my tribe to surrender my rifle." That was in 1881, and the remaining years were not kind to this proud warrior. After a brief stint with Buffalo Bill, he retired to a cabin on the Grand River in Standing Rock, near the place where he was born. Fearful that he would lend his prestige to the rebellious Ghost Dance movement, which had sprung up elsewhere, a band of reservation policemen dragged him from his cabin. In the ensuing gunfight between the police and his supporters, Sitting Bull died, shot by a tribal policeman, a fellow Lakota—one more of life's ironies.

Texas

Texas State Cemetery

AUSTIN

This eighteen-acre state burial ground is located 3.4 miles east of downtown. Along with its curvaceous hillside, memorial pond with water lilies, interpretive paths, fountains, fields of flowers, obelisks, monuments, and imposing granite entrance, it has a plaza bordered by huge stone markers or tablets delineating events and people important in Texas history. The cemetery is fraught with colorful Texas characters, dating back to its beginnings in 1851. The, uh, spirited cast includes **John B. Connally** (1917–1993), governor of Texas, wounded at the time of the John F. Kennedy assassination, later a presidential candidate; **Maureen Connolly** (1934–1969), the first woman to win a tennis Grand Slam (1953); **William Cooke** (1808–1847), secretary of war in the Republic of Texas; **Jacob de Cordova** (1808–1868), legislator and land developer, who laid out the Waco town plan in 1848; **James Frank Dobie** (1888–1964), professor, author of books on Texas folklore, awarded Medal of Freedom by President Lyndon Johnson; **Miriam "Ma" Ferguson** (1875–1961) and **James "Pa" Ferguson** (1871–1944), larger-than-life governors of Texas; **John Hughes** (1855–1947), Texas Ranger captain with the longest service record, from 1887 to 1915; **Cadwell Raines** (1839–1906), judge, author, publisher of the first bibliography of Texas; **James Sylvester** (1807–1882), one of the captors of General Santa Ana at the Battle of San Jacinto; **Walter Prescott Webb** (1888–1963), author, historian, professor of history at University of Texas for forty years; and **Ralph Yarborough** (1903–1996), lawyer, politician, and the only Southern U.S. senator to vote for the Civil Rights Act of 1964. One of the most unusual mausoleums is a Gothic "church" of metal—the work of Elizabet Ney, an Austin sculptor. Through its white grillwork you can see the sarcophagus and marble statue of the occupant, Confederate general **Albert Sidney Johnston** (1803–1862). He was felled by Union forces at Shiloh and is one of many Confederate soldiers and veterans resting here. *909 Navasota Street, Austin. Tel. (512) 463-0605. Web site: www.cemetery.state.tx.us. Grounds open 8:00 A.M.–5:00 P.M. daily. Office hours: 8:00 A.M.–5:00 P.M. Monday–Friday; map and biographic pamphlet, rest rooms, tours available.*

BARBARA JORDAN
1936–1996

This imposing woman, member of the U.S. House of Representatives, first came to national prominence during the 1974 Watergate hearings of the House Judiciary Committee. Her majestic presence and deep, mellifluous voice and perfect diction commanded attention. Her fellow Houstonians knew her long before that. Born in an inner-city Houston ghetto, the daughter of a minister and warehouse clerk, she proved herself an apt student and earned a B.A. degree (magna cum laude) at Texas Southern University and a law degree at Boston University. Later she scored a number of "firsts": the first African American woman elected to the Texas Senate, the first ever chosen as president pro tempore, and then the first African American woman elected to the U.S. House of Represetatives from the South. In 1976 she was chosen for her brilliant oratory as keynote speaker at the Democratic National Convention. Feminists pro-

moted her as a vice presidential candidate, but she wouldn't pursue the nomination, saying, "It's not my turn. When it's my turn, you'll know it." The word was that she'd have liked to be Jimmy Carter's attorney general, but he had other ideas. So she turned to teaching at the Lyndon B. Johnson School of Public Affairs at the University of Texas in Austin. Her turn never came for the vice presidency: she died of cancer at age fifty-nine.

Hillcrest Memorial Park

D A L L A S

On prime Dallas real estate, distinguished by shade trees, a pond in which koi fish shuttle to and fro, stately mausoleums, and angel statuary, Hillcrest Memorial Park caters to an A-list of permanent residents. Their numbers include **E. Paul Crume** (1912–1975), popular columnist in the *Dallas Morning News;* **Greer Garson** (1904–1996), English movie star, winner of best actress Oscar for *Mrs. Miniver* in 1942; **Sarah Tilghman Hughes** (1896–1985), congresswoman and district judge who swore in Lyndon B. Johnson as president after J. F. Kennedy's assassination; **Tom Landry** (1924–2000), celebrated coach of the Dallas Cowboys for twenty-nine years, known as a defensive genius with thirteen division titles, five Super Bowls; **Clint Murchison** (1923–1987), first owner of the Dallas Cowboys; **Field Scovell** (1907–1992), public relations expert, known as Mr. Cotton Bowl for his decades of work promoting this event; and **John Tower** (1925–1991), U.S. senator, and his daughter, **Marian** (1955–1991). *7405 Northwest Highway, Dallas. Tel. (214) 363-5401. Grounds and office open 8:00 A.M.–5:00 P.M. daily; map, rest rooms.*

H. L. HUNT
1 8 8 9 – 1 9 7 4

With a fancy name like Haroldson Lafayette Hunt, Jr., it is no wonder that such a rough-and-tough hombre as oil wildcatter Hunt would want to be called by his initials only. Hunt was born of Southern parents (his father a Confederate veteran and farmer) near Vandalia, Illinois. Imbued with his father's Darwinian view of life, Hunt was a self-made man, working a bunch of jobs: shepherd, mule-team driver, crop picker, concrete pourer, lumberjack, and professional gambler among them, before he discovered oil. Having gone to Arkansas to farm cotton, he began dabbling in oil, drilling in the nearby boomtown of El Dorado, Texas. From 1911 to 1942, when he was dubbed the richest man in the world, Hunt's life was oil (and gambling to find more oil). His game was to rush to the source of a strike, buy up surrounding leases, and offer to buy the wells of the man who had made the strike, but who often lacked capital to develop the well. During the Depression the oil boom was in danger of becoming a bust, with overproduction a major threat. So Hunt and other oil men persuaded the federal government to limit oil production and the number of barrels that could be taken from the ground. Note the irony that such a devout political reactionary as Hunt, who railed vociferously against government (as well as Catholics, Jews, Democrats, the United Nations, and the State Department), wouldn't hesitate to use it when it could help him. One other anomaly in this outsized Texan's life: He was a bigamist, with a family in El Dorado and another in Shreveport, Louisiana. By the time he died, he had acquired a mistress and a third family. You can imagine the, ah, spirited fun when all three families contested his will, not quite forever and a day, but throughout the 1970s. You'd never know all this turmoil now from his peaceful, cross-imbued headstone and flowery footstone, in which his entire name is etched.

MICKEY MANTLE
1 9 3 1 – 1 9 9 5

By the time "the Mick's" baseball career was winding down, he was thirty-three going on seventeen emotionally, but thirty-three going on seventy physically. He viewed himself as born to play baseball (he was mightily encouraged in this by his miner father who didn't want Mickey to spend his life in the Oklahoma mines). His eighteen years with the New York Yankees were golden ones for him and the team, which played in twelve World Series and won seven of them during that time. Mantle himself amassed an amazing record, winning the Triple Crown (for best batting average, most home runs, and most runs-batted-in) two years in a row. In the first year in which he was eligible, he was voted into the Hall of Fame. But in the process of his career, he suffered many injuries and lived a fast, reckless, alcohol-driven life. Later he blamed his careless lifestyle on the fact that Mantle males died young (his father died at forty-one from Hodgkin's disease), saying, "If I had known I would live past forty, I'd have taken care of myself." Well, maybe. Yankee fans were shocked when Mantle and fellow Hall of Famer Willie Mays were banned from baseball by Commissioner Bowie Kuhn for doing public relations for an Atlantic City gambling casino. Both were later reinstated. Beloved as he was by baseball fans, Mantle caused some more controversy in 1995, when he was able to get a liver transplant, leapfrogging over ordinary people ahead of him in line. But it was too late. All those years of road-trip happy hours finally took their toll. His cancer had spread. His charmed all-star life was over.

The Whitehead Museum

DEL RIO

Behind a small fence in back of the replica of the Jersey Lily Saloon lies the headstone of one of the Old West's most famous characters, Judge Roy Bean, and that of his son, Sam. Both the saloon and graves are part of the Whitehead Memorial Museum property, which also includes a hacienda, chapel, doctor's office, barn, and cabins. Bean was moved here from a nearby cemetery because too many visitors to his grave had played havoc with the grounds. *1308 South Main Street, Del Rio. Tel. (830) 774-7568. Hours: 9:00 A.M.-4:30 P.M. Tuesday-Saturday, 1:00 P.M.-5:00 P.M. Sunday, closed holidays; fee for museum, but free access to the graves.*

"JUDGE" ROY BEAN
1823–1904

It's no wonder so many western movies have featured Bean. He was one of a kind, whose prime stock-in-trade was enhancing his own legend. At age fifteen, he left his Kentucky home, following two older brothers westward in search of adventure. One brother became the first mayor of San Diego, the other a sheriff in New Mexico, but Roy did odd jobs: trader, bartender, gambler on cockfights. Eventually he married a Mexican teenager, settled down in San Antonio, and supported his family of five children by selling stolen firewood and watered-down milk. That was just phase one of a long life. The next phase came after he abandoned his family, fled San Antonio, and became a saloon keeper all too fond of his own product. How he was ever chosen to be a justice of the peace says something about Texas law enforcement in the late 1880s. But he was—in the tiny town of Langtry in Pecos County, Texas. The town was really named for a railroader, but Bean had taken a fancy to the British actress Lily Langtry and built a saloon named "Jersey Lily" after her. Most of the time the saloon was his

courtroom, where he dispensed more drinks and tall tales than justice. He liked to project a tough guy image, but there's no evidence that he actually hanged anyone. Bean justice was to tap the bar with his pistol, holler sternly at the culprit, and fine and expel him from town. In spite of his erratic record, Bean was actually elected to the office he had first been appointed to and reelected again and again from 1882 to 1902 (another commentary on oldtime Texas justice). Truth was a stranger to him, but one fact is provable: He was not gunned down on the streets of Laredo, as legend had it; he died peacefully in his bed, after an all-night drinking spree. As for the real Jersey Lily, Bean never met her but wrote inviting her to visit. Months after his death, she stopped by Langtry on her way to San Francisco. Too bad Bean couldn't have bean there to see his idol.

Forest Park Lawndale

HOUSTON

In the parklike setting its name suggests, Forest Park Lawndale has offered residents and visitors repose and tranquility since the 1920s. Those finding such peace fulltime include **Larry Blyden** (1925–1975), actor; **Ted Daffan** (1912–1996), singer and composer of "Born to Lose," which won a gold record and was recorded by more than 120 artists; **Ernest Ford** (1916–1991), lyricist who collaborated on more than 200 country music songs; **Sam "Lightnin'" Hopkins** (1912–1982), blues singer-guitarist, with more than 600 recordings, who embodied Texas country blues; **Richard "Dickey" Kerr** (1893–1963), pitcher for the notorious 1919 Chicago White Sox; and **Gus Mancuso** (1905–1984), major league catcher for the St. Louis Cardinals and five other teams. *6900 Lawndale, Houston. Tel. (713) 928-5141. Grounds open 7:00 A.M.–5:30 P.M. daily. Office hours: 8:00 A.M.–9:00 P.M. daily; rest rooms.*

Glenwood Cemetery

HOUSTON

Opened in 1871 in the garden mode, this beautiful eighty-acre burial ground overlooks Buffalo Bayou and sports an abundance of pine and oak trees, shrubs, and rolling hills, making it a favorite haunt of birders, joggers, and walkers. Full-time inhabitants include **Maria Franklin Gable** (1884–1966), Clark Gable's first wife; **Oveta Culp Hobby** (1905–1995), first secretary of health, education and welfare (1953–1955), and husband **William P. Hobby** (1878–1964), governor and publisher of the *Houston Post*; **Glenn McCarthy** (1907–1988), Texas oil man known as "King of the Wildcatters," developer of Shamrock Hotels; and **Gene Tierney** (1920–1991), Hollywood actress, best known for her leading role in *Laura*. *2525 Washington Avenue, Houston. Tel. (713) 864-7886. Grounds open 7:00 A.M.–6:00 P.M. Office hours: 8:00 A.M.–5:00 P.M. Monday–Friday; rest room, tours available through Greater Houston Preservation Alliance (713-216-5000).*

HOWARD HUGHES
1905–1976

It's too late to ask the real Howard Hughes to stand up, but the mysterious behavior of this eccentric multimillionaire continues to be the stuff that films are made of. Those who remember Hughes only in later life as reclusive, elusive, feeble, and germophobic might be surprised at the glamorous Hughes in his prime. Orphaned at age eighteen, Hughes inherited a million dollars and his father's successful Hughes Tool Company, which in five years—under the guidance of Noel Dietrich, a young accountant Hughes hired to manage it—would bring in $75 million more. This gave young Hughes a chance to do what he wanted, when he wanted. And did he! First he turned to movie making and produced *Scarface* (with his discovery Jean Harlow, as lead), *Hell's Angels* (another Harlow vehicle), and *The Outlaw* (with another sexy Hughes newcomer, Jane Russell). Hughes then turned his attention to flying and his dream of breaking the air speed record. He did this within a year, flying a plane he had designed. He next flew the plane non-stop across the country, setting another record, then from New York to Paris in half Lindbergh's air time, and

from Paris to Moscow, Siberia, and Alaska. Bingo! Another record broken! In 1938 he invested in Trans World Airways, and TWA became one of the first successful major commercial airlines. Meanwhile Hughes's numerous affairs and marriages gave tabloid writers a heyday. Then followed investments in Las Vegas real estate and gaming properties. Little by little Hughes retreated from public life, shuttling in great secrecy from one hotel to another, from Las Vegas to the Bahamas, Mexico, Canada, and England. The public wasn't sure whether he was alive or dead, and Hughes's entourage wasn't telling. Hughes look-alikes surfaced in the oddest places. His "autobiography" turned out to be a forgery, as did the spate of wills that surfaced after his death. A dead ringer? We may never know. One thing is clear: Hughes is as shrouded here as in life, his grave tucked away, above ground level, enclosed by a wrought-iron fence (painted apple-green, which helps locate it). A semicircular concrete "wall" in the rear of the enclosure is another identifier, but his flush-to-the-ground name marker (along with his parents') is too far inside the locked fence to be read.

Lyndon Baines Johnson Ranch

JOHNSON CITY

The Lyndon Baines Johnson National Historical Park consists of two elements. At the first, the Johnson City one, are LBJ's boyhood home, the 1860s Johnson family settlement, and a visitors center. The second element contains the LBJ birthplace, Texas White House, ranch, and sizable family graveyard. The thirty-sixth U.S. president lies here, along with his mother, **Rebeckah Baines Johnson** (1881–1958), his father, **Sam Early Johnson** (1877–1937), and other relatives. As he did in life, LBJ's hefty granite headstone with rough-hewn sides, towers above the others, all lined up in a row, shielded by sculptural live oak trees, and protected by a wrought-iron fence, hedge, and stone fence. The grave can be seen only on tour. *Just off U.S. Highway 290 west, 13 miles between Johnson City and Fredericksburg. Tel.(830) 868-7128. Hours: 10:00 a.m.–4:00 p.m. daily; 1½-hour National Park Service bus tour (fee).*

LYNDON BAINES JOHNSON
1 9 0 8 – 1 9 7 3

All these years after his presidency, certain visceral images, not necessarily positive ones, of our first Texas president remain intact: hunting deer from a pickup truck on his ranch, pulling his hound dogs up by the ears, lifting his shirt to show reporters his appendectomy scars. A different image also lingers: of the sadness in his tired voice as he announced on the radio and TV that he would not seek a second term. There was much about Johnson that was double life size: his reputation as a wheeler-dealer, his ability to twist arms and wheedle votes when he was majority leader of the U.S. Senate, and his astonishing domestic achievements during his first months as president, after the John F. Kennedy assassination: passage of major civil rights, welfare, antipoverty, and tax reduction laws. If his term in office hadn't been diminished by the Vietnam War, it is widely believed that he might have been one of the great presidents of the twentieth century. But that war and its toll remain an albatross around his reputation to this day, tarnishing his last hurrah.

City of Lubbock Cemetery

LUBBOCK

In this city-owned burial ground (which dates back to 1892), as flat as the terrain throughout these high plains, one grave is more heavily trafficked than most: that of native son Buddy Holly. Located right in front of the office, the flat marble stone is etched, appropriately, with a guitar. *2011 East 31st Street, Lubbock. Tel. (806) 767-2270. Grounds open all the time. Office hours: 8:00 A.M.–5:00 P.M. Monday–Friday (closed for lunch 12:00 N.–1:00 P.M.); map, rest room.*

BUDDY HOLLY

1936–1959

Though his career was a short one, his memory lingers on. Always musical, Holly played the violin and guitar as a child, but by age thirteen he had shifted entirely to the guitar and with a friend, Bob Montgomery, played what they called "western bop." Later, with his own band, the Crickets, he played guitar and sang in an excited voice that became his signature. Their songs— "Maybe Baby," "Oh Boy!" and his solo hit "Peggy Sue"—were marketed as rhythm and blues, a field that at the time was the sole (soul?) preserve of black musicians. In fact they were once booked into Harlem's Apollo Theater, and it took them three days to prove they could make it as rhythm-and-blues artists. After successful tours abroad and a new marriage, Holly left the group and moved to New York. He joined a rock show and toured with Ritchie Valens and J. P. Richardson, but the tedious bus trips got them down and one fateful day in Mason City, Iowa, they chartered a small plane, which almost immediately crashed, killing everyone aboard. Holly was seven months short of his twenty-third birthday. But, oh boy!— the melody lingers on, maybe baby forever.

Utah

Brigham Young Burial Site

SALT LAKE CITY

Inside a small area, enclosed by a cast-iron fence, the founder of Salt Lake City is buried. Not exactly a real park nor cemetery, the tiny, immaculately cared-for space holds the grave of Brigham Young and several of his family members, along with a bronze statue of Young sitting on a bench. Young's gravesite is in the far left corner from the entrance gate. *150 East 1st Avenue, Salt Lake City. Grounds open 8:00 A.M.–10:00 P.M.*

BRIGHAM YOUNG
1801–1877

Considering his modest beginnings as the ninth of eleven children of an impoverished Vermont family of drifters, one might not have guessed at Brigham Young's hidden talents. As a young man living in upper New York State, he was a house painter, glazier, and general handyman, showing no sign of his future greatness. But once he converted to Mormonism, he seemed to acquire a purpose in life, soon becoming a wizard at missionary work. Working his way up the church hierarchy, he traveled with leader Joseph Smith and the group to Missouri and later to Nauvoo, Illinois. When Smith was arrested and subsequently killed, the Mormons were on the verge of disintegration, but then Young stepped in and pushed them westward. He was only forty-three at the time, but quickly proved his leadership. Once the group relocated and settled in Salt Lake City, Utah, his organizational abilities became even more impressive, as he taught the group survival skills needed to deal with intense opposition from the federal government and other religious groups. The Mormons' isolated location (at the time) helped them become fiercely independent and a political and social force to be reckoned with. Although short on spiritual pieties, Young was a master at transforming a disparate group into a model fiscal and social community. An ardent practitioner of polygamy, Young reputedly had either nineteen or twenty-seven wives, no one knows for sure. Not in doubt, though, was the fact of his fifty-six children. When death came at age seventy-six, it may have been nature's way of slowing him down.

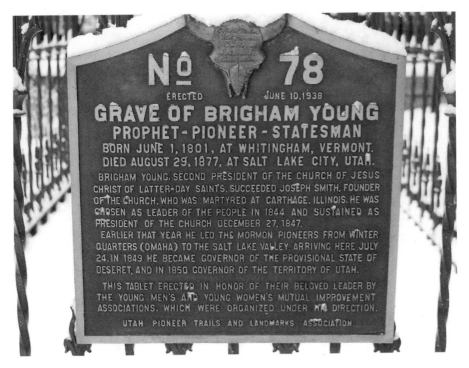

California and the Northwest

There are so many notables in California that a book could be written on the permanent residents of this state's graveyards alone. My son, who lives in Los Angeles, said that when out-of-town friends visit and want to see celebrities, he takes them to the nearest cemetery. It's a sure thing—cheaper and more predictable than Spago's or a Burbank movie studio.

California burial grounds reflect the western migration of our country's population. Surprising people, those we associate with the East or Midwest, show up in their final hours in this sunnier climate. Who would have expected Indiana-born author Theodore Dreiser or New York–bred playwright Clifford Odets to take up final residence in Forest Lawn in Glendale? Or that Truman Capote, born in Louisiana, but a star of New York's glitterary world, would end up in Westwood Memorial Park, Los Angeles? American mobility notwithstanding, graveyard visits are full of surprises, as many of the ones that follow indicate.

California

Mission San Carlos Borromeo de Carmelo

CARMEL

Often called the jewel of the twenty-one Spanish missions strung along the California coast from San Diego north to San Francisco, this is the second one founded by Fray Junipero Serra, and it is where he is buried, on the altar in the sanctuary. The mission began in 1770 and became the headquarters of the entire mission chain. It is especially notable for its eighteenth-century Renaissance reredos. *3080 Rio Road (U.S. Highway 1), Carmel. Tel. (831) 624-1271. Grounds open 9:30 A.M.–4:30 P.M. Monday–Saturday, 10:30 A.M.–4:30 P.M. Sunday. Modest donation requested.*

FATHER JUNIPERO SERRA
1713–1784

This remarkable Spanish Franciscan priest, humbly born on the Balearic island of Mallorca, first arrived in the Americas in 1749. Over the course of a long life (for that time), he walked thousands of miles up and down the California coast—which was part of Mexico then—establishing missions. Though only five feet two inches, he was indomitable, braving few roads, limited supplies, and unfriendly local inhabitants to accomplish his notable achievements. His iron constitution finally gave in to a tubercular infection, and he died at his favorite mission and lies buried in its sanctuary.

Desert Memorial Park

In this flat, desertlike landscape, it is only to be expected that the burial ground would be level land, dotted by palm trees, with all the graves flush with the terrain. Even so, a visitor will find a celebrity harvest here, beginning with **Sonny Bono** (1935–1998), rock singer, later U.S. congressman; **Magda Gabor** (1918–1997), one of the glamorous Hungarian Gabor sisters; **Frederick Loewe** (1904–1988), composer of Broadway hit musicals, *My Fair Lady* among them; and **William Powell** (1892–1984), debonair movie actor with a comic flair, best known for *The Thin Man* series. *69920 Ramon Road, Cathedral Springs. Tel. (760) 328-3316. Grounds open 7:00 A.M.–5:00 P.M. daily in winter, 7:00 A.M.–7:00 P.M. daily in summer. Office hours: 9:00 A.M.–4:30 P.M. daily (but closed 12 N.–1:00 P.M. for lunch); map, rest rooms.*

FRANK SINATRA
1915–1998

Love him or loathe him, and some people did both simultaneously, Francis Albert Sinatra was difficult to ignore. His vocal style—jaunty, intimate, throaty, as though singing just to you—was the most instantly recognizable of any popular musical artist (along with Bing Crosby's) in the past fifty years. It's difficult to think of "My Funny Valentine," "Love and Marriage," "New York, New York," "Fly Me to the Moon," "The Lady Is a Tramp," "My Way," and scores of other popular ballads without inwardly hearing Sinatra's version. Few could quarrel with "Old Blue Eyes"'s way with a song. Nor could you fault his acting. In a second career, launched when his singing days had temporarily faded, Sinatra made *From Here to Eternity* and won a best supporting actor Oscar for it, then went on to give first-rate performances in serious dramas like *The Manchurian Candidate, The Man With the Golden Arm,* and *The Detective,* plus making movie musicals like *Guys and Dolls, On the Town,* and *Pal Joey.* All in all he made more than sixty movies, including some "throwaway" ones with his pals in the so-called Rat Pack. What earned Sinatra disdain from many was his lifestyle: his friendship with known mobsters, high profile marriages and divorces, well-publicized bullying threats to anyone who got in his way in public places. In spite of all the negative baggage, Sinatra continued to sing, make records, play Las Vegas, and tour. Even in later years, when his singing voice was a hoarse travesty of what it had been, his upbeat, joshing performance style lived on and fans still adored him. Part of it was nostalgia for the skinny kid from Hoboken who made it big. Like it or not, he did it *his* way. His prudent gravestone evokes yet another Sinatra melody/memory, with the words, "The Best Is Yet to Come."

Cypress Lawn Cemetery

C O L M A

South of San Francisco, in San Mateo County, is Colma. And in Colma's Cypress Lawn, beyond the Romanesque castlelike entrance portal, are rolling hills, monumental trees, and an impressive number of stately mausoleums of California pioneer families. The Hearsts are here, and the company they keep includes **Hubert Howe Bancroft** (1832–1918), historian; **Laura Hope Crews** (1879–1942), actress; **Francis "Lefty" O'Doul** (1897–1969), major league outfielder with the New York Yankees and other teams; **Claus Spreckels** (1815–1908), sugar magnate; and **Lincoln Steffens** (1866–1936), muckraking journalist and author. *1370 El Camino Real, Colma. (650) 755-0580. Grounds open 8:00 A.M.–4:30 P.M. daily. Office hours: 8:00 A.M.–5:00 P.M. Monday–Friday, 8:30 A.M.–5:00 P.M. Saturday–Sunday; map, rest rooms.*

WILLIAM RANDOLPH HEARST

1 8 6 3 – 1 9 5 1

Citizen Kane is one of Hollywood's great all-time movies, but it certainly muddies the waters in sorting out the real life of newspaper magnate Hearst, on which much of the reel life was ostensibly based. Hearst's father, George, a geologist who made a fortune in mining, owned the *San Francisco Examiner* newspaper and became a U.S. senator. Mother Phoebe's cultural interests started young William on the road to art collecting at age ten, which culminated in San Simeon, the Spanish Renaissance castle that became his refuge later in life. It was Phoebe who sent him from San Francisco to an eastern preparatory school (St. Paul's) and to Harvard in 1882. Although much of his college time was spent goofing around, he actually learned about newspapering on the *Harvard Lampoon*. Later he apprenticed on Joseph Pulitzer's *New York World*, a paper that would become his most serious rival. In 1887 Hearst took over his father's paper,

the *Examiner*, and from then on, ferociously competing with Pulitzer, he swallowed up newspaper after newspaper, transforming himself into the major press baron of the age. He called his style the "new journalism": shorter, snappier, cutting-edge stories with appeals to a mass readership with sensational, not always factual reporting. Others called it "yellow journalism" for many of the same reasons and blamed the Hearst papers' inflammatory rhetoric for pushing the United States into the Spanish-American War. Like his father, Hearst became interested in politics, but despite many campaigns, the only office he ever won was as a U.S. congressman from New York's eleventh district, not the power platform such an ambitious man craved. From Democratic leanings as a young man, Hearst became steadily more conservative as he grew older. In his personal life he was always attracted to the theater, marrying one showgirl, Millicent Willson, and taking another as a mistress—Marion Davies, with whom, from 1917 onward, he spent the rest of his life. Though he inherited one fortune and made another, his imperial lifestyle brought him serious financial problems late in life, forcing him to relinquish control of his numerous properties. His mausoleum, a magnificent Grecian temple with Ionic columns, reflects the exuberance he had for living—and dying. Here he resides in style, along with his mother, **Phoebe** (1840–1919), father, **George** (1820–1891), and one of his five sons, **Randolph Apperson Hearst** (1915–2000), Patty Hearst's father.

Hills of Eternity Memorial Park

C O L M A

This Jewish cemetery, which dates back to 1892, is down the road from Cypress Lawn, with the opportunity for combining visits. *1301 El Camino Real, Colma. Tel. (650) 756-3633. Grounds open 8:30 A.M.–4:00 P.M. Sunday-Friday. Office hours: 8:30 A.M.–4:00 P.M. Sunday-Friday; map, rest room.*

WYATT EARP
1 8 4 8 – 1 9 2 9

As has been said, death is full of surprises. One is to find Wyatt Barry Stapp Earp, the famous gun-toting marshal of the Wild West, resting peaceably in a Jewish cemetery in northern California. The explanation is simple: Lying with him—under a granite upright—is his wife, or common-law wife (depending on which source you believe), **Josephine Marcus** (1861–1944), daughter of a Jewish San Francisco merchant. Like so many old western tales, the Earp legend is as shifting as desert sand. This much seems accurate: He was born in Illinois, grew up in Iowa, and kept tilting westward. He hunted buffalo, drove a stagecoach, and worked for the railroad. As a U.S. marshall, in Witchita, Dodge City, and finally Tombstone, Arizona, Earp was reportedly a fast thinker with a fast gun. His celebrated battle at the O.K. Corral in 1881, in which he, his brothers, and Doc Holliday killed outlaws Billy Clanton and the McLowery brothers, has been so mythologized it is almost impossible from this distance to separate fact from serious exaggeration. In any case in 1897 he headed to Alaska during the gold rush, returned to the United States three years later, and continued prospecting in northern California. His later years were reportedly marked by poverty; he died before his legend was firmly cemented in Hollywood western movies.

Holy Cross Catholic Cemetery

C O L M A

A 230-acre Catholic burying ground, Holy Cross opened in 1887 and is the oldest and largest burial ground in town. Its rolling hills and greenswards are dotted with eucalyptus, palms, pine, and oak trees, shrubs, flowers, and religious statuary. In this restful landscape can be found **Edmund G. "Pat" Brown, Sr.** (1905–1996), two-time governor of California and patriarch of one of the state's leading Democratic families; **Abigail Anne Folger** (1943–1969), Folger coffee heiress and victim (with Sharon Tate among others) in the Manson murders; **Vince Guaraldi** (1928–1976), jazz pianist; and **George Moscone** (1929–1978), San Francisco mayor killed by disgruntled supervisor Dan White for his pro-gay rights policies. *1500 Old Mission Road, Colma. Tel. (650) 756-2060. Grounds open 8:00 A.M.–dusk daily. Office hours: 8:30 A.M.–5:00 P.M. Monday–Saturday; map and self-walking tour, rest rooms.*

JOE DIMAGGIO
1914–1999

"Joltin' Joe" DiMaggio, the "Yankee Clipper," was a baseball-playing Olympian. As an outfielder for the New York Yankees, he won three Most Valuable Player awards, had a career batting average of .325, was easily elected to the Hall of Fame, and for his modest, hardworking, no-high-jinks playing style was one of the all-time most popular Yankees. His 1941 streak of hitting in fifty-six straight games still stands as a record. In 1969 sportswriters named him "the Greatest Living Player," though Ted Williams fans might disgree. He was so proud of this accolade that in his innumerable public appearances at Yankee Stadium and elsewhere, he insisted that this title be included in his introduction. His brief marriage to Marilyn Monroe and the crush he supposedly had on her even after her death became near-legendary. Lesser known was DiMaggio's extreme stinginess and his longtime estrangement, at his insistence, from his only son. On his headstone, which is just southwest of the Clergy circle, is the inscription, "Dignity, Grace and Elegance Personified." All certainly true, but not quite the whole story.

Hillside Memorial Park and Mortuary

CULVER CITY

On fifty well-kept grassy acres that roll and dip, this Jewish sacred ground has been the final home, since its beginning in 1942, of many prominent Hollywood bigwigs, entertainers, producers, comedians, with grave sections named Valley of Remembrance, Garden of Rachel, Mount Sholom, Mount of Olives, and the like. Many residents are to be found in wall crypts in the imposing hilltop mausoleum: **David Begelman** (1921–1995), talent agent, producer, and movie studio head, implicated in a major financial scandal and embezzlement; **Milton Berle** (1908–2002), comedian, TV pioneer; **Eddie Cantor** (1892–1964), singer, comedian, longtime staple of vaudeville, stage, movies, radio, and television; **Hank Greenberg** (1911–1986), baseball's first Jewish superstar, first baseman for the Detroit Tigers, an all-time top hitter; **Lorne Greene** (1915–1987), character actor, famous for his role as Ben Cartright in the television series *Bonanza;* **Moe Howard** (1897–1975), one of the Three Stooges comedy team; **David Janssen** (1931–1980), actor, known for his role in television's *The Fugitive* series; **George Jessel** (1898–1981), vaudeville comedian; **Harry Richmond** (1895–1972), song-and-dance man in vaudeville's heyday, whose signature song was "Puttin' on the Ritz"; **Dick Shawn** (1923–1987), comedian and comic actor, whose most hilarious performance was as the actor playing Hitler in the movie *The Producers;* **Allan Sherman** (1924–1973), satiric songwriter, also the voice of Dr. Seuss's animated *Cat in the Hat;* and **Dinah Shore** (1916–1994), radio singer, star of an NBC television variety show. **Michael Landon** (1936–1991), heartthrob as Little Joe on the television series *Bonanza,* later on *Little House on the Prairie,* has his own private room,

lavish with fresh flowers and messages, visible through a gated glass door. **Jerry Rubin** (1938–1994), 1960s Yippie turned 1980s Yuppie, can be found on the grounds in the Mount of Olives. Dead last, notorious mobster **Mickey Cohen** (1913–1976), who survived every imaginable type of murder attempt to die of natural causes, reposes now in—can it be?—the Alcove of Love. *600 Centinela Avenue, Culver City. Tel. (310) 641-0707; fax (310) 641-3472. Grounds open 8:00 A.M.–5:00 P.M. daily, but closed Saturday. Office hours: 8:00 A.M.–5:00 P.M. daily, but closed Saturday. Mausoleum open 8:00 A.M.–4:00 P.M. daily except Saturday; map, rest room.*

JACK BENNY
1894–1974

As a comedian with split-second timing, Benny began his career as a humorous monologist and master of ceremonies. He found his natural milieu as the star of his own radio show. Later television allowed him to expand the persona he had developed on radio as a vain miser from Winnetka, Illinois, and would-be violinist whose screechy scratchings with the bow drew countless laughs. In fact Benny, born Benjamin Kubelsky in Chicago,

Illinois, did grow up in the Chicago suburb and played the violin well enough to tour vaudeville. Everything else was invented for laughs, including his radio feud with Fred Allen, star of another radio show, which both comics milked further in a 1940 movie, *Love Thy Neighbor.* What gave the Benny show such appeal, besides his own flawless timing, was excellent writing—with Benny as the butt of all jokes—and a superb cast, headed by Eddie Anderson as Benny's valet Rochester; bandleader Phil Harris as a good-natured, truth-dodging drunk; and Mary Livingstone as Benny's wry, sharp-tongued wife. In several movies, notably *To Be or Not to Be, Charley's Aunt,* and *The Horn Blows at Midnight,* Benny showed his comic talents again. His imposing black marble sarcophagus, which is also home to his wife, **Mary Livingstone Benny** (1906–1983), notes that he was a "beloved husband, father and grandfather, a gentle man." Not hard to believe.

AL JOLSON
1886–1950

Eat your heart out, fellow residents, the star spot at Hillside belongs to Al Jolson. Visible from across the freeway miles below and illuminated by spotlights at night, Jolson's monumental memorial, lined by cypress trees, with a bright mosaic ceiling supported by six towering pillars, was designed by Los Angeles architect Paul Williams. It stands high on a hill in front of the main mausoleum, with a 120-foot waterfall cascading down in front and a polished black granite sarcophogus inside. There is a bronze statue of Jolson kneeling on one knee, with arms outstretched, as when he sang his famous song "Mammy." Jolson, born Asa Yoelsom in a Russian (later Lithuanian) village, emigrated to America in 1890 with his family, settling in Washington, D.C. The son of a synagogue cantor, young Jolson made money early by singing on street corners. By age fifteen he had left school, and with his distinctive singing voice and agreeably brassy personality, became a fixture on the vaudeville circuit, then in Broadway musicals. His rendition of "California, Here I Come," "Toot, Toot, Tootsie," and

"April Showers" became signature numbers. When talking movies came, Jolson was ready, starring in the very first, *The Jazz Singer*. During World War II Jolson gave freely of his time to USO shows, and in 1946 *The Jolson Story*, a romanticized movie about his life, revived his sagging career. Ever the entertainer, Jolson died of heart failure after a return from a strenuous USO tour to Korea. Toot, toot, tootsie, goodbye.

Holy Cross Cemetery and Mausoleum

CULVER CITY

Over the grassy land and rolling hills of this Catholic burying ground are grottoes, religious statuary, shrines, and sections with such names as Holy Innocents, Sacred Heart, and Crucifixion. The well-kept grounds are celebrity hideaways, for good, but with a map the well-marked graves are easy to locate. Here you'll find **Mary Astor** (1906–1987), movie actress, star of *The Maltese Falcon;* **Alfred S. Bloomingdale** (1916–1982), businessman who launched Diners Club, the first credit card company; **Ray Bolger** (1904–1987), dancer, entertainer, best known as the Scarecrow in the 1939 movie *The Wizard of Oz;* **Charles Boyer** (1899–1979), French-born Hollywood leading man; **Jackie Coogan** (1914–1984), actor from childhood to old age, most famous as Uncle Fester in *The Addams Family;* **Johnny Desmond** (1919–1985), vocalist with Glenn Miller band; **Jimmy Durante** (1893–1980), comedian in movies, radio, and on stage, known for his lovable personality and genuine humility; **John Farrow** (1904–1963), director, husband of actress Maureen O'Sullivan, father of Mia Farrow; **Jack Haley** (1898–1979), comedian, singer, forever remembered as the Tin Man in *The Wizard of Oz;* **Jose Iturbi** (1895–1980), pianist-composer; **Spike Jones** (1911–1965), zany band leader known for goofy renditions of *Carmen* and other classics; **Jim Jordan** (1896–1988), better known as "Fibber McGee," star of a popular 1930s–1940s radio show of the same name; **Mario Lanza** (1921–1959), Italian singer; and **Fred MacMurray** (1908–1991), versatile movie actor who could play comedy and drama, star of television show *My Three Sons*. Also here are **Audrey Meadows** (1926–1996), actress-comedienne, best known for her role as Alice in television's evergreen series *The Honeymooners;* **Helen O'Connell** (1920–1993), singer with the big swing bands of the 1940s; **Barney Oldfield** (1878–1946), racing car driver who set a land-speed record in 1910; **Walter O'Malley** (1903–1979), owner of baseball's Brooklyn Dodgers, who earned the eternal enmity of New York fans by moving "dem bums" to Los Angeles, making the L.A. team one of the sport's most

successful franchises; **Louella Parsons** (1880–1972), powerful gossip columnist of the 1930s–1940s; **Zasu Pitts** (1898–1963), comic actress who played flaky roles; **Mack Sennett** (1880–1960), actor, writer, movie producer, and director, known for his hilarious slapstick comedies in silent movies, whose tombstone reads, appropriately, "beloved king of comedy"; and **Sharon Tate** (1943–1969), movie actress, wife of Roman Polanski, who was savagely murdered in her home by members of the Charles Manson gang. *5835 West Slauson Avenue, Culver City. Tel. (310) 670-7697. Grounds open 8:00 A.M.–5:00 P.M. daily. Office hours: 8:00 A.M.–5:00 P.M. Monday–Friday, 8:00 A.M.–4:00 P.M. Saturday, 10:00 A.M.–3:00 P.M. Sunday; map, rest rooms.*

JOHN CANDY
1950–1994

Not all fat men are natural comedians, but John Candy really was, bringing a sweetness to his deadpan humor that made fans love him even as they laughed at him. Anyone who watched the Canada-based *Second City TV* and *SCTV* will remember fondly his comic characters: clarinetist-polka bandleader Yosh Schmenge, talk show host Johnny LaRue, Mayor Tommy Shanks, Mr. Mombo, and Gil Hodges, host of the "Fishin' Musician." Canadian Candy was one SCTV member who scored really big in Hollywood, making over forty films, some of which were "throwaways," some keepers. Candy died in the saddle, so to speak, on location in Durango, Mexico, while filming *Wagons East!*, leaving a wife, two children, and legions of bereft fans.

BING CROSBY
1904–1977

"Der Bingle," as this popular singing star of more than five decades was sometimes called, began life in Spokane, Washington, as Harry Lillis Crosby. His nickname "Bing," from a newspaper comic strip, the *Bingville Bugle*, which he loved as a kid, fit his easygoing public personality. He loved to sing, though never learned to read music, and in high school formed a small band. By the time he was twenty-one, he and a friend went to Los Angeles. The friend's sister was singer Mildred Bailey, who helped them get a vaudeville contract. By the late 1920s, with a third partner, they became the Rhythm Boys, but in 1930 CBS offered Crosby his own solo radio show. He was off and running. Using "Where the Blue of the Night Meets the Gold of the Day" as his new theme song, he performed live for twenty straight weeks at New York's Paramount Theatre, a run that ended in contracts with Paramount Pictures and Decca Records. Although he made some one hundred movies, including the popular but trivial "Road" series with Bob Hope, Crosby made his fortune on radio, singing in a relaxed, jazzy style every imaginable type of pop song, from ballads and blues to westerns and star-spangled patriotic songs. A warm, engaging public personality added to the Crosby charm, and he remained Mr. Popularity decade after decade, though posthumous reports suggest he was a stern taskmaster to the four sons of his first marriage to Dixie Lee. Thanks to royalties, lucrative contracts, and smart investments, he died with a fortune of more than $80 million. Not bad for a happy-go-lucky kid from Spokane. His simple granite gravestone, located in the grotto area, bears his etched name—Harry Lillis Bing Crosby—a cross and the words, "BELOVED BY ALL."

JOHN FORD
1895–1973

From Ford's first breath in Cape Elizabeth, Maine, to his last in his home near Palm Desert, California, stretched a continental and cultural divide of great magnitude. Ford (whose given name was Feeney), was the son—the last of thirteen children—of Irish immigrants. He went west as a young man and bridged that cultural divide by making movies, becoming one of the best directors of the twentieth century. His films read like a syllabus of great movies: *The Grapes of Wrath, The Informer, The Quiet Man, Stagecoach, How Green Was My Valley, Drums Along the Mohawk, What Price Glory?, The Searchers, The Man Who Shot Liberty Valance, Mister Roberts.* That's for starters. In a career that spanned sixty years, he made 136 feature films and documentaries, for which he collected six Oscars (two were for World War II documentaries). Movie westerns are still measured against standards he set, using the vast panorama of open space as a backdrop for epic themes of justice, revenge, and chivalry. Ford was a movie monomaniac, saying once, "If I had my way, every morning of my life I'd be behind that camera at nine o'clock, waiting for the boys to roll 'em, because that's the only thing I really like to do." He did, however, between films, enjoy booze and binges with his buddies. In a movie culture where spouses were shed as often as underwear, he was married to the same woman from 1920 to the day he died, despite a brief passionate relationship with Katharine Hepburn. During World War II he served in the U.S. Navy and was awarded a Purple Heart for war wounds received in the Battle of Midway. In life he lobbied for an admiral's rank. Note his gravestone: "Admiral John Ford."

RITA HAYWORTH
1918–1987

In her prime this beautiful dancer-turned-actress seemed to have everything—fame, looks, an electric screen presence. She moved quickly from dancing and roles in B movies (typecast as a Latin type) to serious drama. But to do so she changed her name from Margarita Carmen Cansino to Rita Hayworth, learned how to sing, dyed her hair blond, and raised her hairline by electrolysis. Before long she was a pinup girl for GIs in World War II. Then followed movies like *You'll Never Get Rich* with Fred Astaire, *You Were Never Lovelier* (Astaire again),

Gilda (which established her as a femme fatale), *Lady from Shanghai, Pal Joey,* and scores of others. Late in her career (1955), she won plaudits for *Separate Tables* and *They Came to Cordura* (1959). Her five marriages were also legendary, all to high profile men: wealthy Texan Edward Judson, Orson Welles, Prince Aly Khan of Iran, pop singer Dick Haynes, and producer James Hill. For fifteen years before she died, Hayworth was imprisoned by Alzheimer's disease. Knowing this makes her polished black granite gravestone, situated below a kneeling angel in the grotto area, especially poignant: "Beloved mother . . . to yesterday's companionship and tomorrow's reunion."

BELA LUGOSI
1882–1956

It wasn't easy being Dracula. Lugosi Bela Ferenc Dezs Blasko, born in Lugos, Hungary, was a classical actor, singer, handsome heartthrob at the National Theater of Hungary in Budapest and in Hungarian movies. After emigrating to

the United States in 1921, he won a few romantic roles on Broadway, but in 1927 he was cast as Count Dracula in a play of the same name. It was a huge success, and four years later he reprised the role in *Dracula*, Hollywood's first talking horror film. It too was a hit and the die was cast. For the rest of his life, despite his good looks and penchant for romantic and comic roles, he was destined to play villains. Even then, disappointments plagued his career. Unwilling to don the ugly makeup, he turned down the role of Frankenstein's monster, which went to the lesser-known Boris Karloff, who from then on surpassed Lugosi as Hollywood's favorite monster-you-love-to-hate. In a career of peaks and valleys, one of Lugosi's peaks was as Igor in the 1939 *Son of Frankenstein*. Four years later he finally played the monster in *Frankenstein Meets the Wolf Man*. Smaller roles, a series of cheap films, drug addiction, four failed marriages, touring in second-rate shows, a final fifth marriage, hospitalization for drug abuse, insolvency, that pretty well sums up a sad, lost life. Ironically, at the end, having fought against stereotyping much of his career, he asked to be buried in his Dracula cape. Dracula lives, or does he?

ROSALIND RUSSELL
1 9 1 2 – 1 9 7 6

In the course of more than fifty movies, Russell never became typecast. Born in Waterbury, Connecticut, she began her career in summer stock, followed by a few Broadway shows, which led to a Hollywood screen test and a movie career that stretched from the early 1930s to the late 1960s. Although playing a wise-cracking, brainy career woman was her forte, she could play serious roles—*Night Must Fall, Sister Kenny, Picnic,* and *Mourning Becomes Electra* come to mind—with equal aplomb. Still, she'll probably be best remembered for her screwball performance as the fast-talking reporter in *The Front Page,* as the bitchy Sylvia in *The Women,* and as the irrepressible Mame in both the movie and Broadway show *Auntie Mame.* This was the role of her life, and at age forty-four she played it with the vigor and energy she brought to all her parts. When her movie career sagged in the late 1940s, she spunkily turned to the stage, touring with great success in *Bell, Book and Candle,* followed by even greater raves in *Wonderful Town,* in which she danced and sang, despite limited skills in both. "I don't sing, I gargle," she said. One of the few big movie stars to keep her personal life private, she was the wife of Danish-born producer Frederick Brisson, and devoted much time to fundraising for worthy causes. For this effort, she received the Gene Hersholt Humanitarian Award at the 1973 Oscar ceremonies. Nominated four times for an Oscar, she never won. Go figure.

Forest Lawn Memorial Park

G L E N D A L E

There are now four Forest Lawns, but this one is the mother church, so to speak, the burial ground for so many stars, it can take days to hunt them all down. And I mean *hunt,* for the map lists no celebrity graves, and office personnel are instructed not to divulge where anyone famous is buried. It's a privacy issue. Grounds workers are not so discreet, and they are your best bet for finding special favorites. But don't have your hopes up about visiting **W. C. Fields** (1880–1946), **Clark Gable** (1901–1960), **Jean Harlow** (1911–1937), or **Carole Lombard** (1908–1942). They are locked away in the Great Mausoleum—Fields in the Hall of Inspiration's Columbarium of Nativity, Gable and Lombard in the Sanctuary of Trust, Harlow in the Sanctuary of Benediction—areas roped off-limits except to families and friends. Content yourself with the beautiful plantings, ponds, and hilltop grounds, offering the best of all possible views of Los Angeles spreading below. Forest Lawn is not your little old-fashioned neighborhood burial ground; it's big business. It is also a tourist attraction. Live people come here to be married, as Ronald Reagan and Jane Wyman did in the Wee Kirk o' the Heather church. The names of permanent guests here could fill a book on the entertainment industry. Here's a sampling who, with some persistence, can be, ah, uncovered: **L. Frank Baum** (1856–1919), author of the *Oz* books; **Gutzon Borglum** (1867–1941), sculptor of Mount Rushmore; **Clara Bow** (1905–1965), the "It" girl of silent movies; **Godfrey Cambridge** (1933–1976), comedian; **Lon Chaney, Sr.** (1880–1930), actor in horror films, best known for *The Hunchback of Notre Dame* and *Phantom of the Opera;* **Nat "King" Cole** (1919–1965), jazz pianist and singer with his own King Cole Trio; **Dorothy Dandridge** (1922–1965), singer and actress, who starred in *Carmen Jones* and *Porgy and Bess;* and **Sammy Davis, Jr.** (1925–1990), showbiz personality whose imposing tombstone sums it up, "The entertainer—he did it all." Also here are **Theodore Dreiser** (1871–1945), author of *Sister Carrie, An American Tragedy, The Titan,* and other realistic novels; **Don Drysdale** (1936–1993), Hall of Fame pitcher with the Los Angeles Dodgers; **Samuel Goldwyn** (1882–1974), major Hollywood producer of quality films, known for his legendary "Goldwynisms" in fractured English; **Errol Flynn** (1909–1959), swashbuckling actor; **Ted Knight** (1923–1986), comic actor, a favorite on television's *Mary Tyler Moore Show;* **Alan Ladd** (1913–1964), "tough guy" movie actor, whose pivotal performance was as the loner in *Shane;* **Harold Lloyd** (1893–1971), acrobatic silent film comedian; **Jeanette MacDonald** (1901– 1965), actress-singer, star of movie musicals; **Aimee Semple McPherson** (1890–1944), evangelist; **Tom Mix** (1880–1940), popular cowboy actor; **Clifford Odets** (1906–1963), playwright, whose works include *Golden Boy, Waiting for Lefty,* and *The Country Girl;* **Charlie Ruggles** (1886–1971), comic character actor; and **Jimmy Stewart** (1908–1997), a Hollywood star for decades, known for his service in the U.S. Army Air Force and genuine nice-guy persona. *1712 South Glendale Avenue, Glendale. Tel. (323) 254-7251. Grounds open 8:00 A.M.–5:00 P.M. daily. Office hours: 8:00 A.M.–5:00 P.M. daily; map, rest rooms, gift shop, flower shop, museum.*

GRACIE ALLEN
1902–1964
GEORGE BURNS
1896–1996

The best thing that ever happened to small-time vaudeville comic Burns, as he was the first to admit, was meeting Gracie Allen, an unemployed actress. They soon began a partnership and marriage that lasted until her death forty-one years later. Their schtick as a comedy team was for George to play straight man, Gracie—as a dizzy dame—to get the laugh lines (written by him). Their act was so popular they soon had their own radio show, which lasted twenty-one years, followed by eight years on television and a number of movies for Paramount Studios. After Gracie died, Burns went on to yet another career, performing serious roles (well, sort of) in movies such as *The Sunshine Boys, Oh God!,* and *Going in Style*, playing Las Vegas as a single act, writing his memoirs, and holding forth as a wise oldster. He scheduled one hundredth anniversary shows at the London Palladium and Caesar's Palace in Las Vegas, joking that he couldn't die because he had engagements. Unfortunately, a bad fall, surgery, and life in a wheelchair intervened, and he missed his own big birthday party. He made it to one hundred all right, but three months later he left to join Gracie. Their joint crypt in the wall in the Freedom Mausoleum reads "TOGETHER AGAIN." Could any words be more appropriate?

HUMPHREY BOGART
1899–1957

To look at Bogart's early movies, you'd think he grew up on grim city streets. His tough guy demeanor in *Kid Galahad, Dark Victory,* and *Brother Orchid,* all made in the mid-1930s, was incredibly effective. Yet "Bogie," as he was called, was born Humphrey DeForest Bogart, son of a prominent New York doctor and his artist wife. He attended the posh Phillips Academy in Andover, Massachusetts, and at age seventeen enlisted in the navy and served briefly in the military police, a stint that affected him for life. He was hit in the mouth by a handcuffed prisoner trying to escape. The result: a faint scar and a slight lisp, both of which made him a natural for villainous roles. His breakthrough parts as an actor were as a killer, of course, with some sensitivity in *High Sierra,* and, the same year, as Sam Spade, a hard-boiled detective with integrity in *The Maltese Falcon.* By the time he met Lauren Bacall, his costar in *To Have and Have Not* in 1944, he had been through three tumultuous marriages. His fourth—to her—turned out to be his lucky number, leading to two children and, for once, a settled life. The early 1950s were the golden years of his career, showing range and versatility, with *The Treasure of the Sierra Madre, The African Queen* (for which he won an Oscar), *The Caine Mutiny, Sabrina,* and *The Desperate Hours.* Cancer caught up with him, and he died just after completing *The Harder They Fall.* Look for his marble wall crypt in the Columbarium of Eternal Light inside the Gardens of Remembrance.

WALT DISNEY
1 9 0 1 – 1 9 6 6

With Disneyland and Disney World, the cartoon lands of Mickey and Minnie Mouse, Donald Duck, and Goofy, and all the films produced by Walt Disney Productions, it sometimes seems there never was a time B.D.—before Disney. But the fact that much of the world is now Disneyfied didn't just happen. The genius behind it all was Walt Disney, a Chicago-born, Missouri-raised farm boy with a vision and talent as a commercial artist, who was a pioneer in cartoon animation and adept at marketing. Disney moved to Hollywood in 1923 and soon created Mickey Mouse, who starred in the first synchronized sound cartoon, a breakthrough that led to other cartoons and, in short order, Disney's own studio. Other "firsts" followed: the first cartoon in full color, the first full-length animated film—*Snow White and the Seven*

Dwarfs in 1937—followed by scores of other feature-length cartoon stories: *Pinocchio, Fantasia, Dumbo, Bambi* and *Cinderella.* Disneyland and Disney World have been around so long it is hard to realize they were the world's first theme parks, created by Disney's yearning for amusement parks that could be wholesome entertainment for the entire family. (One wonders what he would think of some of the decidedly unfamily-type films produced these days under the Disney aegis.) Disney won scores of awards: five Oscars, one honorary, and the Presidential Medal of Freedom. With all of this, Disney's final address is surprisingly discreet. On the far right side of the long Court of Freedom is a secluded, flower- and vine-bedecked Disney corner. Its wall crypt's plaque lists Walter Elias Disney and various family members.

MARY PICKFORD
1 8 9 3 – 1 9 7 9

Don't let those golden curls fool you. Nor the soubriquet "Little Mary." Mary Pickford, née Gladys Smith, developed from a six-year-old un-schooled Canadian child performer to one of the most successful film actresses of her time, a scenario writer, and film producer with her own company. She began her career in 1898, acting in stock company melodramas. Years of arduous one-night stands led finally to Broadway and stardom—at age fifteen. Two years later she began making movies, hundreds of them over the next twenty-four years, well into the sound era. By 1917 she was earning $1 million or more a year, no small sum for that time. One of her four talkies, *Coquette,* won her an Oscar. Meanwhile she and her second husband, popular actor Douglas Fairbanks, reigned as Hollywood's royal couple at Pickfair, their Tudor mansion in Beverly Hills. When the marriage ended after sixteen years, in 1936, Mary married (happily) actor-bandleader Buddy Rogers, produced movies, and thrived on her shrewd investments. But by 1976, when she received a special Academy Award, she was an eighty-four-year-old alcoholic recluse. Three years later "America's Sweetheart" was gone. Her imposing white marble tomb, rife with cherubs, doves, and grandiosity speaks of another era; it—and she— rest in the Garden of Remembrance, along with her mother, sister, brother, aunt, and two cousins.

CHARLES DILLON "CASEY" STENGEL
1890 –1975

Though a middling major league ballplayer, Casey (named "KC" for his hometown, Kansas City, Missouri, then renamed "Casey" when the poem "Casey at the Bat" became popular),

Stengel really "hit for average" as a manager. In twenty-five years, he managed some of the best and worst teams, but earned his stripes with a Yankee team that won seven of the ten World Series in which they played during his twelve-year managerial reign. His tortured prose—Stengelese—made him a press and fan favorite. He was fired in 1960 because of his age, but managed the last word: "I'll never make the mistake of being seventy again." Four years later he signed to lead a new National League team, the New York Mets, noting, "Most people my age are dead at the present time." During Stengel's four-year tenure, the Mets lost 452 games, winning only 194, causing him to dub them "my amazin' Mets." After retiring, Stengel was immediately, unanimously elected to the Hall of Fame, without the usual five-year wait. His marker here, on the left wall of the Court of Freedom, beyond a statue of Justice by Daniel Chester French, is pure Stengelese: "There comes a time in every man's life and I've had plenty of them."

SPENCER TRACY

1900–1967

Anyone who has enjoyed Spencer Tracy in such films as *Test Pilot*, *Adam's Rib*, or *Bad Day at Black Rock*, with his rugged "liveable" good looks and manly appeal, might be surprised to learn that when he went to Hollywood after a few big hits on Broadway, the 20th Century Fox studio bosses thought he was too "ugly" to be a leading man. His eighteen films for Fox, as a bad guy or gangster, were mostly discards. A perfectionist, given to fierce arguments over script changes, a heavy and belligerent drinker, he was finally released by Fox. When he signed with MGM, and stayed with them for twenty years, his real movie career took off. Three roles really did it: *San Francisco*, Fritz Lang's *Fury*, and the comedy *Libeled*

Lady. From then on he was able to demonstrate his range, acquired in his early training at New York's American Academy of Dramatic Arts, in a variety of films. Tracy's style, so natural it didn't look like acting, came from painstakingly careful preparation. The nine films he made with Katharine Hepburn put him—and her—in the superstar class, especially *Adam's Rib, Woman of the Year, State of the Union*, and *Pat and Mike*. Through working together professionally, they developed one of Hollywood's most enduring private relationships, which lasted until Tracy's death. Outside the Freedom Mausoleum, in his own tiny secluded "garden," Tracy's mottled gray granite marker is embedded in a tan limestone wall, as low key and unpretentious as his acting style.

Jack London State Historic Park

GLEN ELLEN

The knoll in the Valley of the Moon seems a perfect backdrop for the grave of writer London, who loved this land and began acquiring pieces of it in 1911. It is now an 800-acre park with hiking trails; a man-made lake created by the author himself; canopies of trees—oak, madrones, and a redwood grove—and views of Sonoma Mountain and the Mayacamas Mountains. Also in the park are the Jack London cottage, The House of Happy Walls museum, and the ruins of Wolf House, a home he was building that burned down and was never finished. London's grave, and that of his wife, **Charmian**, are marked by a massive, pitted red lava boulder, covering the small, sealed copper urn that bears his ashes. The boulder is surrounded by a wood-slatted fence, which also encloses the simple wooden headboards of two pioneer children (**David** and **Lilly Greenlaw**) who died in 1876 and 1877, graves that were here when London bought the land. *2400 London Ranch Road, Glen Ellen. Tel (707) 938-5216. Grounds open 9:30 A.M.–5:00 P.M. in winter, 9:30 A.M.–7:00 P.M. in summer. Museum hours: 10:00 A.M.–5:00 P.M. daily; fee (per vehicle), brochure (fee), rest rooms.*

JACK LONDON
1876–1916

Some authors just write about adventure, but London lived it first—then he wrote about it. Although London's parents both came from pioneer stock, his father's decline from farming to an impoverished life on the Oakland waterfront forced young Jack to quit school early and take a series of hard-scrabble jobs: delivering newspapers, working in a cannery and on an ice wagon. All the while he spent his spare time in the public library, feeding his imagination with books on travel and adventure. No mere Walter Mitty, he put in time as an oyster pirate, on fish patrol, and as a seaman, hunting seals off the Siberian coast. Tramping all over the country, he was arrested and spent a month in prison. By then he had written and sold a few stories and decided to change his life. He finished a year of high school and, through heavy cramming, was admitted to the University of California at Berkeley. He lasted half a year, then began writing again, but to earn money he joined the gold rush mania and headed for the Klondike. Beset by scurvy, he had to go home. By now it was 1898, and he was writing in earnest. Between 1899 and 1903 he had a period of frenzied productivity: stories, essays, juveniles, poetry, serials, newspaper work—as well as eight books. One of these was *The Call of the Wild*, usually considered his finest work. By now he was becoming famous and in great demand on the lecture circuit. In 1904 the *San Francisco Examiner* sent him to cover the Russo-Japanese War. The next year he divorced his wife and married again (Charmain Kittredge). They took off on a voyage round-the-world in a forty-five-foot yacht, but by the time they reached Australia, London was so ill they had to return to California. From then on London the wanderer became London the landlubbing rancher, though he took time out to sail around the Horn and go to Vera Cruz, Mexico, as a war correspondent. In a sixteen-year period he published forty-three volumes, with seven more published posthumously. When he died—having lived a life and a half—he was just forty years old.

Inglewood Park Cemetery

INGLEWOOD

This spacious park of rolling hills, shade trees, mausoleums, and obelisks began life, as it were, in 1905. Just south of Los Angeles in the suburb of Inglewood, the cemetery contains many notables. They include **Edgar Bergen** (1903–1978), ventriloquist, entertainer, father of Candice Bergen; **Charles Brown** (1923–1999), performer and composer of "Merry Christmas Baby" and "Drifting Blues"; **Curt Flood** (1938–1997), St. Louis Cardinal outfielder, who lost his job and career when he challenged baseball's reserve clause but was indirectly responsible for free agency; **Betty Grable** (1916–1973), top movie star of the 1940s, the most popular GI pinup in World War II; **Ferde Grofe** (1892–1972), composer and conductor; **James J. Jeffries** (1875–1953), heavyweight boxing champion of the world from

1895 to 1905, who retired undefeated, but later challenged Jack Johnson and lost; **Gypsy Rose Lee** (1914–1970), striptease artist, entertainer, subject of the movie and play, *Gypsy;* **Louis Meyer** (1904–1995), racing driver in Indianapolis 500; and **Cesar Romero** (1907–1994), movie actor who played gigolos and Latin lovers. *720 East Florence Avenue. Tel. (310) 412-6500. Grounds open 8:00 A.M.–5:30 P.M. daily. Office hours: 8:30 A.M.–5:00 P.M. Monday–Friday, 8:30 A.M.–4:00 P.M. Saturday, closed Sunday; map, rest rooms, flower shop.*

ELLA FITZGERALD
1918–1996

The brown bronze name plaque with gilded trim on Ella Fitzgerald's white marble wall crypt, which states "beloved mother and grandmother" with a few musical notes on one side, hardly seems adequate as a memorial to "the first lady of song." But in truth anyone who has heard her fabulous voice, with its great clarity, precise diction, and exuberant spirit, carries the memory forever. She was unique as a popular performer: She didn't dance, wiggle, jiggle, or flirt, and she was no great beauty, but her voice could do it all: jazz, popular songs, blues, calypso, bossa nova. For almost sixty years she sang and sang, on records, in live concerts, at jazz festivals, on radio and television, even in a few movies, and did so with the best bands, from Chick Webb, who was her mentor and helped shape her style, to Louis Armstrong, Count Basie, Duke Ellington, Earl Hines, Errol Garner, and Oscar Peterson. She sang everywhere, on tours to Europe, Asia, and all over the United States. In all she made almost 150 albums, singing everything from George Gershwin and Cole Porter to the Beatles, and won twelve Grammy awards, an honorary doctorate in music from Yale University, and just about every other honor imaginable. From her birth in Newport News, Virginia, and upbringing in Yonkers, New York, to her later home in Beverly Hills, California, when complications from diabetes forced her to retire at last in the 1990s, she sang in a voice that remained strong and true. "Sweet Georgia Brown," "How High the Moon," "A-tisket, A-tasket," and "Don't Be That Way" are just a few of the songs that bear her imprint. "Oh, Lady Be Good"—Ella, you always were.

SUGAR RAY ROBINSON
1921–1989

In a sport with few bona fide heroes, Sugar Ray Robinson—born Walker Smith, Jr., in Detroit—stood out. Known for his grace, brains, and style, he was a major force in boxing for over twenty years, from 1940 to 1965 (with some time out from the sport). During that time he won three middleweight titles and was considered one of the greatest boxers ever. Not that he won all the time: He lost nineteen matches, had six draws, and was briefly suspended for not reporting a bribe attempt. One reason he fought into three decades was that he couldn't handle money. He blew his huge fortune—estimated at nearly $4 million—and got in trouble with the IRS for not paying income tax. He had to return to the ring to pay his debts. Yet as an all-around personality, he was a sweetie. Never count him out.

Calvary Cemetery and Mausoleum

LOS ANGELES

Although the flat grassy grounds, dotted with an occasional palm or pine tree, of this 137-acre Catholic burial site are unspectacular, the main mausoleum is fabulous, a cream-and-tan edifice of rounded domes and stained-glass windows, with an entrance right out of a Cecil B. DeMille movie. Near the top of the steep set of steps leading up to the door, hosts of stone angels on the upper left and right walls seemingly trumpet your arrival. Inside is a serene and restful chapel, with soothing choir music piped in. Marble crypts are located in side passages off the chapel. Here can be found all three Barrymore siblings, **Ethel Barrymore** (1879–1959), **John Barrymore** (1882–1942), and **Lionel Barrymore** (1878–1954), stage and screen royalty for decades; **Lou Costello** (1906–1959), half of the Abbott and Costello movie comedy team (buried under his family name "Louis Francis Cristillo," along with his wife); and **Edward L. Doheny, Sr.** (1856–1935), oil magnate and candidate for vice president in 1920. On the grounds are **Jimmy McHugh** (1894–1969), popular music composer; **Pola Negri** (1899–1987), silent movie star; **Mabel Normand** (1894–1930), beautiful comic actress of the silent screen; **Ramon Novarro** (1899–1968), singer, silent movie actor, star of *Ben Hur* and *The Prisoner of Zenda;* and **Harry Sinclair** (1876–1956), founder of Sinclair Oil Company, involved in the Teapot Dome scandal of the Harding administration. *4201 Whittier Boulevard, Los Angeles. Tel. (323) 261-3106. Grounds open 8:00 A.M.–5:00 P.M. daily. Office hours: 8:30 A.M.–4:30 P.M. Monday–Friday, 8:00 A.M.–4:00 P.M. Saturday, 10:00 A.M.–3:00 P.M. Sunday; map, rest rooms.*

IRENE DUNNE
1898–1990

Her elegant and ladylike demeanor didn't make headlines, but Irene Dunne was one of the most versatile movie actresses of the 1930s–1940s. Not only was she a gifted comedienne (*Theodora Goes Wild, The Awful Truth, My Favorite Wife*), but she could emote with the best of them (*Love Affair, Anna and the King of Siam, I Remember Mama, Cimarron*). And she could sing! In fact, from childhood in Louisville, Kentucky, until she tackled Broadway, she was trained as an opera singer. But her light, clear soprano was better suited to musical comedy, and her star debut was as Magnolia in *Showboat*. She loved playing comedy, once saying, "Big emotional scenes are much easier to play than comedy. An onion can bring tears to your eyes, but what vegetable can make you laugh?" Her career eventually ended, but she still had a busy life, as a Republican activist and supporter of many charities and Catholic causes, and recipient of a Kennedy Center honor given by President Reagan. Her medals as a Dame of Malta and Knight of the Order of the Holy Sepulchre are attached to the front of her marble crypt. Similar medals adorn the crypt next to hers, that of her husband of thirty-seven years, **Francis D. Griffin**. Theodora may have gone wild, but Irene never did.

Forest Lawn Memorial Park

LOS ANGELES

As pristine and immaculately tended as the mother ship in Glendale, this Forest Lawn, which opened in 1948 on about 400 acres, has the same rules: no specifics, no information, no help. Here also, one must rely on the kindness of strangers, that is, grounds workers. Wander the curving road up to the Courts of Remembrance, which is a harvest of well-known names. A few among hundreds: **Gene Autry** (1907–1998), singing cowboy star, later owner of the California Angels baseball team; **Lucille Ball** (1911–1989), gifted television comedienne; **Clyde Beatty** (1902–1965), animal trainer whose wall crypt features a bronze plaque with a beautiful bas relief of a reclining lion; **Roy Campanella** (1921–1993), much-loved baseball player with the Brooklyn Dodgers, three-time winner of Most Valuable Player award; **Leo Durocher** (1905–1991), pugnacious baseball manager who coined the phrase "nice guys finish last"; **Ernie Kovacs** (1919–1962), gifted television comic known for innovative satire and irreverence, who died too young in a car accident; **Dorothy Lamour** (1914–1996), glamorous movie star, famous as the love interest in the Bob Hope–Bing Crosby "Road" movies; **Fritz Lang** (1890–1976), German-born director of *M, Western Union, Ministry of Fear*, many other films; **Charles Laughton** (1899–1962), celebrated English character actor; **Harriet** (1909–1994), **Ozzie** (1906–1975), and **Ricky Nelson** (1940–1985), wife, husband, and son, part of family sitcom in early television; **Freddie Prinze** (1954–1977), first Latino star of a television sitcom; **George Raft** (1895–1980), tough guy of 1930s movies; **Telly Savalas** (1921–1994), best known as the star of television's *Kojak* series; and **Jack Webb** (1920–1982), the star of television's police drama *Dragnet*. *6300 Forest Lawn Drive, Hollywood Hills, Los Angeles. Tel. (800) 204-3131. Fax: (323) 769-7317. Open 8:00 A.M.–5:00 P.M. daily; rest rooms, flower shop, gift shop.*

BETTE DAVIS
1908–1989

Even in death Ms. Davis manages to be the center of attention, as her imposing tomb testifies. Against the backdrop of the outer wall of the Courts of Remembrance, between two elongated evergreens, is her white marble sarcophagus, ornamented with Renaissance flourishes and a stately, full-standing female statue on top. Below her name and those of her mother and sister, is the inscription, "SHE DID IT THE HARD WAY." That's probably true, for she fought hard and often with Jack Warner, head of Warner Brothers, who held her contract, battling for better roles, better scripts, better directors, and better pay—and she usually won. Her fights paid off in roles that showcased her enormous talent, making her Hollywood's leading actress of the late 1930s. Some of her roles were blockbusters: as a sluttish waitress in *Of Human Bondage* (for which she should have won an Oscar), as an actress in *Dangerous* (for which she did), as a gangster's moll in *Kid Galahad*, as a dying society girl in *Dark Victory*, and as an English queen in *The Private Lives of Elizabeth and Essex*. In a fifty-eight year career she made some eighty-seven films and demonstrated she could play comedy, tragedy, and most emotions in between. In the process she won eight Oscar nominations. (Trivial pursuits: It was she who gave the award its nickname, saying the statuette's backside resembled that of her then-husband's, Ham Oscar Nelson.) One of her greatest performances came later in life, as Margo Channing, an aging actress in *All About Eve*. Many a comedian used her mannered speech, big fluttery eyes, and distinctive handling of a cigarette to comic effect. But that doesn't diminish the fact that she was one of Hollywood's greatest. She may have done it the hard way—but it was worth it.

BUSTER KEATON
1895–1966

Arguably the very best silent movie comedian, Joseph Frank Keaton was often overshadowed by Charlie Chaplin, but he has proved his staying power for his acrobatic skills, his incredible stunts (which he did himself), his nuanced deadpan, and his all-round creativeness. Anthony Lane, a *New Yorker* critic, once wrote that "he was just too good, in too many ways, too soon." Certainly Keaton peaked early. He had his training from age three as part of his parents' vaudeville act. His nickname came from a fall down a flight of stairs as a baby, which left him miraculously unharmed. Harry Houdini, a fellow performer, said, "That's some buster your baby took!" Buster took far worse, as part of the family act was for his father to throw little Buster all over the stage, what today would be called child abuse. In 1917, at age twenty-two, Keaton met Roscoe "Fatty" Arbuckle, a big silent star at the time, and they collaborated on two-reelers, with Keaton's roles becoming bigger and bigger. Soon he was producing his own films at his own studio, including, from 1920 to 1929, most of his best and most celebrated films. Among them: *The General, The Navigator, Sherlock Jr.,* and *The Cameraman*. One of his innovations as a director was the use of a split screen. In the 1930s Keaton went into decline as a performer, due to poor luck, a bad deal with MGM that didn't recognize the extent of his talent, his alcoholism, and a bad marriage. By the 1940s he bounced back and the 1950s brought a new appraisal of his remarkable talents. There were television appearances and cameos in such movies as *Around the World in 80 Days* and *A Funny Thing Happened on the Way to the Forum*.

STAN LAUREL
1890–1965

It's something of a surprise, on discovering the white marble memorial marker ensconced in the fieldstone wall, up a few steps behind the massive statue of George Washington in the Court of Liberty, to see "Stan Laurel, A Master of Comedy" with no Hardy in sight. Laurel and Hardy: One always thinks of this comedy team in tandem, so it's only natural to expect them to be buried side by side. What made them special were the contrasts: tall, skinny, perpetually perplexed, English-accented Laurel and fat, bumptious, blowhard, know-it-all American Oliver Hardy (1892–1957). Laurel, born in Ulverston, in the lake country of England, had only a grammar school education and was in show business from the get-go; Hardy, Georgia born, studied law briefly and trained as a singer at the Atlanta Conservatory of Music. Director Leo McCarey brought this disparate twosome together and directed all their shorts, which are acknowledged as their comic masterpieces. Laurel's early training in pantomime shows clearly in

his clever business and perfect timing. He did much of the writing for their skits. They shared a proclivity for marriage: Laurel six times, Hardy three. Two years older than Hardy, Laurel outlived his thirty-year partner by eight years but stopped working after Hardy's death. If you want to find Ollie, he's at Valhalla Memorial Park in North Hollywood. Separated at last.

LIBERACE
1 9 1 9 – 1 9 8 7

Don't expect Wladziu Valentino Liberace—Lee to friends—to hide discreetly in some hillside locale. This flamboyant showman continues to call attention to himself. You'll find him residing in a splendid white marble sarcophagus in the Courts of Remembrance, ornamented with Florentine designs and a black metal rendering of his signature and a piano with the candelabra on it, his trademarks in life. Above the tomb stands a draped marble figure (his muse per-

haps). With him are his mother ("our beloved mom") and older brother, **George**. Trained as a classical pianist, Liberace debuted with the Chicago Symphony Orchestra in 1940, but he wasn't sure he would make it in that field. Drawn to popular music, he created a persona that grew more outrageous every passing year and made him the star of supper clubs and his own television show, which won one Emmy as the best entertainment show and another for Lee as the best male performer. Critics scoffed, calling him the "Candelabra Casanova." Such criticism prompted him to quip, "I cried all the way to the bank," a remark later copied by others. Critics also questioned his sexual orientation. Growing up in a era of closet dwellers, he constantly denied his homosexuality, while mincing, winking, and flaunting pink tuxedos and a hot-pink llama fur coat covered in sequins and rhinestones. He basked in outrageous parodies of himself, one time flying across the stage in the guise of a purple bird. Even so, he made and spent millions and was dear to the fluttering hearts of fans, mostly older women.

Hollywood Forever Park

LOS ANGELES

A medium-size burial ground of sixty acres in the heart of Hollywood, this is as crowded with celebrities as Oscar night, a virtual pantheon of movie gods and goddesses. There are blue-chip local notables as well, such as **Harry Chandler** (1864–1944) of the *Los Angeles Times* newspaper family and philanthropist **William A. Clark, Jr**. (1877–1934), whose Greek temple mausoleum occupies its very own island in the graceful pond, around which blue herons and white egrets swoop. Pines, palms, cypresses, ancient oaks, and various weeping trees, white marble mausoleums and monuments are rampant, and the flat grounds are so walkable, with graves so well marked that the map sold in the office isn't a necessity. The cemetery, which opened in 1889, had a period of not-so-benign neglect, but new ownership seems to have made a difference in its upkeep. In a large Hollywood Cathedral Mausoleum, with beautiful Tiffany-like windows, are wall crypts of note: in 1224 is **Peter Finch** (1916–1977), English actor who starred in *Sunday, Bloody Sunday* and scores of other films; in corridor C, niche 5, tier 1 is **Peter Lorre** (1904–1964), character actor with an unmistakable spooky whisper, who provided chills in *Casablanca*, *The Maltese Falcon,* and other thrillers; and in 1205 is **Rudolph Valentino** (1895–1926), heartthrob of female fans for his sultry "Latin lover" looks in *The Sheik* and other romantic silent movies. The long list of stars at rest throughout the park includes **Marion Davies** (1897–1961), actress, better known as the longtime mistress of publisher William Randolph Hearst; **Nelson Eddy** (1901–1967), robust singing star of musicals with Jeanette MacDonald; **Douglas Fairbanks, Sr.** (1883–1939), and **Douglas Fairbanks, Jr.** (1909–2000), both movie actors in the flashy acrobatic style (though Jr. could also do debonair comedy), together in one of the park's most serene setting by a reflecting pool; **Victor Fleming** (1883–1949), film director; **Woody Herman** (1913–1987), bandleader and jazz clarinetist; **Adolphe Menjou** (1890–1963), suave character actor of the 1930s and 1940s; **Paul Muni** (1895–1967), star of *The Good Earth* and other films, and his screen-writer wife, **Bella** (1898–1971), sharing the same modest memorial stone in the Beth Olan Jewish section. **Benjamin "Bugsy" Siegel** (1906–1947), notorious gangster, has gone underground here as well. **Hattie McDaniel** (1895–1952), African American character actress, winner of a best supporting actress Oscar for her role as Mammy in *Gone with the Wind,* was denied burial here in 1952—which she had requested—but now has a distinctive memorial prominently located next to the pond full of waterlilies. *6000 Santa Monica Boulevard, Los Angeles. Tel. (323) 469-1181. Grounds open 7:00 A.M.–5:00 P.M. daily, but Beth Olam section is closed Saturday. Office hours: 8:30 A.M.–5:00 P.M. Monday–Friday, 10:00 A.M.–4:00 P.M. Saturday–Sunday; map (fee), rest room, flower shop.*

MEL BLANC
1908–1989

As a child in Portland, Oregon, Melvin Jerome Blank was the class clown, always mimicking accents. A teacher said, "You'll never amount to anything. You're like your last name: blank." At age sixteen, Mel began spelling his name Blanc and later changed it legally. Radio led to the movies, and when he auditioned at Warner Brothers, he was hired to do the voice of a drunken bull in a 1937 Porky Pig short. This led to being Porky himself. Porky's final line, "That's all folks!" was supposedly a Blanc ad-lib that took. "What's up, Doc?" was another Blanc idea, this one for Bugs Bunny. In time Blanc's was the voice of Daffy Duck, Elmer Fudd, the Road Runner, Yosemite Sam, Sylvester the Cat, Tweety Pie, and the original voice and irritating

laugh of Woody Woodpecker. In a lifetime of cartoon voices, he did more than 3,000 cartoons and was the first such actor to receive on-screen credit for his work. He had other jobs from time to time: on Jack Benny's radio and television shows, small roles in films, and as a coach of accents for Warner Brothers actors. But he preferred working behind the scenes. It seems fitting that his headstone would read: "That's all folks." Too bad there's no soundtrack to go with it.

CECIL B. DEMILLE
1881–1959

How soon we forget! Cecil who? From the 1930s through the 1950s, when you thought of movie extravaganzas, only one name leaped out at you: C. B. DeMille. Each of his high-budget films was made with "a cast of thousands," as the ads proclaimed. Although his movies began larger than life and grew from there, his personal beginnings were sedately middle class. But both parents had theatrical leanings, and Cecil became an actor, then managed his mother's theatrical agency. Through the agency he met Jesse L. Lasky and Samuel Goldfish (later Goldwyn), Lasky's brother-in-law. The three men became partners and DeMille had the chance to direct his first movie, *The Straw Man*, in 1912 on a budget of $15,000. The film made $225,000 and De Mille was off and running. He bought out his partners, and began directing the epics with gargantuan sets and lavish props for which he became famous. The list is awesome—and so were the profits—what with *The Ten Commandments*, *The King of Kings*, *Cleopatra*, *The Crusades*, *The Greatest Show on Earth* (his only film to win an Oscar, for best pic-

ture). Then there were his panoramic westerns: *The Plainsman* and *Union Pacific*. Today, with all the electronic wizardry and special effects in movies, DeMille's panoramic wonders seem almost archaic. Yet he scored a number of "firsts": first to list the actors' names at the start of a film (in *The Squaw Man*); first to sign Hal Roach, Hopalong Cassidy, and Gloria Swanson; first to do several versions of a popular film; first to show sneak previews to test audiences; first to use camera booms and artificial "effect" lighting. The DeMille sarcophagi are among the cemetery's most imposing. With Cecil Blount DeMille is **Constance Adams DeMille** (1874–1960), his wife of fifty-seven years—a Hollywood rarity—who outlived him by a year. Brother **William DeMille** (1878–1955) and their mother, **Matilda** (1853–1923), are also present and accounted for.

JOHN HUSTON
1906–1987

A mere marker in the ground doesn't do justice to the Huston achievements, which began with *The Maltese Falcon* in 1941 and ended, as he did, with *The Dead* in 1987. The son of character actor Walter Huston and Rhea Gore, a newspaper reporter, John came upon his multiple talents naturally. His father helped get him a job as a screenwriter, and he subsequently worked on scripts for *Jezebel* and *Wuthering Heights*. But he wanted to direct as well, so after one more script, *High Sierra*, he was given the chance. That's where *The Maltese Falcon* came in, and with it a whole new career. In 1948, he directed Humphrey Bogart again in another blockbuster, *The Treasure of the Sierra Madre*, which brought him

Oscars for screenwriting and directing and his father one for best supporting actor. Success mostly followed success with *The African Queen* (bringing Bogart an Oscar for best actor), *Moulin Rouge, Beat the Devil,* and *Moby-Dick.* In 1983 he received a lifetime achievement award from the American Film Institute, which spurred him on to direct three more first-rate films: *Under the Volcano, Prizzi's Honor,* and *The Dead.* In contrast to his crisp, well-made movies, which were always within budget, Huston's personal life was in frequent disarray. Five marriages, various liaisons, an assortment of children (including the talented actress Angelica Huston), and frequent wanderings sum it up. After wrapping *The Dead,* Huston was in Rhode Island (where he was born), helping his son Danny direct his first movie, when he died. Life had come full cycle. John Huston the scriptwriter would have appreciated the tidy ending.

TYRONE POWER
1 9 1 4 – 1 9 5 8

With his darkly handsome looks and the fact that he was the third generation of a theatrical family, Power was only twenty-two years old when he signed a seven-year contract with 20th Century Fox. That was 1936, and within seven years he had made twenty pictures, becoming a matinee idol. From 1942 to 1946, he took time out for real life and the U.S. Marine Corps. He went from private to flight officer on some dangerous missions in the South Pacific. When the war ended, he had a first lieutenant's rank and a new maturity that suited him for the leads in *The Razor's Edge* and *Nightmare Alley,* offbeat movies that proved he was more than just a pretty face. Like his father, who died with his acting boots on, Power suffered a fatal heart attack in the midst of a duel on the set of *Solomon and Sheba* in Madrid. His friend, fellow actor David Niven, said, "He was that great rarity—a man who was just as nice as he seemed to be."

His monument here, next to the pond, is surely more pretentious than he was: Its three shallow steps of white marble lead to a marble funeral urn, marble bench, and marble book—standing upright—with bas relief masks of the Greek gods of Comedy and Tragedy and Shakespeare's line in Hamlet that "THERE'S A SPECIAL PROVIDENCE IN THE FALL OF A SPARROW."

Home of Peace Memorial Park and Mausoleum

LOS ANGELES

The grounds at this old Jewish cemetery, which dates back to 1855, are lovely, if crowded, shaded by palms, pines, and other trees. There are many substantial private mausoleums and scores of upright headstones lined in tight rows. Resting here are **Shemp Howard** (1895–1955), part of the Three Stooges slapstick comedy team; **Louis Mayer** (1885–1957), renown head of Metro-Goldwyn-Mayer; and the **Warner brothers**, together in their own mausoleum (except Jack). **Jack L. Warner** (1892–1978), one of the most powerful studio heads of the 1930s and 1940s, was also one of the most combative with his stars. His gravesite here, with private garden, trees, fountain, and walkway, is serenity itself. *4334 Whittier Boulevard, Los Angeles. Tel. (323) 261-6135. Grounds open 8:00 A.M.–4:00 P.M. daily except Saturday. Office hours: 9:00 A.M.–4:00 P.M. daily, except Saturday; map, rest room.*

Westwood Village Memorial Park

LOS ANGELES

Talk about big things in small packages! This tiny, hard-to-find burial ground, just off Wilshire Boulevard and surrounded by high-rise buildings in Westwood, is easily overlooked. If you enter the driveway to the AVCO Theater parking lot, the cemetery is to the right. Once found, it is a mother lode of celebrity sightings and the easiest of any burial ground to explore in a very short time. The main area resembles a grassy village square, punctuated by pepper trees and pines. Clustered among the inhabitants are **Eve Arden** (1909–1990), character actress known for wise-cracking roles, which she perfected in the television series *Our Miss Brooks;* **Jim Backus** (1913–1989), movie and television actor, whose voice was used for the cartoon character Mr. Magoo; historians **Will** (1885–1981) and **Ariel Durant** (1898–1981); **Eva Gabor** (1919–1995), one of the publicity-happy Hungarian sisters; **Armand Hammer** (1898–1990), businessman-entrepreneur, investor in Occidental Petroleum; **James Wong Howe** (1899–1976), award-winning cinematographer; **Stan Kenton**

(1911–1979), jazz band leader; **Burt Lancaster** (1913–1994), a megastar of major movies like *Elmer Gantry, Sweet Smell of Success,* and *Seven Days in May;* **Irving "Swifty" Lazar** (1907–1993), noted actors' agent; **Peggy Lee** (1920–2002), popular songstress for more than five decades; and **Oscar Levant** (1906–1972), classical pianist and actor. Also here are **Dean Martin** (1917–1995), laid-back crooner, actor, and "Rat Pack" pal of Frank Sinatra; **Walter Matthau** (1920–2000), talented actor in comic and serious roles, known for *Charade, Cactus Flower,* and as Oscar Madison in *The Odd Couple,* with his friend Jack Lemmon; **Nader Naderpour** (1929–2000), respected Iranian poet ; **Gregor Piatigorsky** (1903–1976), cellist; **Buddy Rich** (1917–1987), brilliant jazz drummer; **G. David Schine** (1929–1996), the once-

infamous friend of Roy Cohn and Senator Joe McCarthy, who later became a respectable producer; **Natalie Wood Wagner** (1938–1981), movie actress from age five, died too young by drowning mysteriously; and **Darryl F. Zanuck** (1902–1979), award-winning movie producer. **Roy Orbison** (1936–1988), rockabilly singer and songwriter, is tucked into an unmarked grave on the grassy green, between actor **Lew Ayres** (1908–1996) and Jim Backus on the west edge of the green. Popular rock musician and bandleader **Frank Zappa** (1940–1993) is here as well, also unmarked and unnoticed. Unearthing him is an undercover job, but he is just to the right of Lew Ayres by a large tree. The large headstone of **George C. Scott** (1927–1999), actor and Oscar winner for *Patton,* is also unmarked, but you'll find it just left of Walter Matthau along the south side of the park, next to the drive-way. Nearby is newly arrived **Jack Lemmon** (1925–2001), versatile movie and stage actor, two-time Oscar winner. **Fanny Brice** (1891–1951), comedienne of stage and radio, was recently reinterred here from Home of Peace Memorial Park and now resides in quiet splendor in a rose garden sanctuary behind the path where Matthau rests. *1218 Glendon Avenue, Los Angeles. Tel. (310) 474–11579 or (800) 966–5113. Open 8:00 A.M.–5:00 P.M. daily; map, rest rooms.*

TRUMAN CAPOTE
1924–1984

It is difficult to think of Capote—wispy, lispy, and fey, with a little boy voice and five-foot three-inch height—as a ladies' man, but for many years after his first success as a novelist he was the darling—witty, gossipy, and clever—and confidante of prominent New York society belles. His first book, *Other Voices, Other Rooms,* published in 1948, was a best-seller within weeks, pushing its twenty-three-year-old New Orleans–born author into the limelight, a place he never willingly left. *The Grass Harp* followed, establishing him as a Southern novelist, though he lived most of his life, from age eight, in New York City, with time out for school in Ossining, New York, and Greenwich, Connecticut. For a while, success followed success. He won two O. Henry Awards for short stories, of which he was a master. He also wrote some superb nonfiction: articles in the *New Yorker* magazine and *In Cold Blood,* a book about the brutal murder of a family in Kansas. This was often called his very best book and was a pacesetter of the nonfiction novel genre. With *Breakfast at Tiffany's,* he was back with his light touch and returned to the South and memories of childhood in two charming memoirs. Television talk shows, readings, and social extravaganzas like his "Black and White Ball" followed, and with them a pattern of alcoholism, drug use, and nervous breakdowns. Capote died of a liver disease complicated by multiple drug use and phlebitis. There was much controversy about Capote's ashes, half of which were brought east in an urn and ended up in Crooked Pond, Bridgehampton, New York, where a huge boulder commemorates the locale. But his work lives on, as clever and creative as when he burst like a gamin on the New York literary scene.

MARILYN MONROE
1926–1962

Hers is the grave most tourists seek, rushing to her beige marble wall crypt (which usually has fresh flowers in the built-in vase attached to it) at the north end of the park, barely glancing at the other intriguing residents. A marble bench, dedicated to her, rests opposite her crypt. Even in death this blond siren, who began life as Norma Jean Mortensen, continues to lure admirers. From her early impact films, *The Asphalt Jungle* and *All About Eve,* to *The Seven Year Itch, Bus Stop, Some Like It Hot,* and *The Misfits,* she filled the screen with her presence, her voluptuous figure, wiggle when she walked, innocent smile, and breathy, little girl voice. She proved she could do comedy in *How to Marry a Millionaire,* but wanted to be taken seriously as a dramatic actress and studied at the Actors Studio in New York. She had big yearnings, which three marriages, numerous affairs, psychiatry, and the adulation of fans couldn't satisfy. Her short life was star-crossed by drugs, insecurities, insomnia, habitual tardiness—she'd be hours late, both in life and on movie sets—and bouts with mental illness (probably hereditary). Her final curtain, a mysterious suicide after she'd been fired from her last movie, then reinstated, has been the stuff of movies, plays, biographies, and endless gossip. Was it really suicide, murder, or a fake attempt for attention that went awry? We'll never know.

San Fernando Mission Cemetery and Mausoleum

MISSION HILLS

In this one-hundred-acre Catholic graveyard, the terrain is level, with most tombstones flush with the ground. Religious statues are interspersed with a few trees, and the tan brick walls and buildings with red tile roofs are in the Spanish mission style, which echos the authentic old San Fernando Mission in the same town. There are no superstars resting here, but there are a number of remarkable character actors who were the joy of many devout fans of movies of Hollywood's golden age. Here you'll encounter **Edward Arnold** (1890–1956), who played bankers, corrupt politicians (as in *Meet John Doe*), and pompous white-collar villains in more than 150 movies; **Ed Begley, Sr.** (1901–1970), who won a best supporting actor Oscar for *Sweet Bird of Youth;* **William Bendix** (1906–1964), who played thugs, often with a heart of gold, as well as Riley in the television series *Life of Riley;* **Jerry Colonna** (1904–1986), comic actor best known as Bob Hope's buddy in many films; **William Frawley** (1887–1966), who was Fred Mertz on television's *I Love Lucy;* **George Gobel** (1919–1991), "Lonesome George," the comedian; and **Henry O'Neill** (1891–1961), who was in more than 200 movies. Other residents are **Chuck Connors** (1921–1992), of television's *The Rifleman;* and **Ritchie Valens** (1941–1959), rock musician, who died in the same plane crash that killed Buddy Holly. *11160 Stranwood Avenue, Mission Hills. Tel. (818) 361-7387. Grounds open 8:00 A.M.–5:00 P.M. daily. Office hours: 8:00 A.M.–5:00 P.M. Monday–Friday, 8:00 A.M.–4:00 P.M. Saturday, 10:00 A.M.–3:00 P.M. Sunday; map, rest rooms.*

WALTER BRENNAN
1894–1974

Character actors may not bring you to a movie theater, but they're often the ones you remember when you leave. Look at all the great westerns—most were ensemble works, dependent on a cast of believable characters. Walter Brennan was one of the best. In a forty-five-year career, he appeared in over 450 movies and won a best supporting actor Oscar three times (for *Come and Get It, Kentucky,* and as Judge Roy Bean in *The Westerner*), the first actor to do so. Directors liked Brennan's reliability as much as his talent, and he worked for many top-notch ones: Howard Hawks, Fritz Lang, John Ford, and Henry Hathaway, holding his own with actors like Gary Cooper, Henry Fonda, Spencer Tracy, John Wayne, Jimmy Stewart, and Gregory Peck. Married for fifty-four years to his high school sweetheart, Brennan continued to work right into his seventies, moving easily into television—and the sitcom *The Real McCoy*—when movie roles dried up. No question about it, he *was* the real McCoy.

Mountain View Cemetery

OAKLAND

Established in 1863 in the Oakland hills—and designed by Frederick Law Olmstead—Mountain View, with its beautiful 220 acres, is in the garden tradition of burial grounds. Its hallmarks are splendid vistas of the bay, broad avenues encompassing the slopes of six hills, sheltering shade trees, grassy knolls, a "Millionaires' Row" of substantial mausoleums shaped like pyramids and Gothic churches, and obelisks topped by winged angels and funereal urns. The crème de la crème of the settlers and powers of the Bay Area reside here. Among them are **Warren A. Bechtel** (1872–1933), industrialist and engineer; **Charles Crocker** (1822–1888), a founder of the Southern Pacific Railroad; **Domingo Ghirardelli** (1815–1894), founder of the chocolate company that bears his name; **Thomas Hill** (1828–1908), a famous landscape painter of Yosemite Valley; **Henry J. Kaiser** (1882–1967), founder of Kaiser Steel & Aluminum, builder of World War II's Liberty ships, and pioneer in health care insurance for employees, which later led to Kaiser Permanente, an innovator in managed health care; and **Frank Norris** (1870–1902), author of *The Octopus, The Pit,* and other influential realistic novels. *5000 Piedmont Avenue, Oakland. Tel. (510) 658-2588. Grounds open 7:30 A.M.–5:00 P.M. Monday–Friday, 9:00 A.M.–5:00 P.M. weekends and holidays. Office Hours: 8:00 A.M.–4:30 P.M. Monday–Friday, 10:00 A.M.–4:00 P.M. weekends and holidays; map, rest rooms.*

JULIA MORGAN
1872–1957

Don't tell Julia Morgan that Women's Lib began in the 1960s. This pioneering San Francisco architect was one of the first women to enroll in the University of California's School of Engineering and receive a B.S. She was also the first woman to be admitted to the Ecole des Beaux-Arts in Paris and one of the earliest architects—perhaps the first woman—to be licensed by examination in California. Later, in 1921, she was one of the first women admitted to the American Institute of Architects. One of her first jobs was to work on the new Greek Theatre and the Hearst Memorial Mining

Building at the University of California at Berkeley. This led to a lifelong association with the Hearst family. Over a long professional life, which included some 700 projects, she is best known for San Simeon, the Hearst Castle south of Monterey, the most famous of many Hearst estates she worked on. Her rough-hewn granite headstone, on which various family members' names are included, rests on a quiet slope, as unostentatious as she herself was—a quiet success story for all time.

Santa Barbara Cemetery

SANTA BARBARA

With a sweeping view of the Pacific Ocean, situated amidst beautifully groomed green lawns, punctuated by stately pines, eucalyptus, and a Romanesque-style chapel (where the office is located), this relatively small cemetery is the last address of "whiz kid" educator **Robert Maynard Hutchins** (1899–1977), president of the University of Chicago, and of nature writer and botanist **Donald C. Peattie** (1898–1964), among others. *901 Channel Drive, Santa Barbara. Tel. (805) 969-3231. Grounds open 8:00 A.M.–5:00 P.M. daily. Office hours: 8:30 A.M.–4:45 P.M. Monday-Friday; map, rest room.*

RONALD COLMAN

1891–1958

You'd probably have to be a fan of old movies to remember Ronald Charles Colman nowadays, but in his 1930–1940s heyday, he was the romantic lead in such movies as *A Tale of Two Cities, Lost Horizon, The Prisoner of Zenda, If I Were King, The Light That Failed,* and *Random Harvest.* His upper-middle-class English family; prep school; years in an exclusive British regiment in World War I, during which he was wounded, decorated, and medically discharged; his training for the diplomatic corps, all were fodder for his acting career. After minor successes in London and Broadway, he arrived in Hollywood in 1925, where his distinctive, plummy voice and upper-class English accent were ideally suited to nuanced roles of experienced, sometimes world-weary heroes. Colman's

large polished black granite headstone features, appropriately, a theater curtain half-opened to reveal a quote from Prospero's speech in *The Tempest:* "WE ARE SUCH STUFF AS DREAMS ARE MADE ON, AND OUR LITTLE LIFE IS ROUNDED WITH A SLEEP."

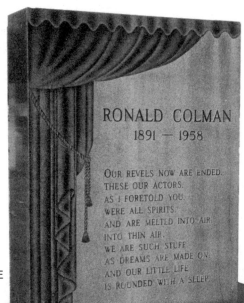

RONALD COLMAN
1891 — 1958

OUR REVELS NOW ARE ENDED.
THESE OUR ACTORS,
AS I FORETOLD YOU,
WERE ALL SPIRITS,
AND ARE MELTED INTO AIR,
INTO THIN AIR.
WE ARE SUCH STUFF
AS DREAMS ARE MADE ON,
AND OUR LITTLE LIFE
IS ROUNDED WITH A SLEEP.

Washington

Greenwood Memorial Park

RENTON

In this suburb southeast of Seattle, the rolling hills and wooded pathways of Greenwood are home to local dignitaries, among others. *350 Monroe Avenue NE, Renton. Tel. (425) 255-1511. Grounds open from dawn to dusk. Office hours: 8:30 A.M.–5:00 P.M. Monday–Friday, 9:00 A.M.–5:00 P.M. Saturday, 11:00 A.M.–4:00 P.M. Sunday; map, rest rooms.*

JIMI HENDRIX
1942–1970

More than just a wild man of the guitar, James Marshall Hendrix —alias Jimi— was uniquely talented. He rocked, he rolled, he leaped, he swiveled, he bumped and ground, he rolled sideways, he picked the strings with his teeth, he sometimes set the guitar on fire, and for a change of pace threw it against his amplifiers. At his peak, 1968, when he was named artist of the year by *Billboard* and *Rolling Stone,* he could do anything, and often did, incorporating elements of blues, rock, and jazz into his music for a totally new sound. "The world's a bringdown," he once said, "if we play loud enough, maybe we can drown it out." For someone who flamed out and died young, he packed a lot into twenty-eight years. Having perfect pitch, he got his first guitar at eleven and taught himself to play by listening to blues artists B. B. King, Muddy Waters, and "T-Bone" Walker. He trained by playing in backup bands for the Isley Brothers, King, and Ike and Tina Turner, and later played with a number of blues greats. When he toured Europe with his own group, the Jimi Hendrix Experience, he was an enormous success, which was made even bigger in his American debut at the Monterey International Pop Festival in 1967. Sometimes hyped as the "black Elvis," he scored because of his music—albums like *Axis: Bold as Love* and *Electric Ladyland*—his theatrical flair, and, especially, the sheer uniqueness of his sound. He died in London of a drug overdose complication. The only guitar in the vicinity in this silent city on a hill is etched into the left side of Hendrix's granite gravestone. But his hits—"Hey Joe," "Purple Haze," "Foxy Lady," and many more—are as alive and fresh as ever.

Lakeview Cemetery

SEATTLE

On grounds dotted with shrubbery and aged evergreens, this old burial ground dates back to 1872. There are now some 40,000 gravesites, including a Nisei Memorial, honoring Japanese American servicemen killed in action in World War II. Resting here also are prominent Seattle settlers such as **Colonel Alden J. Blethen** (1846–1916), founder of the *Seattle Times* newspaper; **Elisha P. Ferry** (1825–1895), first governor of the state; **John W. Nordstrom** (1871–1963), Klondike adventurer who opened a shoe store, the origins of Nordstrom Department Stores; and **Dorothea G. E. Ohben**, big-time madame, whose estate funded the start of the Seattle public school system. *1554 15th Avenue East, Seattle. Tel. (206) 322-1582. Grounds open 9:00 A.M.–4:30 P.M. daily in winter, 9:00 A.M.– 8:00 P.M. daily in summer; map, rest rooms.*

BRUCE LEE
1940–1973

Bruce Lee's life was short and his fame as brief as a sputtering candle. Born in San Francisco, he grew up in Hong Kong, attended college briefly in Seattle, and made his name and fortune in Hong Kong movies as a master of martial arts. In his brief time, he set new standards for complex dancer-like acrobatics, and his fight scenes were like a vigorous form of ballet. His intense good looks, physical grace, and charisma appealed to audiences East and West. His mysterious death, whether from a kidney infection, drugs, or at the hands of Chinese gangsters—nobody knows for sure—came suddenly and too soon. His polished red granite headstone, with his photograph at the top, rests in an elegant site in the shade of a tall pine tree. On his right a similar black granite stone commemorates his son, **Brandon Bruce Lee** (1965–1993), a budding actor and martial arts expert killed on a movie set by live bullets fired accidentally.

APPENDIX

In case you have been wondering about certain missing persons in these pages, the following entries may answer some of your questions.

Gone With the Wind

Bud Abbott (1895–1974), comedian, part of Abbott and Costello comedy team; ashes scattered in Pacific Ocean

Desi Arnaz (1917–1986), entertainer; ashes scattered

Cliff Arquette (1918–1974), comedian; ashes scattered by Telophase Society

Jean Arthur (1900–1991), actress; ashes scattered off Point Lobos, California

Richard Boone (1917–1981), actor; ashes scattered in the Hawaiian Islands

John Carradine (1909–1988), actor; buried at sea in Catalina Channel, California

Rachel Carson (1907–1964), biologist-ecologist, author; ashes scattered along the Maine coast near Sheepscott

Kurt Cobain (1967–1994), musician; ashes scattered in the Wishkah River, Washington State

Irvin S. Cobb (1876–1944), writer, editor, humorist; ashes fertilized a tree in Padukah, Kentucky

Charles Coburn (1877–1961), character actor in movies; ashes scattered in Georgia, Massachusetts, and New York

Aaron Copeland (1900–1990), composer; ashes scattered throughout Tanglewood Music Center, Berkshires, Massachusetts

Wally Cox (1924–1973), comedian; ashes scattered at sea

Dennis Crosby (1935–1991), actor, son of Bing Crosby; ashes scattered in northern California

Bobby Darin (1936–1973), singer, performer; body donated for research purposes to the UCLA Medical School, Los Angeles, California

Clarence Darrow (1857–1938), lawyer, famous for the Scopes Trial; ashes scattered from bridge into Jackson Park Lagoon, Chicago

Andy Devine (1896–1977), cowboy singer-actor; ashes scattered at sea

Eddie Duchin (1909–1951), orchestra leader; ashes scattered in Atlantic Ocean

Ann Dvorak (1924–1979), movie actress; ashes scattered

Albert Einstein (1879–1955), scientist, physicist; ashes scattered over unknown river in New Jersey

Margaret Fuller (1810–1850), educator, first American woman journalist; lost at sea, body never recovered

Jerry Garcia (1942–1995), musician; ashes scattered: half in the Ganges River, India, half beneath the Golden Gate Bridge in San Francisco

Marvin Gaye (1939–1984), singer; ashes scattered in Pacific Ocean

Theodore Geisel (1904–1991), aka Dr. Seuss, author of children's books; location of ashes unknown

Cary Grant (1904–1986) actor, perennial Hollywood star; ashes scattered in California

Walter Gropius (1883–1969), architect; ashes scattered behind Authors' Ridge in Sleepy Hollow Cemetery, Concord, Massachusetts

Woody Guthrie (1912–1967), folk singer, composer; ashes scattered in Atlantic Ocean

George Harrison (1943-2001), rock musician, one of the Beatles; ashes scattered over several rivers in India

Marsden Hartley (1877–1943), painter; ashes scattered in Androscoggin River, Maine

Phil Hartman (1948–1998), comedian; ashes scattered over Catalina Island's Emerald Bay, California

Howard Hawks (1896-1977), director-producer; ashes scattered

Dick Haymes (1918–1980), popular singer; ashes given to family

Van Heflin (1910–1971), actor; ashes scattered in Pacific Ocean

Joe Hill (1879–1915), labor leader; as requested by him, his ashes scattered in every state except Utah, where he was executed by firing squad for killing a businessman

Alfred Hitchcock (1899–1980), director; ashes scattered

William Holden (1918–1981), movie actor; ashes scattered in Pacific Ocean

Rock Hudson (1925–1985), movie actor; ashes scattered at sea

Christopher Isherwood (1904–1986), author; body donated for research to UCLA Medical School, Los Angeles, California

William James (1842–1910), Harvard professor/psychologist/philosopher; ashes scattered in mountain stream in Chocorua, New Hampshire

Janis Joplin (1943–1970), singer, rock star; ashes scattered in Pacific Ocean along northern California coast

Andre Kostelanetz (1901–1980), conductor, composer; ashes scattered in Pacific Ocean off Kauai, Hawaii

Veronica Lake (1919–1973), movie actress; ashes scattered in the Caribbean off the Virgin Islands

Elsa Lanchester (1902–1986), movie actress; ashes scattered at sea

Peter Lawford (1923–1984), actor; ashes scattered, memorial at Westwood Cemetery, Los Angeles, California

Frank Loesser (1910–1969), composer of Broadway musicals; ashes scattered in Atlantic Ocean

Herbert "Zeppo" Marx (1901–1979), one of the Marx Brothers comedy team; ashes scattered at sea

Steve McQueen (1930–1980), movie star; ashes scattered in Santa Paula Valley, California

Ethel Merman (1908–1984), musical comedy star; ashes scattered on Broadway

Charles Mingus (1922–1979), jazz musician/composer; ashes thrown into the Ganges River

Georgia O'Keeffe (1887–1986), painter; ashes scattered at The Pedernal, Abiquiu, New Mexico

J. Robert Oppenheimer (1904–1967), physicist; ashes scattered in the Caribbean

Dorothy Parker (1893–1967), writer, poet, screenwriter, all-round wit; ashes in a special memorial garden at NAACP headquarters, Baltimore, Maryland

Walter Pidgeon (1897–1984), actor; body donated for research to UCLA Medical School, Los Angeles, California

Walter Reuther (1907–1970), labor leader, head of United Auto Workers union; ashes scattered over Black Lake at UAW Family Education Center, Onaway, Michigan

Richard Rodgers (1902–1979), composer; ashes scattered

Damon Runyon (1884–1956), author of humorous stories about Broadway; ashes scattered from a plane over Times Square, New York City, New York

E. W. Scripps (1854–1926), publisher of Scripps-Howard newspaper chain; died in Liberia, body buried at sea

Ted Shawn (1891–1972), modern dance pioneer; ashes scattered at Jacob's Pillow Festival, Lee, Massachusetts

John Sloan (1871–1951), painter; ashes scattered in Lock Haven, Pennsylvania

General Joseph W. "Vinegar Joe" Stilwell (1883–1946), commander of the China-Burma-India theater in World War II; ashes scattered in Pacific Ocean

Billy Strayhorn (1915–1967), jazz pianist and arranger; ashes scattered in New York City

Norman Thomas (1884–1968), Socialist; ashes scattered in Long Island Sound, New York

Paul Tillich (1886–1965), German-born Christian theologian; ashes scattered among pine trees in park named after him at New Harmony, Indiana

Thorstein Veblen (1857–1929), philosopher; ashes scattered in Pacific Ocean

Carl Van Vechten (1880–1964), author; ashes scattered in Shakespeare Gardens, Central Park, Manhattan, New York

Doak Walker (1927–1998), Detroit Lions football player, Heisman Trophy winner; ashes scattered at Long's Peak, Estes Park, Colorado

Fats Waller (1904–1943), jazz musician; ashes scattered in Harlem, New York

Edward Weston (1886–1958), photographer; ashes scattered in Pacific Ocean

Victoria Woodhull (1838–1927), suffragette, political activist; ashes scattered in Atlantic Ocean

Return to Sender

WHEREABOUTS UNKNOWN

Jim Bowie (1795–1836), **Davey Crockett** (1786–1836), and **William Travis** (–1836), frontiersmen, all killed in the battle against Mexican forces at the Alamo, their bodies thrown into a mass grave. (Whether the bones reburied near the railing of San Fernando Cathedral in San Antonio, Texas, are theirs is conjecture.)

Wilt Chamberlain (1936–1999), basketball player; location of ashes unknown

Roberto Clemente (1934–1972), baseball player; killed in a plane that crashed minutes after takeoff in San Juan, Puerto Rico, body never found

Hart Crane (1899–1932), much acclaimed American poet; seriously depressed, jumped overboard in Florida waters from a Mexican ship en route to New York, body never recovered

Crazy Horse (ca. 1842–1877), Sioux Indian chief; body returned to family, believed to be in the Panhandle, Oklahoma, or near Wounded Knee, Montana

Amelia Earhart (1898–1937), aviator; presumed to have crashed in the Pacific, body never found

Jimmy Hoffa (1913–1975), head of the Teamsters union, believed to be in league with organized crime; disappeared from a Bloomfield, Michigan, parking lot, where he had gone to meet a Mafia boss, body never recovered

Leslie Howard (1890–1943), movie actor; airplane crashed during World War II, body never recovered

Henry Hudson (1575–1611), English explorer, discoverer of Hudson River and Hudson's Bay; set adrift after a mutiny of his crew, never seen again

Anne Hutchinson (1591–1643), exiled by the Massachusetts Bay Colony and killed by Indians; believed to be buried somewhere in the Bronx, New York

Ring Lardner, Sr. (1885–1933), sportswriter and humorist; location unknown

Glenn Miller (1904–1944), band leader and trombonist; airplane downed over English Channel during World War II, body never recovered

Lee Harvey Oswald (1939–1963), alleged assassin of President John F. Kennedy; supposedly buried in Rose Hill Park in Fort Worth, Texas, but body allegedly stolen, recovered in Oklahoma, and reburied in the same cemetery under an assumed name

Thomas Paine (1737–1809), American revolutionary, author of *Common*

Sense; his coffin was stolen from his New Rochelle, New York, farm, shipped to England, and the bones vanished

Michael Rockefeller (1938–1961), son of Nelson Rockefeller, lost at sea while on a film expedition in New Guinea, his forty-foot catamaran capsized in shark-infested offshore waters; body never recovered

Hernando de Soto (1500–1542), Spanish explorer; somewhere along the Mississippi River

Dr. Benjamin Spock (1903–1998), pediatrician, author of medical advice to parents, political activist; location of ashes unknown

Jim Thompson (1906–1967), onetime OSS (Office of Strategic Services) officer in World War II in Thailand, stayed to develop the Thai silk industry, became major exporter; disappeared into the jungle in the Cameron Highlands of Malaysia on Easter Sunday, never seen again, foul play suspected but unproved

Nat Turner (1800–1831), African slave, leader of slave uprising; hanged when captured, body dissected by surgeons, whereabouts of remains unknown

Wish You Were There

B U R I A L S   A B R O A D

Benedict Arnold (1741–1801), American patriot, then traitor; buried in the crypt of St. Mary's Church, Battersea, London, England

Josephine Baker (1906–1975), African American entertainer, star of *Folies-Bergeres* and Paris nightlife; buried in Monaco

Ingrid Bergman (1915–1982), Swedish movie actress of the 1940s–1950s; buried in Stockholm, Sweden

Maria Callas (1923–1977), famous opera singer; buried in Pere Lachaise Cemetery, Paris, France

Charlie Chaplin (1889–1977), British-born comic of silent movies; buried in Corsier Cemetery, Corsier, Switzerland

W. E. B. DuBois (1868–1963), African American social reformer, writer; buried outside Government House, Accra, Ghana

Isadora Duncan (1878–1927), American modern dancer; buried in Pere Lachaise Cemetery, Paris, France

Marcus Garvey (1887–1940), social reformer, leader of the "Back to Africa" movement for African Americans; buried in King George VI Memorial Park, ·Kingston, Jamaica

Princess Grace (Kelly) of Monaco (1929–1982), movie actress, later princess of Monaco; buried in Cathedral of Monaco

Jim Morrison (1943–1971), American rock musician; buried in Pere Lachaise Cemetery, Paris, France

Robert Leroy Parker (1866–) and **Harry Longabaugh** (1865–), the originals of Butch Cassidy and the Sundance Kid; somewhere in Bolivia

General George S. Patton, Jr. (1885–1945), commander of Third Army in World War II; buried in Luxembourg American Cemetery, Hamm, Luxembourg

Pocahontas (1595–1617), American Indian who married an English colonist; buried in St. George's Churchyard, Gravesend, England

John Reed (1887–1920), journalist, subject of the movie *Reds;* buried in Kremlin wall, Moscow, Russia

Artur Rubenstein (1887–1982), world-renown classical pianist; buried in a special plot outside Jerusalem, Israel

Gertrude Stein (1874–1946), author and expatriate, famous for her Paris literary salon; buried in Pere Lachaise Cemetery, Paris, France

Orson Welles (1915–1985), actor, director, writer; ashes buried in a well in Ronda, Spain

Benjamin West (1738–1820), American painter, loyal to England, went to live there after the American Revolution; buried in St. Paul's Cathedral, London, England

Edith Wharton (1862–1937), author of *Ethan Frome, House of Mirth,* and other social novels; buried in Versailles, France

Richard Wright (1908–1960), African American writer, author of *Black Boy* and *Native Son;* buried in Pere Lachaise Cemetery, Paris, France

Privacy Then, Now, and Forever

Certain of the following are more reticent in death than in life. But all are resting on their own terms: in private, on family estates or other property, usually with no access to the public.

Bennett Cerf (1898–1971), humorist, publisher; ashes scattered at his Mount Kisco, New York, home

Claudette Colbert (1903–1996), movie star; buried in an unmarked grave at Woodlawn Cemetery, Bronx, New York

Quentin Crisp (1908–1999), actor-author; ashes given to executor of his estate

Dale Earnhardt, Sr. (1951–2001), race car driver; Earnhardt estate, Mooresville, North Carolina

Florence Eldridge (1901–1988), actress, wife of Frederick March; buried on March estate, New Milford, Connecticut

Greta Garbo (1905–1990), reclusive Swedish movie actress; ashes given to a niece, Gray Reisfield

Will Geer (1902–1978), movie and television actor; in Shakespeare Garden at Will Geer estate, Topanga Canyon, California

Walter Huston (1884–1950), character actor in movies; ashes given to his family

John Lennon (1940–1980), singer/guitarist/songwriter/writer; ashes given to family or friend

Ida Lupino (1918–1995), movie actress; ashes buried at her Burbank, California, residence

Frederick March (1897–1975) movie and stage actor; buried on the March estate in New Milford, Connecticut

Edna St. Vincent Millay (1892–1950), poet; buried in Steepletop cemetery on Millay family estate, Austerlitz, New York

Robert Montgomery (1904–1981), movie actor; ashes given to his family

John Muir (1838–1914), naturalist; at Muir private cemetery, Martinez, California

Edward R. Murrow (1908–1965), CBS radio and television reporter, newscaster; ashes scattered at his Glen Arden Farm, Pawling, New York

Larry Parks (1914–1975), movie actor, portrayed Al Jolson in *The Jolson Story;* ashes buried at his home in Studio City, California

River Phoenix (1970–1993), promising young actor; ashes scattered at family's ranch in Florida

Otto Preminger (1906–1986), movie director; buried in an unmarked grave at Woodlawn Cemetery, Bronx, New York

Nelson Rockefeller (1908–1979), New York governor, U.S. vice president; ashes scattered on family estate, Westchester, New York

Jacqueline Susann (1921–1974), author of *Valley of the Dolls,* other popular novels; ashes given to family

John Wayne (1907–1979), movie actor; buried in an unmarked grave at Pacific View Memorial Park, Newport Beach, California

No Longer at the White House

Last known addresses of all deceased former presidents of the United States. Presidents are listed in the order of their presidencies.

George Washington (1732–1799), Mount Vernon, Virginia

John Adams (1735–1826), United First Parish Church, Quincy, Massachusetts (see p. 24)

Thomas Jefferson (1743–1826), family cemetery, Monticello, Charlottesville, Virginia

James Madison (1751–1836), Montpelier Estate, Montpelier Station, Virginia

James Monroe (1758–1831), Hollywood Cemetery, Richmond, Virginia (see p. 120)

John Quincy Adams (1767–1848), United First Parish Church, Quincy, Massachusetts (see p. 24)

Andrew Jackson (1767–1845), The Hermitage, Nashville, Tennessee (see p. 168)

Martin Van Buren (1782–1862), Kinderhook Dutch Reformed Church, Kinderhook, New York

William Henry Harrison (1773–1841), William Henry Harrison State Park, North Bend, Ohio

John Tyler (1790–1862), Hollywood Cemetery, Richmond, Virginia (see p. 121)

James Polk (1818–1849), State Capitol grounds, Nashville, Tennessee

Zachary Taylor (1784–1850), Zachary Taylor National Cemetery, Louisville, Kentucky (see p. 145)

Millard Fillmore (1800–1874), Forest Lawn Cemetery, Buffalo, New York

Franklin Pierce (1804–1869), Old North Cemetery, Concord, New Hampshire

James Buchanan (1791–1868), Woodward Hill Cemetery, Lancaster, Pennsylvania

Abraham Lincoln (1809–1865), Oak Ridge Cemetery, Springfield, Illinois (see p. 133)

Andrew Johnson (1808–1875), Andrew Johnson National Cemetery, Greeneville, Tennessee

Ulysses S. Grant (1822–1885), General Grant National Memorial, Riverside Drive, New York City, New York

Rutherford B. Hayes (1822–1893), Spiegel Grove, Rutherford B. Hayes's home, Freemont, Ohio

James Garfield (1831–1881), Lake View Cemetery, Cleveland, Ohio (see p. 163)

Chester Arthur (1829–1886), Albany Rural Cemetery, Menands, New York

Grover Cleveland (1837–1908), Princeton Cemetery, Princeton, New Jersey (see p. 96)

Benjamin Harrison (1833–1901), Crown Hill Cemetery, Indianapolis, Indiana (see p. 138)

William McKinley (1843–1901), McKinley Memorial, Canton, Ohio

Theodore Roosevelt (1858–1919), Youngs Memorial Cemetery, adjacent to Theodore Roosevelt Sanctuary and Trailside Museum, Oyster Bay, Long Island, New York (see p. 69)

William Howard Taft (1857–1930), Arlington National Cemetery, Arlington, Virginia

Woodrow Wilson (1856–1924), Washington National Cathedral, Washington, D.C. (see p. 83)

Warren Harding (1865–1923), Harding Memorial, Marion, Ohio

Calvin Coolidge (1872–1933), Plymouth Cemetery, Plymouth, Vermont (see p. 32)

Herbert Hoover (1874–1964), Herbert Hoover Historic Site, West Branch, Iowa (see p. 141)

Franklin D. Roosevelt (1882–1945), Rose garden of Franklin D. Roosevelt Historic Site, Hyde Park, New York (see p. 62)

Harry S. Truman (1884–1972), Harry S. Truman Library and Museum, Independence, Missouri (see p. 154)

Dwight D. Eisenhower (1890–1969), Eisenhower Center, Abilene, Kansas (see p. 177)

John F. Kennedy (1917–1963), Arlington National Cemetery, Arlington, Virginia (see p. 114)

Lyndon B. Johnson (1908–1973), Lyndon Baines Johnson Ranch, Johnson City, Texas (see p. 197)

Richard M. Nixon (1913–1994), Nixon Library, Yorba Linda, California

End Notes

‡ The ashes of songwriter **Steve Goodman** can be found under home plate at Wrigley Field, Chicago, Illinois.

‡ **David Kennison** (1734–1852), supposedly the last survivor of the Boston Tea Party (1773), died in 1852 at age 115. His last address is a huge boulder with a bronze plaque in Lincoln Park, Chicago, Illinois.

‡ The vertebrae of **John Wilkes Booth** (1838–1865), assassin of President Abraham Lincoln, are on display at the National Museum of Health and Medicine, Walter Reed Medical Center, Washington, D.C.

‡ The skeleton, spleen, and brain of **Charles Guiteau** (1841–1882), assassin of President James Garfield, are at the National Museum of Health and Medicine, Walter Reed Medical Center, Washington, D.C.

‡ The ashes and death masks of **Nicola Sacco** (1891–1927) and **Bartolomeo Vanzetti** (1888–1927), electrocuted anarchists, are in Boston Public Library. For years the whereabouts of the ashes was kept secret because of the inflammatory nature of their case.

INDEX

TO'MB IT MAY CONCERN

Patricia Brooks admits to a limitless fascination with cemeteries dating back, she says, to early exposure to "Tales From the Crypt." Her long experience as a restaurant critic (for the *New York Times'* Connecticut section) and freelance food writer (for *Bon Appétit, Food and Wine,* and many other national publications) whetted her appetite for more than just desserts. Years of travels have taken her across the United States, Europe, North Africa, the Middle East, India, Asia, and Down Under. Researching and writing articles and guidebooks and, yes, even a little ghostwriting, she has inevitably found herself soul-searching in the sepulchral solitude of a benign burial ground, observing statuary and other graven images. Her seventeen books (including guides to Spain, Britain, New York State and New England) have not deadened her enthusiasm for spirited subjects—even those who are out of sight, but not out of mind. One thing special in writing about graveyards, she avers, is that "you never run out of subjects. It doesn't take much digging—so to speak—to find them."